Getting Help

▶ **With items on-screen:** Choose Help⇨What's This and click the part of the screen you need help with

▶ **With dialog boxes:** Click the question mark in the upper-right corner of the dialog box and click an option

▶ **With Office 97 programs features:** Choose Help⇨Contents and Index. On the Contents tab of the Help Topics dialog box, double-click book icons and question marks to get to a topic. On the Index tab, type the topic's name and double-click it in the box in the lower-half of the tab.

▶ **Using the Office Assistant:** Click the Office Assistant button or press F1, type a question in the box, and click the Search button

Doing the Microsoft Office 97 Basics

▶ **Starting an Office 97 program:** Click the Start button, choose Programs, and choose the program you want to start from the menu

▶ **Exiting an Office 97 program:** Choose File⇨Exit or click the Close button

▶ **Creating a new file:** Choose File⇨New, press Ctrl+N, or click the New button

▶ **Saving a file:** Choose File⇨Save, find the folder in which you want to save the file, enter a name in the File Name box, and click the Save button

▶ **Opening a file:** Choose File⇨Open, press Ctrl+O, or click the Open button; find the folder the file is in; select the file that you want to open and then click the Open button or press Enter

▶ **Closing a file:** Click the Save button, choose File⇨Save, or press Ctrl+S to save the file and then choose File⇨Close

Progress Check

Unit 1: Getting Acquainted with Word 97 and the Other Office 97 Programs

❏ Lesson 1-1: Starting and Closing an Office 97 Program

❏ Lesson 1-2: Opening and Closing a File

❏ Lesson 1-3: Ways of Viewing Documents

❏ Lesson 1-4: Moving Around in Documents

❏ Lesson 1-5: Getting Help When You Need It

Unit 2: Creating a Document

❏ Lesson 2-1: Creating, Saving, and Naming a New Document

❏ Lesson 2-2: Entering and Editing Text

❏ Lesson 2-3: Selecting Text

❏ Lesson 2-4: Copying and Moving Text

❏ Lesson 2-5: Deleting Text

❏ Lesson 2-6: Changing Fonts and Character Styles

Unit 3: Polishing and Printing Your Document

❏ Lesson 3-1: Laying Out Margins

❏ Lesson 3-2: Indenting Text

❏ Lesson 3-3: Handling Line Spacing

❏ Lesson 3-4: Aligning Text in Documents

❏ Lesson 3-5: Checking Your Spelling (and Grammar)

❏ Lesson 3-6: Printing a File

Unit 4: Learning the Ropes

❏ Lesson 4-1: Creating a Worksheet

❏ Lesson 4-2: Finding Your Way around a Worksheet

❏ Lesson 4-3: Entering and Editing the Data

❏ Lesson 4-4: Copying, Moving, and Deleting Data

❏ Lesson 4-5: Viewing Worksheets

❏ Lesson 4-6: Printing a Worksheet

Unit 5: Making a Worksheet Look Just Right

❏ Lesson 5-1: Formatting Numbers and Text

❏ Lesson 5-2: Changing the Width and Height of Columns and Rows

❏ Lesson 5-3: Inserting and Deleting Columns and Rows

❏ Lesson 5-4: Aligning Numbers and Text

❏ Lesson 5-5: Applying Borders, Patterns, and Colors

Dummies 101:™ Microsoft® Office 97 For Windows®

CHEAT SHEET

Selecting Stuff

▸ **In Microsoft Word 97:** Double-click a word to select it. Click and then drag across text to select it. Double-click in the left margin to select a paragraph. Press Ctrl+A to select an entire document.

▸ **In Microsoft Excel 97:** Click and drag over cells to select them. To select a block of cells, click one corner and drag to the other.

▸ **In Microsoft PowerPoint 97:** Click and drag over text on slides to select them. To select a slide, switch to Slide Sorter view and then click the slide. To select a slide in Outline view, click a slide icon.

▸ **In Microsoft Access 97:** To select records, drag across the small squares to their left in Datasheet view. To select a field, switch to Design view and click the box to the left of the field.

Accessing the CD-ROM Files

See Appendix B for all the CD-ROM details. Here's a quick-reference guide to accessing the CD files (but remember that you should wait until the appropriate lesson before opening any of the files).

Note: The CD-ROM does not contain any of the Microsoft Office 97 program or Windows 95. The Microsoft Office 97 programs and Windows 95 must already be installed on your computer.

With the appropriate Office 97 program running:

1. **With the program window on-screen, choose File in the upper-left corner of the window.**
2. **Choose Open.**
3. **In the Open dialog box, click the Office 101 folder.**
4. **Double-click the file that you want to open.**

IDG BOOKS WORLDWIDE

Copyright © 1996 IDG Books Worldwide, Inc.
All rights reserved.
Cheat Sheet $2.95 value. Item 0097-X
For more information on IDG Books,
call 1-800-762-2974

COMPUTER BOOK SERIES FROM IDG

References for the Rest of Us! ®

Are you intimidated and confused by computers? Do you find that traditional manuals are overloaded with technical details you'll never use? Do your friends and family always call you to fix simple problems on their PCs? Then the ...*For Dummies* ® computer book series from IDG Books Worldwide is for you.

...*For Dummies* books are written for those frustrated computer users who know they aren't really dumb but find that PC hardware, software, and indeed the unique vocabulary of computing make them feel helpless. ...*For Dummies* books use a lighthearted approach, a down-to-earth style, and even cartoons and humorous icons to diffuse computer novices' fears and build their confidence. Lighthearted but not lightweight, these books are a perfect survival guide for anyone forced to use a computer.

> *"I like my copy so much I told friends; now they bought copies."*
>
> **Irene C., Orwell, Ohio**

> *"Quick, concise, nontechnical, and humorous."*
>
> **Jay A., Elburn, Illinois**

> *"Thanks, I needed this book. Now I can sleep at night."*
>
> **Robin F., British Columbia, Canada**

Already, hundreds of thousands of satisfied readers agree. They have made ...*For Dummies* books the #1 introductory level computer book series and have written asking for more. So, if you're looking for the most fun and easy way to learn about computers, look to ...*For Dummies* books to give you a helping hand.

IDG BOOKS WORLDWIDE ™

7/96r

DUMMIES 101:™
MICROSOFT®
OFFICE 97
FOR
WINDOWS®

by Peter Weverka

IDG Books Worldwide, Inc.
An International Data Group Company

Foster City, CA ✦ Chicago, IL ✦ Indianapolis, IN ✦ Southlake, TX

Dummies 101™: Microsoft® Office 97 For Windows®

Published by
IDG Books Worldwide, Inc.
An International Data Group Company
919 E. Hillsdale Blvd.
Suite 400
Foster City, CA 94404
http://www.idgbooks.com (IDG Books Worldwide Web site)
http://www.dummies.com (Dummies Press Web site)

Library of Congress Catalog Card No.: 96-80225

ISBN: 0-7645-0097-X

Printed in the United States of America

10 9 8 7 6 5 4 3 2 1

1M/ST/QR/ZX/IN

Distributed in the United States by IDG Books Worldwide, Inc.

Distributed by Macmillan Canada for Canada; by Transworld Publishers Limited in the United Kingdom and Europe; by WoodsLane Pty. Ltd. for Australia; by WoodsLane Enterprises Ltd. for New Zealand; by Longman Singapore Publishers Ltd. for Singapore, Malaysia, Thailand, and Indonesia; by Simron Pty. Ltd. for South Africa; by Toppan Company Ltd. for Japan; by Distribuidora Cuspide for Argentina; by Livraria Cultura for Brazil; by Ediciencia S.A. for Ecuador; by Addison-Wesley Publishing Company for Korea; by Ediciones ZETA S.C.R. Ltda. for Peru; by WS Computer Publishing Company, Inc., for the Philippines; by Unalis Corporation for Taiwan; by Contemporanea de Ediciones for Venezuela. Authorized Sales Agent: Anthony Rudkin Associates for the Middle East and North Africa.

For general information on IDG Books Worldwide's books in the U.S., please call our Consumer Customer Service department at 800-762-2974. For reseller information, including discounts and premium sales, please call our Reseller Customer Service department at 800-434-3422.

For information on where to purchase IDG Books Worldwide's books outside the U.S., please contact our International Sales department at 415-655-3172 or fax 415-655-3295.

For information on foreign language translations, please contact our Foreign & Subsidiary Rights department at 415-655-3021 or fax 415-655-3281.

For sales inquiries and special prices for bulk quantities, please contact our Sales department at 415-655-3200 or write to the address above.

For information on using IDG Books Worldwide's books in the classroom or for ordering examination copies, please contact our Educational Sales department at 800-434-2086 or fax 817-251-8174.

For press review copies, author interviews, or other publicity information, please contact our Public Relations department at 415-655-3000 or fax 415-655-3299.

For authorization to photocopy items for corporate, personal, or educational use, please contact Copyright Clearance Center, 222 Rosewood Drive, Danvers, MA 01923, or fax 508-750-4470.

 is a trademark under exclusive license to IDG Books Worldwide, Inc., from International Data Group, Inc.

About the Author

Peter Weverka is the author of *Word For Windows 95 For Dummies Quick Reference* and *Dummies 101: Word For Windows 95,* both published by IDG Books Worldwide, Inc. He is also the editor of 75 computer books on topics ranging from the Internet to desktop publishing. His humorous articles and stories (none related to computers, thankfully) have appeared in *Harper's* and *Exquisite Corpse.*

ABOUT IDG BOOKS WORLDWIDE

Welcome to the world of IDG Books Worldwide.

IDG Books Worldwide, Inc., is a subsidiary of International Data Group, the world's largest publisher of computer-related information and the leading global provider of information services on information technology. IDG was founded more than 25 years ago and now employs more than 8,500 people worldwide. IDG publishes more than 275 computer publications in over 75 countries (see listing below). More than 60 million people read one or more IDG publications each month.

Launched in 1990, IDG Books Worldwide is today the #1 publisher of best-selling computer books in the United States. We are proud to have received eight awards from the Computer Press Association in recognition of editorial excellence and three from *Computer Currents'* First Annual Readers' Choice Awards. Our best-selling *...For Dummies*® series has more than 30 million copies in print with translations in 30 languages. IDG Books Worldwide, through a joint venture with IDG's Hi-Tech Beijing, became the first U.S. publisher to publish a computer book in the People's Republic of China. In record time, IDG Books Worldwide has become the first choice for millions of readers around the world who want to learn how to better manage their businesses.

Our mission is simple: Every one of our books is designed to bring extra value and skill-building instructions to the reader. Our books are written by experts who understand and care about our readers. The knowledge base of our editorial staff comes from years of experience in publishing, education, and journalism — experience we use to produce books for the '90s. In short, we care about books, so we attract the best people. We devote special attention to details such as audience, interior design, use of icons, and illustrations. And because we use an efficient process of authoring, editing, and desktop publishing our books electronically, we can spend more time ensuring superior content and spend less time on the technicalities of making books.

You can count on our commitment to deliver high-quality books at competitive prices on topics you want to read about. At IDG Books Worldwide, we continue in the IDG tradition of delivering quality for more than 25 years. You'll find no better book on a subject than one from IDG Books Worldwide.

John J. Kilcullen

John Kilcullen
President and CEO
IDG Books Worldwide, Inc.

Eighth Annual
Computer Press
Awards ≥ 1992

Ninth Annual
Computer Press
Awards ≥ 1993

Tenth Annual
Computer Press
Awards ≥ 1994

Eleventh Annual
Computer Press
Awards ≥ 1995

Dedication

For Anne Crowley

Author's Acknowledgments

Many people gave their best to this book, and I am grateful to all of them. I would especially like to thank Acquisitions Editor Gareth Hancock, who graciously offered me the opportunity to write this and other books for IDG Books Worldwide, Inc.

I owe a lot to Mary Goodwin, who cheerfully saw this book through the production stage and offered many suggestions for making this book a better one. Thanks as well go to copy editor William A. Barton.

This book was tech edited by Jim McCarter, who followed in my footsteps and made sure that all the instructions on these pages are indeed accurate.

Finally, I want to thank my family — Sofia, Henry, and Addie — for putting up with my vampire-like working hours and my eerie demeanor at daybreak.

Publisher's Acknowledgments

We're proud of this book; please send us your comments about it by using the Reader Response Card at the back of the book or by e-mailing us at feedback/dummies@idgbooks.com. Some of the people who helped bring this book to market include the following:

Acquisitions, Development, and Editorial

Project Editor: Mary Goodwin

Acquisitions Editor: Gareth Hancock

Product Development Director: Mary Bednarek

Media Development Manager: Joyce Pepple

Copy Editor: William A. Barton

Technical Reviewer: Jim McCarter

Editorial Manager: Mary C. Corder

Editorial Assistants: Constance Carlisle, Chris H. Collins, Michael D. Sullivan

Production

Project Coordinator: Regina Snyder

Layout and Graphics: Cameron Booker, Linda M. Boyer, Dominique DeFelice, Angela F. Hunckler, Drew R. Moore, Mark C. Owens, Brent Savage

Proofreaders: Melissa D. Buddendeck, Joel Draper, Nancy Reinhart, Rachel Garvey, Nancy Price, Dwight Ramsey, Rob Springer, Carrie Voorhis, Karen York

Indexer: Sherry Massey

General and Administrative

IDG Books Worldwide, Inc.: John Kilcullen, CEO; Steven Berkowitz, President and Publisher

Dummies, Inc.: Brenda McLaughlin, Senior Vice President & Group Publisher

Dummies Technology Press & Dummies Editorial: Diane Graves Steele, Vice President and Associate Publisher; Judith A. Taylor, Brand Manager; Kristin A. Cocks, Editorial Director

Dummies Trade Press: Kathleen A. Welton, Vice President & Publisher; Stacy S. Collins, Brand Manager

IDG Books Production for Dummies Press: Beth Jenkins, Production Director; Cindy L. Phipps, Supervisor of Project Coordination, Production Proofreading and Indexing; Kathie S. Schnorr, Supervisor of Page Layout; Shelley Lea, Supervisor of Graphics and Design; Debbie J. Gates, Production Systems Specialist; Tony Augsburger, Supervisor of Reprints and Bluelines; Leslie Popplewell, Media Archive Coordinator

Dummies Packaging & Book Design: Patti Sandez, Packaging Specialist; Kavish+Kavish, Cover Design

◆

The publisher would like to give special thanks to Patrick J. McGovern, without whom this book would not have been possible.

◆

Files at a Glance

ABC 123

The following is a list of the files on the CD that comes with this book. The list tells which lessons offer practice files, what each practice file is meant to help you learn, and the name of each practice file. Appendix B explains how to install the files on your computer.

Part I: Word 97

Part II: Excel 97

Part III: PowerPoint 97

Part V: Access 97

Bonus Stuff (Other Items on the CD)

Bonus units

Unit 13: Bringing It All Together
Unit 14: Office 97 and the World Wide Web

Lesson files for bonus units

Contents at a Glance

Table of Contents

Introduction

This book is written and designed to turn you into an experienced user of the five Microsoft Office 97 programs — Microsoft Word 97, Microsoft Excel 97, Microsoft PowerPoint 97, Microsoft Outlook, and Microsoft Access 97 — in the shortest possible time. The 60-plus lessons in this book cover the most important features of Office 97 in a thorough, step-by-step fashion. After you finish with this book, you will have explored and learned everything you need to know to become one of those people whom others seek out when they have a question about running computer programs.

How you make use of this book is up to you. You can study it from beginning to end or you can dive in where you need instructions for using a particular program or doing a particular task. You decide. The important thing to know is that the lessons are presented so that you can learn at your own pace. If you want to speed through this book, more power to you, and if you're one of those people who learn things slowly but thoroughly (I am), this book's method of presenting instructions will also serve you very well.

By now you may have noticed that a CD comes with this book. (If you haven't spotted the CD yet, you can find it on the back inside cover of the book.) This CD holds practice files for most of the lessons in this book. By using the practice files on the CD and following the instructions in the lessons, you will get hands-on learning experience in the five Office 97 programs. You will acquire skills that would take hours and hours to acquire on your own. And you will discover shortcuts and techniques for doing tasks that you would likely not discover if you didn't have this book.

On the CD are over 50 practice files, including word-processed documents, spreadsheets, slide presentations, and databases. Each file is a stand-in for an Office 97 file that you might work on at home or at an office. As you follow the lessons and work with the practice files, you will encounter the same problems and obstacles that you normally encounter when you use Word 97, Excel 97, PowerPoint 97, Outlook, or Access 97. The only difference is that I will show you how to solve the problems and get around the obstacles. Lucky you — you are about to become the beneficiary of my many years of blind groping and daring experimentation. You are about to become a very proficient, very confident user of the Office 97 programs.

Whom This Book Is For

This book is for beginning to intermediate users of the five Office 97 programs. It is also for neophytes who have never touched a computer. If you've never used any of the programs, you can start right now with this book.

Foolish Assumptions about the Reader

Pardon me, but I made one or two foolish assumptions about you, the reader of this book. I have assumed that you are using the Windows 95 operating system. I have also assumed that you've already loaded at least one Office 97 program on your computer. This book covers five Office 97 programs, but you don't have to load all of them on your computer to read this book or follow the lessons.

If you are having trouble loading an Office 97 program on your computer, I suggest calling the store where you bought Office 97 for technical assistance.

To make good use of this book, you have to use the practice files on the CD-ROM. I've assumed that you have a CD-ROM for loading the practice files on your computer.

How much hard-disk space and computer memory is needed to run an Office 97 program depends on which program you are running. PowerPoint 97 requires a lot of memory, for example, but Outlook does not. I have assumed that your computer has enough hard-disk space to load the Office 97 programs. I have assumed that your computer has enough memory as well. Read "Using the Dummies 101 CD-ROM" to find out how much muscle your computer needs to run the CD that comes with this book.

What's in This Book, Anyway?

This book is a tutorial. It explains, in step-by-step fashion, how to word process with Word 97; work a spreadsheet with Excel 97; create and present slides with PowerPoint 97; send and receive e-mail, as well as schedule yourself and keep a contact list, with Outlook; and wrestle with a database with Access 97. The first unit, which is nominally about Word 97, explains basic tasks you will do in all the programs, including creating, saving, and opening files. As the book progresses, you tackle each of the Office 97 programs in turn.

You will find over 60 lessons in all. The book is divided into six parts, one for each of the five Office 97 programs and a set of appendixes. You'll also find two bonus units on the CD that comes with this book — Unit 13 covers sharing data among programs, and Unit 14 discusses using Office 97 to create a Web page.

Part I: Word 97

Part I explains the basic procedures you must know to run any Office 97 program. It explains how to start a program, create a file, save a file, and open a file. Then it focuses on Word 97, the word processing program in Office 97. In this part, you learn how to edit, lay out, and enter text in a document, as well as how to run the spell-checker and prettify documents.

Part II: Excel 97

Part II tackles Excel 97, the Office 97 spreadsheet program. It explains how to create a *worksheet* (the Excel 97 name for spreadsheets), enter data, and manipulate data in different ways. This part also teaches you how to make a worksheet look good and construct functions and formulas to crunch the numbers.

Part III: PowerPoint 97

Part III explores PowerPoint 97, the slide presentation program in Office 97. Among other things, this part explains how to enter text on slides and change the slides' appearance, and how to give a slide show.

Part IV: Outlook

Part IV delves into Outlook. In this part, you learn how to send and receive e-mail and how to use the "personal organizer" side of Outlook. You learn how to schedule appointments and meetings, maintain a contact list of the people you know and do business with, and track the tasks and projects you need to do.

Part V: Access 97

Part V looks at Access 97, the database program in Office 97. It demonstrates how to create and enter data in a database, as well as how to mine a database for valuable information by querying, filtering, and sorting.

Appendixes

At the end of each part of this book is a test. You can find the answers to the test questions in Appendix A. Appendix B explains how to load the practice files and bonus units that come with this book on your computer.

On the CD: Bonus Stuff

I had so much I wanted to tell you about the Office 97 programs, I couldn't fit it all into the book. Lucky for you, you can still have the benefit of my infinite wisdom, because the CD offers two bonus units. The first unit covers sharing data across the different Office 97 programs, and the second covers creating Web pages with Office 97 programs. The bonus units are just like the other units in the book — they look the same, read the same, and may even taste the same for all I know.

Using the Dummies 101 CD-ROM

The *Dummies 101* CD-ROM at the back of this book contains all the files you need to complete the lessons and exercises in this book. By using the files on the CD-ROM, you avoid having to create practice files of your own. In the CD-ROM files are sample Word 97 documents, Excel 97 spreadsheets, PowerPoint 97 slide presentations, and Access 97 databases. The CD also includes a handy installation program that copies files to your hard disk. After you're done with this book, you can delete the files from your hard disk, if you want.

Check out Appendix B for all the details about the CD-ROM. Remember that the files are meant to accompany the book's lessons, so try to resist the urge to fool around with them before I tell you to.

The *Dummies 101* CD-ROM does *not* include any Microsoft Office 97 programs. The Mighty Microsoft Corporation would get quite angry if IDG Books Worldwide, Inc., gave the programs away illegally. No, you have to buy the programs from a software store or get them as birthday gifts. The CD-ROM on this book does not include Windows 95, either.

To use the CD-ROM, you need the following:

- ◗ A computer with a CD-ROM drive
- ◗ The Microsoft Office 97 programs installed on your computer
- ◗ Microsoft Windows 95 installed on your computer
- ◗ At least 8MB of RAM installed on your computer
- ◗ At least 4MB of free hard-disk space available if you want to install just the exercise files

Here's how to install the files from the Dummies 101 CD-ROM onto your hard disk. The first thing you need to do is install a couple of icons to the Start menu or Program Manager to make the CD easier to use. Then you install the exercise files.

With Windows 95 up and running, follow these steps:

on the CD

1 **Insert the Dummies 101 CD (label side up) into your computer's CD drive and wait about 30 seconds to see whether Windows 95 starts the CD for you.**

If your computer's CD-ROM has the AutoPlay feature, the installation program runs automatically. If the program does not start after 30 seconds, go to Step 2. If it does, go to Step 4.

2 **If the installation program doesn't start automatically, click the Start button and click Run.**

3 **In the dialog box that appears, type** d:\setup.exe **(if your CD drive is not drive D, then substitute the appropriate letter for D) and click OK.**

A message informs you that the program is about to install the icons.

4 **Click OK in the message window.**

After a moment, a program group called Dummies 101 appears on the Start menu, with a set of icons. Then another message appears, asking whether you want to use the CD now.

5 **Click Yes to use the CD interface window or click No if you want to use the CD later.**

If you click on No, you can run the CD later simply by clicking the Dummies 101 - Office 97 For Windows CD icon in the Dummies 101 program group (on the Start menu).

Note: For more detailed installation information, see Appendix B.

heads up

If you have problems with the installation process, you can call the IDG Books Worldwide, Inc., Customer Support number: 800-762-2974 (outside the U.S.: 317-596-5261).

The Cast of Icons

To help you get more out of this book, I've placed icons here and there. Here's what those icons mean:

heads up

Where you see the heads up icon, pay close attention. This icon marks passages that give especially good advice — advice that you should remember. It also alerts you to places where I describe risky techniques or ask you to make decisions that could change the way an Office 97 program works.

on the test

Information that you will need to know for the tests at the end of each part is marked with the on the test icon (questions on the quizzes at the end of each unit are not marked with this icon). I want you to do well on the tests, so prick up your ears when you see this icon. If you stumble on a test question, look in Appendix A to find out which lesson provides the answer to the question, and then turn to the lesson, find the on the test icon, and get the right answer.

on the CD

Most of the lessons in this book require you to use a practice file. When I tell you to open a practice file, you will see the on the CD icon. Also, a list at the beginning of each unit tells which files you need to complete the lessons in the unit.

Stuff You Should Know

To help you learn quickly and get the most out of this book, I've adopted a few conventions.

Where I tell you to click a button, a picture of the button appears in the margin of the book. For example, the button you see in the margin next to this text is the Save button. Where I tell you to click the Save button to save a file, you'll see the Save button in the margin.

Save button

Besides clicking buttons, you can do tasks in the Office 97 programs by pressing combinations of keys. For example, you can also save a file by pressing Ctrl+S. In other words, you press the Ctrl key and the S key at the same time. Where you see Ctrl+, Alt+, or Shift+ followed by a key name (or maybe more than one key name), you press the keys simultaneously.

To show you how to give commands, I use the ⇨ symbol. For example, you can choose File⇨Save to save. The ⇨ is just a shorthand method of saying, "Choose Save from the File menu."

Notice how the *F* in File and the *S* in Save are underlined in the preceding paragraph. Those same characters are underlined in the command names in the Office 97 programs. You can press underlined letters to give commands on menus and press the Alt key and underlined letters to make selections in dialog boxes. Where a letter is underlined in a command name or on a dialog box option in an Office 97 program, it is also underlined on the pages of this book.

Where you see letters and numbers in boldface text in this book, I want you to type the letters or numbers. For example, if you read "type **Annual Report** in the File name text box to name your document," you should do just that: You should type those very same letters.

At the start of each unit is a list of prerequisites. The prerequisites explain what you need to know in order to complete the unit successfully. For example, before you can open a file, you need to know how to create one, so creating a file is a prerequisite for opening a file. Beside each prerequisite on the list is a mention of the lesson in this book you can refer to if you don't know a prerequisite and need to brush up on it.

At the end of each lesson you will find a progress check. Progress checks describe precisely what you need to have learned from each lesson before going on to the next lesson. When you complete a lesson, read the progress check to make sure you are ready to move ahead.

Notes in the margin of this book tell you the names of buttons, provide short-cuts for doing tasks, and give word definitions, among other things. Don't forget to glance at the margin notes to pick up this valuable information.

Last but not least of the conventions in this book are the recesses. This book is packed with information, and no mortal soul could take it in all in one sitting. When I think it is time for a rest, I put a brief recess in the text. Recesses are meant to help you take stock of what you have learned and point to places where you should take a breather.

this is a note in the margin

Word 97

Part I

In this part...

Part I explains the ins and outs of Microsoft Word 97, the Microsoft Office 97 word-processing program. It shows how to edit a Word 97 file. And because appearances count for a lot, Part I also describes how to format a Word 97 file so it looks good on the page.

In Part I, you also delve into a handful of tasks that pertain to all the Office 97 programs, not just Word 97. For example, you learn how to open and exit a program and how to open, close, and save a file as well.

My word, you find a lot of good stuff in Part I.

Getting Acquainted with Word 97 and the Other Office 97 Programs

Prerequisites
▶ Turning on your computer
▶ Installing the program
▶ Being wise and merciful

▶ Open
▶ View
on the CD   ▶ Hurry Up

Objectives for This Unit

✓ Opening and closing Office 97 programs

✓ Opening a file so that you can work on it

✓ Viewing documents in different ways

✓ Moving around in documents big and small

✓ Getting instructions from the Help program

T his unit describes the basics of running a Microsoft Office 97 program, whether the program is Word 97, Excel 97, PowerPoint 97, Outlook, or Access 97. The day is soon coming when you can trade information back and forth across the different programs in Office 97, and to prepare for that happy day, I explain how to open several programs at once and how to switch from one program to the other. In this unit, you also learn how to open a file in any Office 97 program.

I show you the different parts of the Word 97 screen, too. If you ventured into Word 97 already, you know that the screen is cluttered with buttons showing funny symbols, arrows that point every which way, and menus that sport peculiar names. You figure out what some of these interesting items are in Part I and how to get a different view of your work on-screen.

This unit also explains how to move around on-screen and how to get instructions from Office 97 in case you're confronted with a task that you don't know how to handle yet.

Lesson 1-1

Starting and Closing an Office 97 Program

Obviously, you can't write a 100-page report in Word 97, create an elaborate Excel 97 chart, dazzle viewers with a PowerPoint 97 slide-show presentation, sort through e-mail messages in Outlook, or mine for data in an Access 97 database until you start the programs.

Luckily for you, starting an Office 97 program is as easy as falling off a turnip truck. This lesson describes how to start and close down the programs in Office 97. The lesson also explains how to run several programs at once and switch from one to the other.

To learn how to open the Office 97 programs, turn on your computer and follow these steps:

on the test

1 Click the Start button on the taskbar.

Click means to move the mouse pointer over something and press the left mouse button quickly. When you move the mouse pointer over something you can click, the mouse turns into an arrow.

As shown in Figure 1-1, the *taskbar* is located along the bottom of the Windows 95 screen. The Start button is on the left, in the lower-left corner of the screen.

After you click the Start button, the Start menu appears.

2 Choose Programs on the Start menu.

The fastest way to choose Programs is to click the word Programs with the mouse, but you can also press the letter P or press the ↑ key until you highlight Programs.

After you click Programs, another menu appears (if you chose Programs by pressing the ↑ key, press the → key now to see the menu). On this menu is an alphabetical list of the programs installed on your computer. On this menu, if you look closely, you see the name Microsoft Word.

3 Choose Microsoft Word to open Word 97.

To choose Microsoft Word on this menu, either click Microsoft Word or press the ↓ key until you highlight Microsoft Word and then press the Enter key.

After a moment or two, a screen with the words Microsoft Word 97 appears, and then you see the program itself on-screen. If you're running Word 97 for the first time, you also see the Office Assistant — an animated figure (with an ugly face) who invites you to learn about Word 97. Ignore him for now (Lesson 1-5 explains the Office Assistant and how it works).

In the next step, you open Excel 97.

4 Click the Start button, choose Programs, and choose Microsoft Excel.

Now a screen with the words Microsoft Excel 97 appears, and Excel 97 opens. Two programs, Word 97 and Excel 97, are now running, but only Excel 97 appears on-screen. Suppose, however, that you want to get back to Word 97.

mouse pointer turns into an arrow when over something you can click

click = press the left mouse button

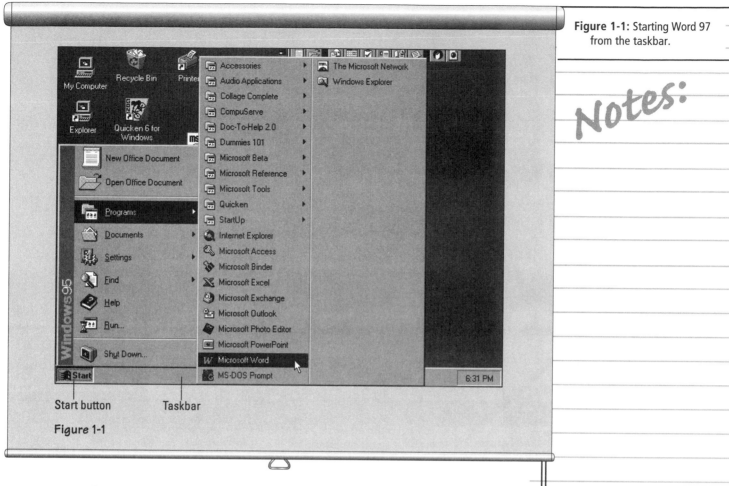

Figure 1-1: Starting Word 97 from the taskbar.

Notes:

Start button   Taskbar

Figure 1-1

5 **Click the Microsoft Word button on the taskbar.**

As soon as you click this button, you see the Word 97 screen again. (If you wanted to copy text from a Word 97 document to an Excel 97 worksheet, you could do so by clicking buttons on the taskbar and switching back and forth between the programs.)

document = Word 97 file

6 **Click the Start button, choose Programs, and choose Microsoft PowerPoint.**

Now three Office 97 programs are running and, not coincidentally, three buttons appear on the taskbar. But how do you *close* these programs? Read on.

7 **Click the Cancel button in the PowerPoint dialog box sitting in the middle of the screen to tell PowerPoint 97 that you don't want to create a presentation and then click the Close button in the upper-right corner of the PowerPoint 97 window.**

☒
Close button

Clicking the Close button (the *X*) in the upper-right corner of a window is the fastest way to close a program, but you have other ways to accomplish the same task, as the following two steps demonstrate.

heads up

Make sure that you click the Close button and *not* either of the two buttons to its left. Those buttons are for minimizing the program window and shrinking the window in size.

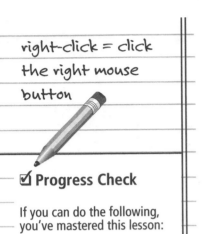

right-click = click
the right mouse
button

☑ **Progress Check**

If you can do the following,
you've mastered this lesson:

❏ Open an Office 97
   program.

❏ Close an Office 97
   program.

8 **Right-click the Microsoft Excel button on the taskbar and, after the shortcut menu appears, click the Close command on the shortcut menu.**

Right-click means to click with the *right* mouse button, not the left one. After you click the Close button, Excel 97 disappears and its button is removed from the taskbar.

9 **Back in Word 97, choose File➪Exit.**

You can always choose File➪Exit to shut down a program. To choose this command, either click File on the menu bar and then click the menu's Exit command or press Alt+F to open the File menu and then press the X key (the underlined letter in the menu's Exit command).

Now you're back where you started, at the Windows 95 desktop. Click the Start button, choose Programs, and then choose Microsoft Word to open the program so that you can go on to the next lesson.

Lesson 1-2

Opening and Closing a File

After you save and close a file (Unit 2 explains how), you must open the file again before you can work on it. This lesson explains how to open a file — in this case, a Word 97 document — and how to close the file after you open it. The techniques for opening files are the same, no matter which Office 97 program you're running.

Throughout this book, I ask you to open practice files in the Office 101 folder. Get good at opening files so that you save yourself a lot of time down the road. To help you get good at this process, this lesson includes an extra credit shortcut for opening files quickly (see "Opening files from the Favorites folder" in this unit for the details).

heads up

If you haven't installed the practice files for this book yet, please see the instructions for installing the files in the introduction, in Appendix B, or on the last page of this book.

Opening a file

on the CD

For this lesson, you open a file called Open that's located in the Office 101 folder. To open this file, make sure that Word 97 is running and then carry out the following steps:

1 **Choose File➪Open.**

You can also press Ctrl+O or click the Open button on the Standard toolbar. Whichever route you take, you see the Open dialog box, as shown in Figure 1-2.

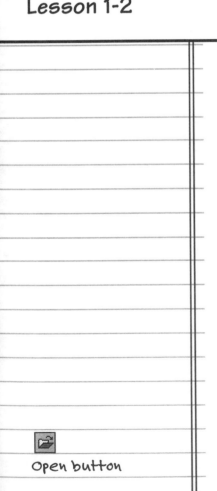

Open button

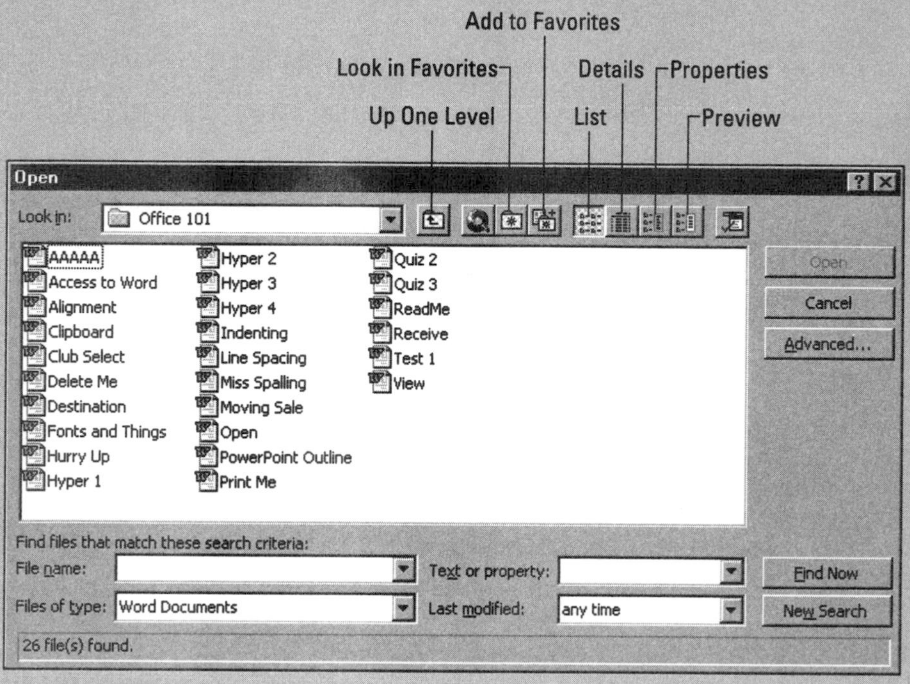

Add to Favorites

Look in Favorites┐   Details ┌Properties

Up One Level   List   ┌Preview

Figure 1-2

Figure 1-2: To open a file, find and click the name of the file that you want to open in the Open dialog box and then click the Open button.

Notes:

From this dialog box, you can access any file on your computer, including the Open file in the Office 101 folder. To access the file you want, you click buttons or double-click folders in the Open dialog box.

2 **Click the Up One Level button as many times as necessary for the C drive to appear in the Look in drop-down list box.**

The Up One Level button is labeled in Figure 1-2. Each time you click this button, you move up in the hierarchy of folders. After the C drive appears in the Look In text box, you know you're at the top of the folder hierarchy. You know you've reached the C drive when you see a computer icon followed by some text and (C:). To move down the hierarchy, you double-click the names of the folders that appear in the Open dialog box.

3 **Double-click the Office 101 folder.**

Now you see the files in the Office 101 folder. To open one of these files, all you need to do is double-click the name of the file in the list or click the filename and then click the Open button. Before doing so, however, check out the different ways of viewing files in the Open dialog box.

4 **Click the Details button.**

The Open dialog box tells you how big each file is, which program was used to create the file, and when the file was last modified. Look in the Type column if you aren't sure which file belongs to which program — the information in that column tells you straightaway.

5 **Click the Properties button.**

Now the Open dialog box tells you who created the file, how many times the file was revised, and how much time was spent creating the file, among other things.

6 **Click the Preview button.**

You get a thumbnail view of the file. Click the Details, Properties, and Preview buttons if you can't quite remember the name of a file you want to open or if you aren't sure what is in a file.

7 **Click the List button.**

Click the List button to access a plain but exhaustive list of the files in the folder you double-clicked.

8 **Select the Open file in the Open dialog box.**

To select a file, click its name. If you do so successfully, the filename is highlighted on-screen.

9 **Click the Open button to open the file.**

If you are a speed demon, you can bypass Step 9 and simply double-click a file in the Open dialog box to open that file straightaway.

on the test

By the way, the bottom of the File menu lists the last four files you opened. To open one of those files, all you need to do is open the File menu and either click a filename in the menu or press 1, 2, 3, or 4 on the keyboard.

Closing a file

Closing a file is pretty simple. All you need to do to close the file you just opened — or to close any file for that matter — is to choose File⇨Close. To do so, click File on the menu bar and then click the Close command or press Alt+F to open the File menu and then press the C key, *C* being the underlined letter in the word Close on the File menu.

heads up

By the way, suppose that you're the adventurous sort and you typed a word or two in the Open file that I had you open just now. If you did type a word or two before closing the file, you see a dialog box that asks whether you want to save the changes you made before you close the file. Saving changes to a file is explained in detail in Lesson 2-2. For now, click the No button to tell Word 97 to close the file without saving any changes.

double-click =
press the left
mouse button
twice quickly

extra credit

Opening files from the Favorites folder

Clicking the Up One Level button and double-clicking folders in the Open dialog box to find a file you want to open can be a hassle, especially if the document is buried deep inside your computer. To make finding and opening files easier, Word 97 offers the Favorites folder.

By putting shortcuts to the folders and files you use most often in the Favorites folder, you can open files and folders much, much faster. Here's how to put a shortcut to the Office 101 folder in the Favorites folder:

1. **Choose File⇨Open, press Ctrl+O, or click the Open button so that the Open dialog box appears on-screen.**

2. **In the Open dialog box, find and display the Office 101 folder (the start of this lesson explains how).**

3. **Click the Office 101 folder to select it.**

4. **Click the Add to Favorites button in the Open dialog box.**

   You can see this button in Figure 1-2. When you click the button, a small menu appears with two options: Add 'Disk_vol1 (c:)' to Favorites or Add Selected Item to Favorites.

5. **Click Add Selected Item to Favorites, because you want to create a shortcut to the Office 101 folder, the item you selected in Step 3.**

6. **Still in the Open dialog box, click the Look in Favorites button (see Figure 1-2).**

   Word 97 takes you to the Favorites folder, where you see a shortcut icon to the Office 101 folder. Shortcut icons have little arrows in the lower-left corner.

7. **Double-click the Office 101 shortcut icon.**

   Word 97 takes you to the Office 101 folder. If you want to open a file in this folder, all you need to do is click the flilename and then click the Open button.

8. **Click the Cancel button or press Esc to leave the Open dialog box.**

Throughout this book, I ask you to open practice files in the Office 101 folder. Now that you have created a shortcut to that folder, you can get to the Office 101 folder quicker than you can say "Microsoft Office 97."

Recess

If you want to take a break right now, I don't blame you in the least. You're free to go to recess. But no pushing in the hallways. And if I catch any of you pulling hair, I'm sending you *straight* to the principal's office. By the way, if you want to turn the computer off, go right ahead (after you have closed all your programs, of course). But be sure to turn it on again and start Word 97 before you begin the next lesson.

Notes:

☑ **Progress Check**

If you can successfully perform the following tasks, you've mastered this lesson:

❑ Open a file.

❑ Use buttons in the Open dialog box.

❑ Close a file.

Lesson 1-3   Ways of Viewing Documents

Lesson 1-3 leaves the other Office 97 programs behind and starts focusing on Word 97, the word-processing program. As a matter of fact, this lesson focuses on the part of the program that your eyes focus on while you're word-processing: the Word 97 screen. This lesson also explains techniques for viewing documents.

You can view Word 97 documents in Normal View, Online Layout View, Page Layout View, and Full Screen View. You can also zoom in or out to make the words and letters bigger or smaller. To learn how to look at documents in different views and decide which view is best for you, follow these steps:

on the CD

1 **Start Word 97 (if the program isn't running already) and then open the View file in the Office 101 folder.**

The previous lesson in this book explains how to open a document, in case you've forgotten.

When I saved the View file after I created it, the document was in Normal View, so the document appears in Normal View when you open the file. When you are writing a first draft of a document and need to focus on the words, Normal View is the way to go.

2 **Click the Online Layout View button in the lower-left corner of the screen to change to Online Layout View.**

on the test

Another way to switch to Online Layout View is to choose View▷Online Layout. Now you see something extraordinary: The document changes color and a pair of scales appear. You can see page backgrounds only in Online Layout View. This view is designed for creating and viewing documents that people see online — that is, on computer screens. Use Online Layout View to design Web pages, for example.

Notice, however, that the scales in the View file appear out of place. In Normal View, you can't see graphics, and in Online Layout View, graphics do not appear in their rightful places. To place graphics correctly, you must view the document in Page Layout View.

3 **Choose View▷Page Layout.**

You can also get to Page Layout View by clicking the Page Layout View button. (In Online Layout View, however, the View buttons aren't available, because Word 97 wants more room for displaying documents.)

In Page Layout View, you can see precisely where the graphic (the scales) will appear when the document is printed. You can also see a header and the top of the page itself. Headers and footers, the lines of text that appear at the top and bottom of pages and list the title of the work, its author, and other pertinent information, only appear in Page Layout view. Do layout work in Page Layout view so you can see what your document will look like when it is printed.

4 **Click the Zoom drop-down list and choose 50%.**

As shown in Figure 1-3, the Zoom drop-down list is on the right side of the Standard toolbar. To open a drop-down list, click the little downward-pointing arrow that appears next to the list box.

Notes:

click the small downward-pointing arrow to open the Zoom drop-down list

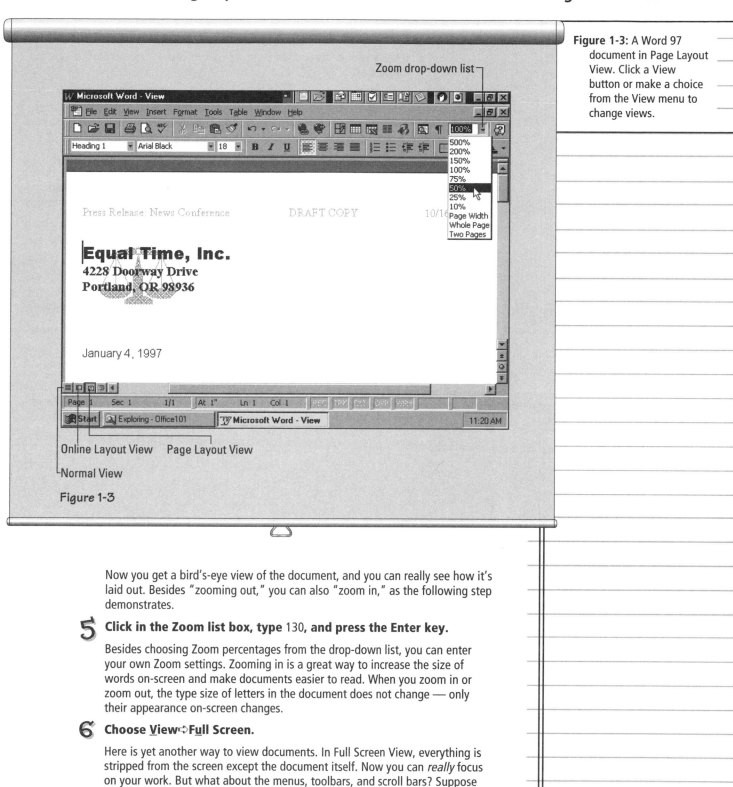

Zoom drop-down list

Figure 1-3: A Word 97 document in Page Layout View. Click a View button or make a choice from the View menu to change views.

Online Layout View   Page Layout View

Normal View

Figure 1-3

Now you get a bird's-eye view of the document, and you can really see how it's laid out. Besides "zooming out," you can also "zoom in," as the following step demonstrates.

5 Click in the Zoom list box, type 130, and press the Enter key.

Besides choosing Zoom percentages from the drop-down list, you can enter your own Zoom settings. Zooming in is a great way to increase the size of words on-screen and make documents easier to read. When you zoom in or zoom out, the type size of letters in the document does not change — only their appearance on-screen changes.

6 Choose View➪Full Screen.

Here is yet another way to view documents. In Full Screen View, everything is stripped from the screen except the document itself. Now you can *really* focus on your work. But what about the menus, toolbars, and scroll bars? Suppose that you want to choose a menu command?

☑ **Progress Check**

If you can perform the following tasks, you've mastered this lesson:

❑ Switch to Normal, Online Layout, Page Layout, and Full Screen Views.

❑ Zoom in and out on documents.

7 **Gently move the mouse pointer to the top of the screen to see the menu bar.**

The menu bar appears as the pointer touches the top of the screen. Now you can choose commands from the menu. Of course, you can also choose commands in Full Screen View by pressing Alt and a letter.

8 **Click the Close Full Screen button to leave Full Screen View.**

You land back where you started, in Page Layout View.

9 **Close the View file by choosing File↓Close and then click the No button when Word 97 asks whether you want to save your changes to the document.**

So ends the tour of views in Word 97. I hope the view was good from where you were sitting.

Lesson 1-4 Moving Around in Documents

Notes:

Word 97 files have a habit of getting longer. And the longer a document gets, the more difficult moving around inside the document becomes. Fasten your seat belt. This lesson explains tried-and-true techniques for getting around in Word 97 and other Office 97 files very quickly.

on the CD

To get from place to place in a document, you can press keys, use the scroll bars, or choose menu commands. Open the Hurry Up file in the Office 101 folder to practice moving around quickly in a file.

Pressing keys to get from place to place

Check out these keyboard techniques for moving around in files:

1 **Press and hold the → key.**

When you do this, the text cursor rockets through the text, first to the right side of the screen and then to the next line.

2 **Press and hold the ← key.**

The cursor rockets in the other direction. You can also press the ↑ or ↓ key to move the cursor up or down on-screen.

3 **With the cursor in the middle of a line, press the Home key.**

The cursor moves to the beginning of the line. To quickly move the cursor to the right side of a line, press the End key.

4 Press Ctrl+End.

The cursor moves to the end of the document. Look at the status bar along the bottom of the screen right above the taskbar. It reads, among other things, Page 18 and 18/18. You can always tell by glancing at the status bar what page the text cursor is on and how many pages are in the document. If the text cursor were on page 15, the status bar would read, Page 15 and 15/18.

5 Press Ctrl+Home.

Now you're at the very beginning of the document. In tandem with the Ctrl key, pressing an arrow key or a direction key such as End or Home gives the cursor an extra boost and makes the cursor travel far. Pressing Ctrl+←, for example, moves the cursor to the left an entire word, and pressing Ctrl+ → moves the cursor right an entire word.

6 Press PgDn and then PgUp.

Your view of the document moves down by the length of one screen and then up by the length of one screen.

Don't close the Hurry Up document just yet. You need this file to try out scroll bar techniques and Word 97 commands for moving around in documents.

Scroll bar techniques and commands for moving around in a document

Besides pressing keys, you can click the scroll bar and choose commands to get around in a long document. The *scroll bar* is the elevator shaft on the right side of the window. By clicking the arrow at the top or bottom, by dragging the *scroll box* — the elevator — you can get from place to place. Figure 1-4 shows the scroll bar. There is a second scroll bar along the bottom of the window for scrolling left and right.

1 Click the arrow that points down at the bottom of the scroll bar on the right side of the screen.

With each click, the screen scrolls down a line.

2 Click the arrow that points up at the top of the scroll bar.

By clicking the up arrow, you scroll the screen upward a line at a time.

3 Drag the scroll box down the scroll bar.

Drag means to click something — the scroll box, in this case — hold down the mouse button, roll the mouse pointer across the screen, and then release the mouse button after you finish dragging.

Now you're really moving. As you drag the scroll box down the scroll bar, a yellow box appears. It tells you to which page you're moving. (In the Hurry Up document, I assigned *styles* to headings, so the yellow box also lists headings as you scroll past them. I don't explain styles in this book, but I can tell you that you can format headings in documents by making choices from the Style menu on the Formatting toolbar.) When you are done dragging and release the mouse button, you see a new part of the document.

on the test

press Ctrl+End to go to the end of document

status bar=bar above taskbar that shows information about your file

press Ctrl+Home to go to the start of the document

drag = to click and hold down the mouse button and then move the pointer

Figure 1-4: Use the vertical scroll bar to move around quickly in a document.

Notes:

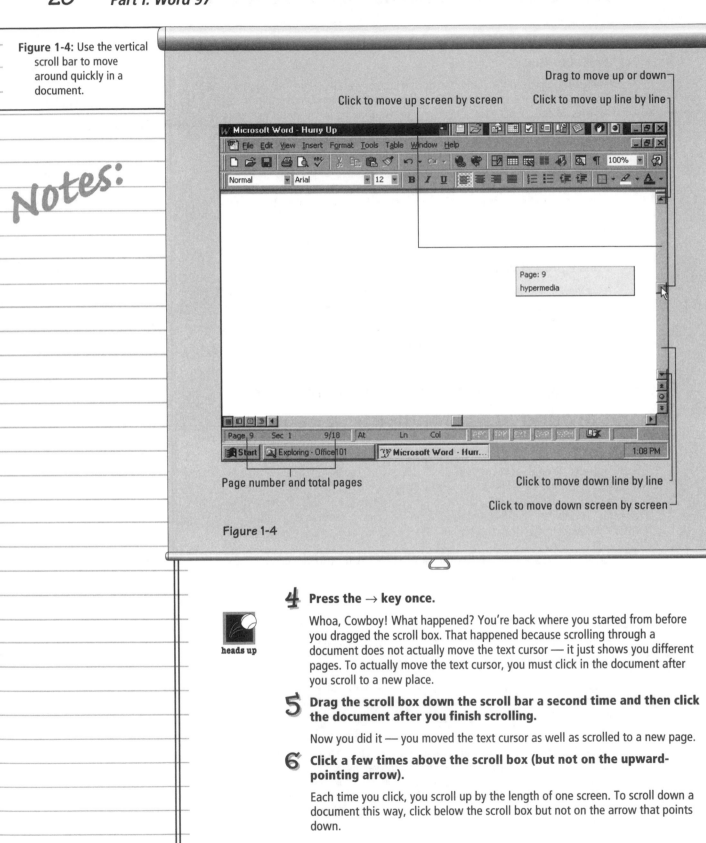

Drag to move up or down

Click to move up screen by screen

Click to move up line by line

Page: 9
hypermedia

Page number and total pages

Click to move down line by line

Click to move down screen by screen

Figure 1-4

4 Press the → key once.

heads up

Whoa, Cowboy! What happened? You're back where you started from before you dragged the scroll box. That happened because scrolling through a document does not actually move the text cursor — it just shows you different pages. To actually move the text cursor, you must click in the document after you scroll to a new place.

5 Drag the scroll box down the scroll bar a second time and then click the document after you finish scrolling.

Now you did it — you moved the text cursor as well as scrolled to a new page.

6 Click a few times above the scroll box (but not on the upward-pointing arrow).

Each time you click, you scroll up by the length of one screen. To scroll down a document this way, click below the scroll box but not on the arrow that points down.

7 **Click the Previous Page button directly below the scroll bar.**

The screen scrolls up by one page. The Previous Page button has two little arrows on it. Below this button lies the Select Browse Object button, a circle, and below that lies the Next Page button. Click the Next Page button to scroll down a page.

By clicking the Select Browse Object, you can scroll, not to the next page, but to other places in a document.

8 **Click the Select Browse Object button and then gently move the pointer over the Browse by buttons on the drop-down list that appears.**

After you click the button, a menu of Browse by buttons appears. By clicking one of these buttons, you can make the Previous Page and Next Page buttons take you through a document to the next field, endnote, footnote, comment, page, heading graphic, or table. You can also tell Word 97 to find text in a document or go to a specific page.

9 **Click the Browse by Heading button.**

As I mentioned earlier, I assigned heading styles to the headings in the Hurry Up document. You must have assigned styles to headings to browse by headings in a document.

10 **Click what used to be called the Previous Page button — the two little upward-pointing arrows.**

Now the button is blue, not black, and it is called the Previous Heading button. After you click it, you move to the previous heading in the document. Try clicking this button and the blue Next Heading button a few times.

If you want to make the buttons take you from page to page again instead of from heading to heading, click the Select Browse Object button again and choose Browse by Page.

11 **Choose Edit⇨Go To to see the Go To tab of the Find and Replace dialog box.**

From this dialog box, you can tell Word 97 to take you to a specific page. Word 97 offers two other ways to open this dialog box: Press Ctrl+G or click the Select Browse Object button and then click the Go To button.

12 **Type 8 in the Enter page number text box, click the Go To button, and then click Close or press Esc.**

You land safely on page 8 of the Hurry Up document. Close the Hurry Up document now and take a deep breath. (If you can't remember how to close a document, see Lesson 1-2.)

Between the keyboard shortcuts, the scroll bar techniques, and the Browse by buttons, you can surely get where you want to go in a hurry with Word 97.

Previous Page
button

☑ **Progress Check**

If you can perform the following tasks, you've mastered this lesson:

❑ Press keyboard shortcuts to move around in a file.

❑ Use the scroll bars to get from place to place.

❑ Use the Edit⇨Go To command.

Figure 1-5: Click the question mark in a dialog box and then click an option you want to know about.

Figure 1-6: The Index tab in the Help Topics dialog box works like the index of a book.

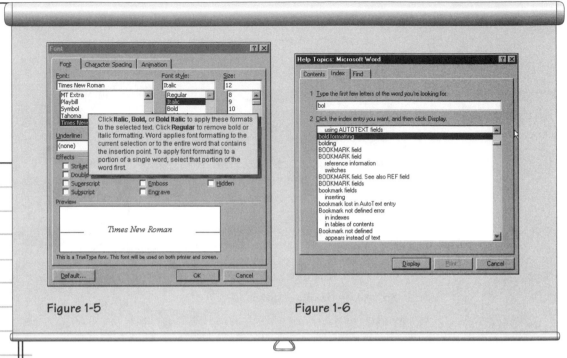

Figure 1-5   Figure 1-6

Lesson 1-5

Getting Help When You Need It

Dare I say that this slender book doesn't explain *every* task you can do in Office 97? I would need another thousand pages to explain everything. All is not lost, however, if you want to try something that isn't explained in this book, because you can always seek guidance from the Help program.

The makers of Office 97 understand the importance of helping the needy, so the Office 97 programs offer many ways to seek help. The following pages describe techniques for getting help with the commands and buttons in an Office 97 program and how to open and get help from the Help programs that come with Word 97, Excel 97, PowerPoint 97, Outlook, and Access 97.

Getting help with buttons and commands

on the test

To explore the ways to get help inside Word 97 and the other Office 97 programs, open Word 97, type a few words on-screen, and follow these steps:

1   Gently slide the pointer over a toolbar button.

The button's name appears in a small yellow or white box. If you know to press a button but aren't sure which one is which, you can find out a button's name this way. (If you don't see the yellow box, somebody's been playing with the toolbar settings. Choose View➪Toolbars➪Customize, click the Options tab in the Customize dialog box, click the Show ScreenTips on Toolbars check box, and then click Close.)

2 **Choose Help⇨What's This or press Shift+F1.**

You see the Help cursor, a pointer with a question mark beside it. As long as you see the Help cursor, you can click a part of the screen to see what it does.

3 **Click a toolbar button.**

A lengthy description of the button appears in a handy yellow box. Besides clicking part of the screen, you can also click text to find out how it has been formatted.

4 **Choose Help⇨What's This or press Shift+F1 again, but this time click the words you typed on-screen.**

A gray box tells you how the paragraph you typed is formatted and in which font the characters appear. If you have trouble telling how text is formatted, click the Help cursor in the text.

5 **Press Esc to shake off the Help cursor.**

Now you're back where you started and can check out another technique for getting Help.

6 **Choose Format⇨Font to open the Font dialog box.**

In the upper-right corner of dialog boxes you see a question mark. By clicking the question mark and then clicking a dialog box option, you can find out what the option is good for.

7 **Click the question mark in the Font dialog box and then click the text box or list box under Font Style.**

As Figure 1-5 shows, a yellow box appears with a synopsis of the Word 97 font styles. If you don't know what an option does or are searching for an option in a dialog box, you can get help this way.

8 **Click Cancel or press Esc to close the Font dialog box.**

Now you will open the Word 97 Help program to seek Help. Read on.

Getting help in an Office 97 program

These techniques for accessing Help in any Office 97 program serve you whether you're working in Word 97, Excel 97, PowerPoint 97, Outlook, or Access 97. To access the Help program, follow these steps:

1 **Choose Help⇨Contents and Index.**

The Help dialog box offers two tabs that are very useful for finding Help: the Contents and Index tabs.

2 **Click the Contents tab, if necessary, and then double-click one of the book icons.**

Beside each book icon is a topic name. After you find a topic that interests you, double-click its book icon. You see either more book icons or question mark icons with subtopic names beside them. I hope the subject you need help with is listed here. If not, click the down arrow on the scroll bar to view more topics and subtopics.

Help cursor

Notes:

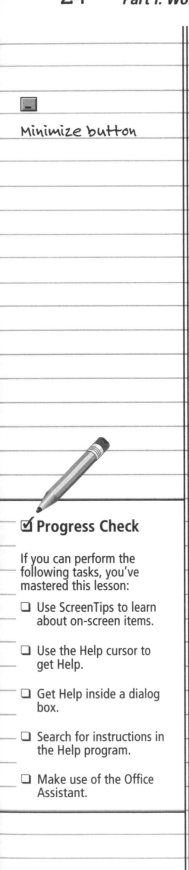

Minimize button

☑ **Progress Check**

If you can perform the following tasks, you've mastered this lesson:

❑ Use ScreenTips to learn about on-screen items.

❑ Use the Help cursor to get Help.

❑ Get Help inside a dialog box.

❑ Search for instructions in the Help program.

❑ Make use of the Office Assistant.

3 Double-click a subtopic icon.

The Help program opens and displays a list of instructions. Notice that the Help program appears in its own window. If you want, you can click the Word 97 document, start working away, and read instructions from the Help window as you go. Or you can click the Help window's Minimize button and, if you need instructions, click the Help program button on the taskbar to see the instructions again.

4 Click the Help Topics button in the Help window.

You return to the Help Topics dialog box, where you can get Help another way.

5 Click the Index tab.

As shown in Figure 1-6, you see the Index tab. On the Index tab, topics are arranged in alphabetical order, as they are in the index of a book.

6 In the text box (box 1), type the name of a topic you are interested in.

The list of topics in box 2 scrolls to the topic you entered — or to a similarly spelled topic if your topic isn't on the list. To get to a topic, you can either type its name or use the scroll bar on the right side of box 2.

7 Double-click a topic in the list in box 2 or click a topic in the list and then click the Display button.

A new set of instructions appears in the Help program window.

8 Click the Back button in the Help program window.

By clicking this nifty button, you can go back to the Help screen you saw previously — in this case, the one you got to by way of the Contents tab. Click the Back button if you're investigating several topics at once and you want to backtrack.

9 Click the Close button to exit the Help program.

Now you can test the Office Assistant, the other means of getting Help in Office 97.

10 Click the Office Assistant button or press F1.

The Office Assistant button is the rightmost button on the Standard toolbar (it has a light bulb and a balloon with a question mark on it). After you click the button, the Office Assistant, an animated figure you're likely to find either indispensable or pesky, depending on your point of view, appears on-screen.

Under `What would you like to do?`, you can type a question, click the Search button, and pray for an answer.

11 Type a question in the white box in the Office Assistant window and hope for the best.

Questions should be short and to the point. The Office Assistant is not particularly intelligent. With luck, an answer to your question appears on-screen. (Personally, I think the Office Assistant is a bother, but you may like the feature.)

12 Click the Office Assistant's Close button (the X in the upper-right corner) to make the Office Assistant leave the screen.

So ends our foray into the Help program. Very soon, you will become a crackerjack user of Office 97 and find yourself delving into the Help program to discover how to do new things. Happy hunting!

Unit 1 Quiz

For the following questions, circle the letter of the correct answer or answers. This short quiz is designed to help you remember what you learned in Unit 1. Each question may have more than one right answer.

1. **Where is the taskbar located?**

   A. Beside the toolbars.

   B. Beside the scroll bar.

   C. In the gym.

   D. Along the bottom of the screen.

   E. In a corner of the garage.

2. **To start an Office 97 program, you perform this action:**

   A. Press F1 and ask the Office Assistant for Help.

   B. Shake the Magic 8-Ball.

   C. Click the Start button on the taskbar, choose Programs, and then choose the Office 97 program you want to open.

   D. Choose File➪Open.

   E. None of the above.

3. **To open a file, you perform the following action:**

   A. Grab the handle on the file cabinet and give the drawer a pull.

   B. Choose File➪Open, find and click the file's name in the Open dialog box, and then click the Open button.

   C. Click the File menu to open it, and if the file is one the four listed at the bottom of the menu, click the file's name in the menu.

   D. Choose File➪New.

   E. B and C.

4. **Where are the Word 97 View buttons on the screen?**

   A. In the lower-left corner of the screen.

   B. On the toolbar below the menu bar.

   C. Where the view is best.

   D. On the View menu.

   E. Way up there in the right corner of the screen.

Notes:

5. **To go quickly to the start of a document, press which of the following:**

   A. F1.

   B. Home.

   C. The ↑ key.

   D. Ctrl+Home.

   E. Close and then open the document real fast.

6. **To move through a document with the scroll bar along the right side of the screen, you perform the following action:**

   A. Click the down arrow to move down a line at a time.

   B. Click the scroll bar to move a screen at a time.

   C. Drag the scroll box.

   D. Click the up arrow to move up a line at a time.

   E. All the above.

7. **Which of the following techniques for getting Help in Office 97 costs $30?**

   A. Pressing F1.

   B. Choosing Help⇨Contents and Index.

   C. Choosing Help⇨What's This.

   D. Calling Microsoft Tech Support at (206) 635-4948.

   E. Clicking the question mark button in a dialog box.

Unit 1 Exercise

on the CD

1. Close and then reopen Word 97.

2. Open the file called Open in the Office 101 folder.

3. Switch to Page Layout View.

4. Move to the bottom of the document by using the vertical scroll bar and then read the secret message in the footer.

5. Move to the top of the document by pressing keys.

6. Get Help on the following topics: fonts, menus, and footers. (You can use any method you want to find Help.)

7. Close the Open document and click No after Word 97 asks whether you want to save your changes.

Creating a Document

Objectives for This Unit

✓ Creating and saving your own documents

✓ Entering text

✓ Selecting, copying, moving, and deleting text

✓ Fixing mistakes in a document

✓ Changing the appearance and size of text

Prerequisites

▶ Starting Word 97 (Lesson 1-1)

▶ Opening a file (Lesson 1-2)

▶ Moving around in documents (Lesson 1-4)

on the CD

▶ Club Select

▶ Moving Sale

▶ Delete Me

▶ Fonts and Things

▶ Quiz 2

The last unit was a bit of a tease. In its pages, I showed you how to start Word 97, open a file, view a file, and move around in a file — but I didn't give you the chance to get your hands dirty and actually do any work. Sorry about that. To make it up to you, this unit plunges right into the nitty-gritty of word-processing. *Word-processing,* by the way, is just a fancy word for writing letters or reports with a computer program.

In this unit, you learn how to create a document of your own, how to save it, and how to name it. Then you discover how to enter text and manipulate words to your heart's content. I show you, for example, how to delete, copy, and move text. I also show you how to change fonts, also known as *typefaces,* and change the size of text as well. You also discover how to fix editing blunders, in case you're prone to making mistakes, and who isn't prone to making mistakes when they are sitting in front of a computer?

Lesson 2-1

Creating, Saving, and Naming a New Document

In this lesson, you create a document, save the document, and name it after a very important person — yourself. When you save a document or file for the first time, Word 97 gives you the opportunity to name it. So you really do two things at once when you save a document: You save it and name it.

heads up

You can use the same techniques for saving and naming a file in all the Office 97 applications. Saving and naming files are to computers what eating bread and drinking water are to humanity.

To follow this lesson, begin by starting Word 97 (if you haven't already done so). The program opens to an empty document with the word *Document1* in the title bar. The *title bar* is the stripe along the top of the screen. It lists the name of the program you are working in and a file. After you are finished saving a document in this lesson, your name will appear in the title bar.

To create, name, and save a document, follow these steps:

1 **Click the New button, the leftmost button on the Standard toolbar.**

You can also create a new document by pressing Ctrl+N or by choosing File⇨New. The New button and Ctrl+N take you straight to a new, empty document. Choosing File⇨New, however, leads to the New dialog box, where you choose a template for creating a document.

After you get good with Word 97, you might experiment with templates. A *template* is a set of formats. Instead of creating formats for headings, tables, indentations, and whatnot yourself, you can let the pros at Microsoft do it for you by creating a document from a template.

Notice that the title bar now reads Document2. You're going to change that in a moment.

2 **Type a word or two in your new document.**

Soon you will see how Word 97 grabs text from documents and uses that text for document names.

3 **Click the Save button on the Standard toolbar to tell Word 97 that you want to save your new document.**

Besides clicking the Save button, you can press Ctrl+S or choose File⇨Save to save a file. The Save As dialog box appears, as shown in Figure 2-1. This dialog box is where you give your new file a name and tell Word 97 in which folder to save the file.

For this lesson, you will save your new file in the Office 101 folder, but you can save a file in any folder you wish. To choose a folder in the Save As dialog box, you use the same techniques you use to locate a folder in the Open dialog box. (Lesson 1-2 explains how to perform that task.)

---

title bar = stripe on top of screen

New button

Save button

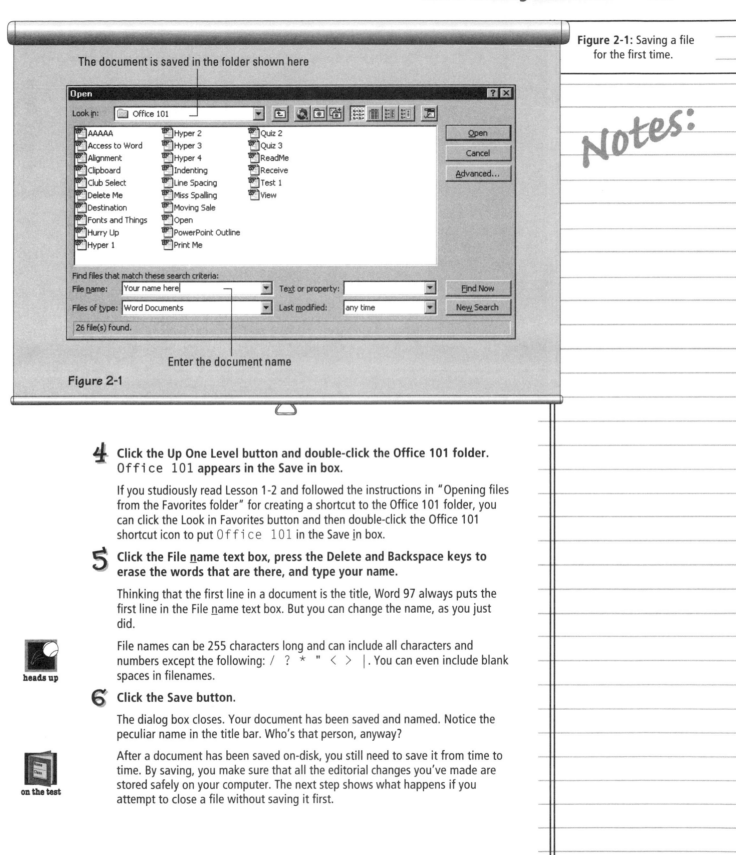

The document is saved in the folder shown here

Enter the document name

Figure 2-1

Figure 2-1: Saving a file for the first time.

Notes:

4 Click the Up One Level button and double-click the Office 101 folder. Office 101 appears in the Save in box.

If you studiously read Lesson 1-2 and followed the instructions in "Opening files from the Favorites folder" for creating a shortcut to the Office 101 folder, you can click the Look in Favorites button and then double-click the Office 101 shortcut icon to put Office 101 in the Save in box.

5 Click the File name text box, press the Delete and Backspace keys to erase the words that are there, and type your name.

Thinking that the first line in a document is the title, Word 97 always puts the first line in the File name text box. But you can change the name, as you just did.

heads up

File names can be 255 characters long and can include all characters and numbers except the following: / ? * " < > |. You can even include blank spaces in filenames.

6 Click the Save button.

The dialog box closes. Your document has been saved and named. Notice the peculiar name in the title bar. Who's that person, anyway?

on the test

After a document has been saved on-disk, you still need to save it from time to time. By saving, you make sure that all the editorial changes you've made are stored safely on your computer. The next step shows what happens if you attempt to close a file without saving it first.

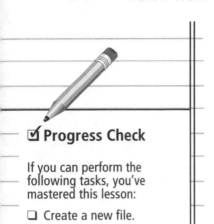

☑ **Progress Check**

If you can perform the following tasks, you've mastered this lesson:

❑ Create a new file.

❑ Save a file.

7 **Type a couple words in the document and then choose File⇨Close — as if you were closing the file.**

You hear a beep, and a dialog box appears on-screen and asks if you want to save the changes you just made before you close the file. This dialog box is the program's way of telling you that you need to save your document if you want it back in its present form the next time you open it. If you click Yes in this dialog box, Word 97 saves the document before closing it, but if you click No, Word 97 closes the document without saving your most recent changes.

8 **Click Cancel or press Esc to tell Word 97 that you want to keep working on the file after all.**

You need this document to complete Lesson 2-2. Good thing you clicked Cancel or pressed Esc.

9 **Click the Save button.**

After you clicked the Save button on the Standard toolbar back in Step 3, Word 97 showed you the Save As dialog box, but not now. You saved and named the document already, so now you hear only the grinding sound of your recent editorial changes being saved. You can also press Ctrl+S or choose File⇨Save to save a document you've saved and named already.

Lesson 2-2   Entering and Editing Text

The last lesson had you create a file, name your document after a very important person, and then save the file. In this lesson, you try out basic editing techniques on your new file. The techniques described here are ones you use whenever you work on a Word 97 document.

Follow these steps to learn how to enter text and make basic editorial changes:

1 **Click somewhere in the middle of the text you entered in the last lesson and then press the Del or Delete key a few times.**

Pressing the Del key or Delete key erases characters to the right of the cursor. The Del key is located in the lower-right corner of the keyboard. You will find the Delete key to the right of the Enter key.

Suppose that you want to erase characters to the left of the cursor.

on the test

2 **Press the Backspace key once or twice.**

Now the characters to the cursor's left disappear. Not coincidentally, the Backspace key is the one with an arrow that points left on it. The Backspace key is right above the Enter key. Pressing Del and Backspace are the principle ways of erasing text. (In Lesson 2-5, I show you a speed technique for erasing gobs and gobs of text at once.)

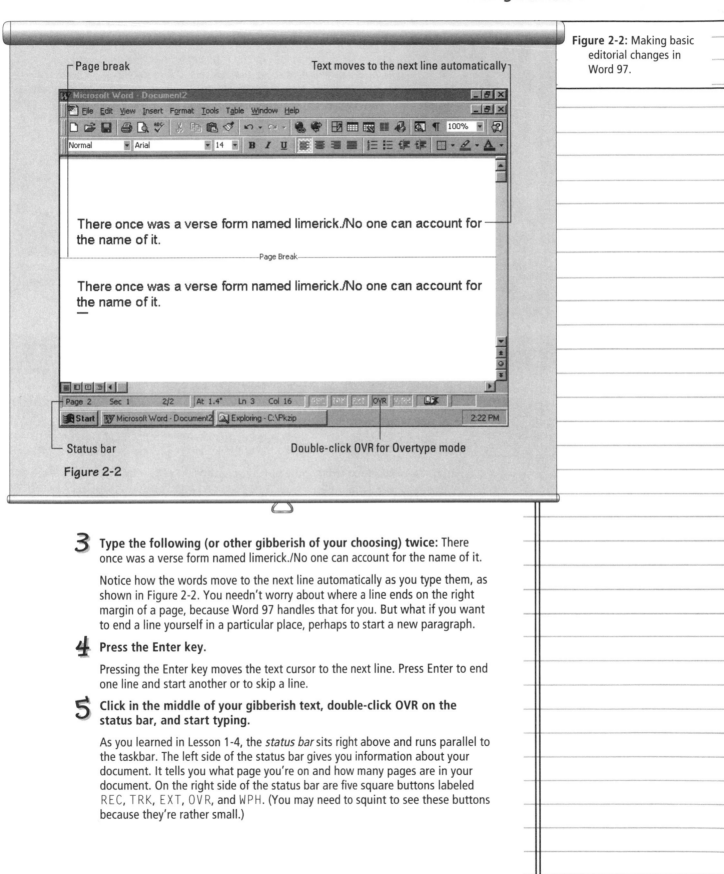

Page break

Text moves to the next line automatically

There once was a verse form named limerick./No one can account for the name of it.

──────Page Break──────

There once was a verse form named limerick./No one can account for the name of it.

Status bar

Double-click OVR for Overtype mode

Figure 2-2

Figure 2-2: Making basic editorial changes in Word 97.

3 **Type the following (or other gibberish of your choosing) twice:** There once was a verse form named limerick./No one can account for the name of it.

Notice how the words move to the next line automatically as you type them, as shown in Figure 2-2. You needn't worry about where a line ends on the right margin of a page, because Word 97 handles that for you. But what if you want to end a line yourself in a particular place, perhaps to start a new paragraph.

4 **Press the Enter key.**

Pressing the Enter key moves the text cursor to the next line. Press Enter to end one line and start another or to skip a line.

5 **Click in the middle of your gibberish text, double-click OVR on the status bar, and start typing.**

As you learned in Lesson 1-4, the *status bar* sits right above and runs parallel to the taskbar. The left side of the status bar gives you information about your document. It tells you what page you're on and how many pages are in your document. On the right side of the status bar are five square buttons labeled REC, TRK, EXT, OVR, and WPH. (You may need to squint to see these buttons because they're rather small.)

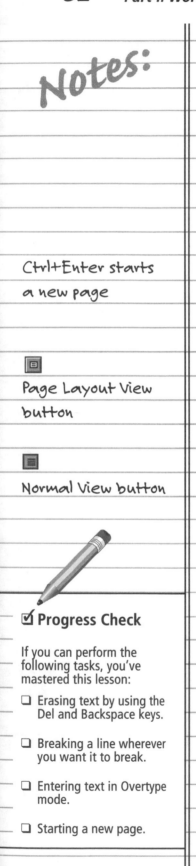

Ctrl+Enter starts
a new page

Page Layout View
button

Normal View button

☑ **Progress Check**

If you can perform the
following tasks, you've
mastered this lesson:

❑ Erasing text by using the
  Del and Backspace keys.

❑ Breaking a line wherever
  you want it to break.

❑ Entering text in Overtype
  mode.

❑ Starting a new page.

heads up

OVR stands for *Overtype*. Normally as you enter text, the characters you enter push aside the ones that are already there, but if you double-click OVR, the letters you type swallow the other letters. Double-click OVR to enter text and erase existing text at the same time. And don't forget to double-click OVR again when you are done. It would be frustrating to watch letters gobble other letters when you don't want that to happen.

6 **Double-click OVR again to get out of overtype mode.**

Now the letters OVR on the status bar grow dim again. In Step 4, you learned how to press the Enter key to end a line abruptly or skip a line. The next step shows how to end a page abruptly.

7 **Press Ctrl+Enter.**

To perform this action, press and hold the Ctrl key as you press the Enter key. In Normal View, the words Page Break and a dotted line appear on-screen in case you have any doubt that you really ended one page and started another, as shown in Figure 2-2. In Page Layout View, you can actually see the top of the new page. Besides pressing Ctrl+Enter, you can create a *page break* by choosing Insert⇨Break and then clicking OK in the Break dialog box.

Pressing Ctrl+Enter does this much faster.

8 **Click the Page Layout View button in the lower-left corner of the screen to switch to Page Layout View, if you are not already in Page Layout View.**

As Lesson 1-3 explained, you can also switch to Page Layout View by choosing View⇨Page Layout. Now you see beyond a shadow of a doubt that you entered a page break, because the top of the second page appears on-screen.

9 **Click the Normal View button to get back to Normal view, click the dotted line that forms the page break, and then press the Del key.**

Your page break is gone and you're back to a single-page document. In this book I'm going to tell you not only how to complete a task, but how to "uncomplete" it, too.

10 **Save and close the document you named after yourself for posterity.**

You don't need the document for the next lesson.

Back in Step 3, I had you type, "There once was a verse form named limerick./No one can account for the name of it. The rest of the limerick goes: Some think from a game/Or from poets it came./If you know please come up to Limerick."

Selecting Text

on the test

Knowing how to select text is very important, because you can't move or copy text until you select it. Nor can you delete gobs of text without selecting all that text first. And if you want to change characters from one font to another, you must select the characters. I could give you 101 reasons why selecting text is important, so knowing the many shortcuts for selecting text is useful indeed.

on the CD

For this lesson in selecting text, open the Club Select document in the Office 101 folder. After each numbered step that follows, click in the document. By clicking, you "unselect" text that the numbered steps that follow tell you to select. After you have "unselected" text, you can go on to the next step and learn another technique for selecting text.

1 Move the pointer into the left margin, hold down the Ctrl key, and then click once to select the entire document.

To do this correctly, you must click when the pointer is aimed toward the upper-right corner of the screen, not the upper-left corner. You know when text is selected because it is highlighted on-screen. You can also select an entire document by triple-clicking in the left margin, choosing Edit⇨Select All, or pressing Ctrl+A.

2 Drag the cursor across a few words to select them.

Drag means to click, hold down the mouse button, and slide the cursor across the screen. Notice how Word 97 selects a word at a time, not a letter at a time, as you drag the mouse.

on the test

3 Click once in the left margin to select a line of text.

Again, the pointer must be aimed at the upper-right corner of the screen as you click for this technique and all other selection techniques to work.

4 Double-click a word to select it.

5 Double-click in the left margin to select an entire paragraph.

6 Click in the left margin and drag the cursor downward or upward to select several lines at once.

As you drag, you select the lines to the right of the mouse pointer.

Suppose you select a bunch of text and realize that you selected too much or too little. In that case, you can call on the EXT button on the status bar. EXT (the letters stand for "extend") is in the middle of the five buttons.

7 Double-click EXT on the status bar and then click different places on-screen or press the ↑ or ↓ key.

Notice how the amount of text you selected changes. Besides double-clicking EXT to "extend" a selection, you can press F8.

Margin note (handwritten):
drag = to click and hold down the mouse button and roll the cursor across the screen

8 **Press Ctrl+End.**

Now you have selected everything from the start of the original selection to the end of the document. Lesson 1-4 described keyboard techniques for moving the cursor up, down, and back and forth in a document. After you press F8 or double-click EXT, the keyboard shortcuts for moving the cursor in a document also work for selecting text.

9 **Double-click EXT or press F8 and then click in the document.**

To stop extending a selection, you must double-click EXT or press F8 again.

Close the Club Select document. In the next two lessons about copying, moving, and deleting text, you find out how useful these selection techniques really are.

Lesson 2-4 # Copying and Moving Text

The last lesson taught you how to select text. After you select text, you can move it elsewhere or copy it to a new place in a document.

Copying and moving text are two of the most common word-processing chores. After this lesson, you will never need to retype text that you entered in the wrong place, because you will simply move it. And instead of retyping long addresses and difficult-to-spell names, you will simply type them once and then copy them to new places.

Moving text to new places

on the CD

Word 97 offers many techniques for moving text. To find out about these techniques, open the Moving Sale document in the Office 101 folder and follow these steps:

1 **Select the second word in the title, Moving, by double-clicking it.**

Obviously, this word is in the wrong place. In the next step, you drag the word to the left of Sale, where it belongs.

2 **Press and hold down the left mouse button, drag the word Moving to the left of Sale, and then release the mouse button.**

on the test

As you drag, a square appears below the pointer, and a vertical line shows you precisely where you are moving the text you selected. Moving text this way is called *dragging and dropping*. It isn't the only way to move text, however.

3 **Select the second paragraph by double-clicking in the margin to its left.**

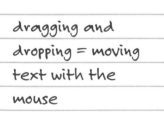

dragging and dropping = moving text with the mouse

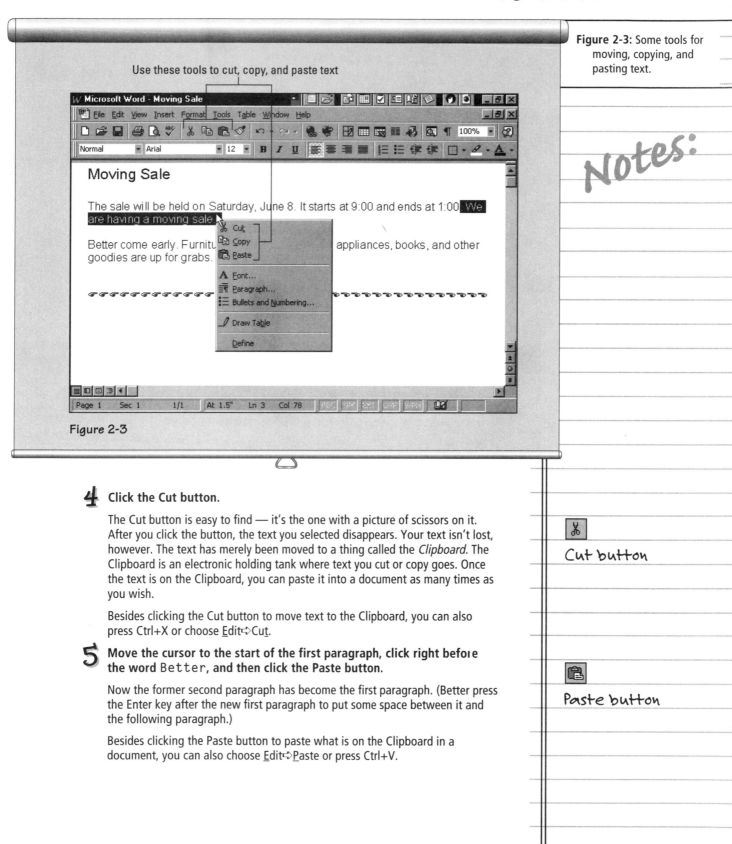

Use these tools to cut, copy, and paste text

Figure 2-3

Figure 2-3: Some tools for moving, copying, and pasting text.

Notes:

4 **Click the Cut button.**

The Cut button is easy to find — it's the one with a picture of scissors on it. After you click the button, the text you selected disappears. Your text isn't lost, however. The text has merely been moved to a thing called the *Clipboard.* The Clipboard is an electronic holding tank where text you cut or copy goes. Once the text is on the Clipboard, you can paste it into a document as many times as you wish.

Besides clicking the Cut button to move text to the Clipboard, you can also press Ctrl+X or choose Edit⇨Cut.

5 **Move the cursor to the start of the first paragraph, click right before the word** Better**, and then click the Paste button.**

Now the former second paragraph has become the first paragraph. (Better press the Enter key after the new first paragraph to put some space between it and the following paragraph.)

Besides clicking the Paste button to paste what is on the Clipboard in a document, you can also choose Edit⇨Paste or press Ctrl+V.

Cut button

Paste button

right-click = press the right mouse button

6 **Drag over the last sentence in the first paragraph,** We are having a moving sale, **to select it and then right-click the sentence you just selected.**

Right-click means to press the right mouse button, not the left one. After you right-click, you see a shortcut menu that includes the Cut, Copy, and Paste commands, as shown in Figure 2-3.

7 **Slide the pointer to the first command on the menu, Cut, and then click.**

You just cut the sentence you selected earlier to the Clipboard.

8 **Click to the left of the word** The **at the start of the paragraph, right-click, and then choose Paste from the shortcut menu.**

Besides cutting and pasting by using toolbar buttons, menu commands, key presses, and drag and drop, you can move text by right-clicking and using the shortcut menu.

Keep the Moving Sales document open. You need this document for the rest of this lesson.

Copying and pasting text

The techniques for copying text work identically to the ones for cutting text. The difference is that text isn't removed from the document when you copy it. The text is copied to the Clipboard, not moved there. Follow these steps to try out techniques for copying text:

1 **Select the title at the top of the document and press Ctrl+C.**

You can also click the Copy button or choose Edit➪Copy to copy text. The title is now copied to the Clipboard.

Copy button

2 **Click the document just below the pointing-finger symbols and press Ctrl+V.**

You just copied the text to a new place. I guess you know by now that you can also paste what is on the Clipboard by clicking the Paste button or by choosing Edit➪Paste. Now try the drag-and-drop method of copying text.

3 **Click the left margin beside the first line of text under the title of the document and then drag the cursor southward until you reach the bottom of the document.**

The text is highlighted and ready to be copied.

4 **Press and hold the Ctrl key, click the selected text, drag the text to the bottom of the screen, below the title that you already copied there, and then release the mouse button.**

press Ctrl to copy text with the drag-and-drop method

Except for holding the Ctrl key, copying text by using the drag-and-drop method works the same as does moving text by using the drag-and-drop method. As you drag, a square with a cross in it appears below the pointer, and the vertical line shows you where the text is going to "drop" after you release the mouse button.

In the next step, you try an experiment that demonstrates how the Clipboard works.

5 **Click the Paste button.**

Interestingly, the text you dragged and dropped in Step 4 isn't pasted into the document. Instead, you see the title that you copied to the Clipboard in Step 1. Why is that?

heads up

Text is cut or copied to the Clipboard after you choose the Cut and Copy commands, click the Cut or Copy button, or press Ctrl+X or Ctrl+C. When you move or copy text by dragging and dropping it, however, the text isn't placed on the Clipboard.

If you copied a complicated graphic or address to the Clipboard, you could keep it there and still copy and move text by using the drag-and-drop method. When you wanted to insert the graphic or address, it would still be on the Clipboard, ready and willing. You wouldn't have to copy it all over again each time you wanted to paste it in your document.

6 **Triple-click in the left margin or press Ctrl+A to select the entire document.**

The next three steps demonstrate a *very* practical application of the copy commands.

7 **Right-click in the document and choose Copy from the shortcut menu.**

8 **Click the New button or press Ctrl+N to start a new document.**

9 **Right-click in the new document and choose Paste from the shortcut menu.**

You just copied an entire document. In "Copying one document into another," you discover a cleaner way to copy an entire file, but in any case, you should know that text can be cut or copied and pasted into other documents and even into other Windows-based programs. You could, for example, copy a long-winded passage from a Word 97 document and paste the passage into Excel 97 or PowerPoint 97.

10 **Close the Moving Sale document and click No after Word 97 asks whether you want to save your changes.**

If you intend to read "Copying one document into another," don't close the Moving Sales document. Otherwise, go ahead and close the file now.

extra credit

Copying one document into another

The fastest, cleanest, most wholesome way to copy an entire document into another is to choose Insert⇨File. Here's how:

1. Put the cursor where you want the file to be inserted.

2. Choose Insert⇨File.

You see the Insert File dialog box. (I hope it looks familiar. This dialog box looks like and works exactly

the same as the Open dialog box you learned about in Lesson 1-2.)

3. Click the Up One Level button and double-click folders until you arrive at the folder where the file you want to copy is located.

4. To insert the file, either double-click its name in the dialog box list or click the name and then click the OK button.

Notes:

New button

☑ **Progress Check**

If you can perform the following tasks, you've mastered this lesson:

❏ Move and copy text by using toolbar buttons, menu commands, and keystrokes.

❏ Move and copy text by using the shortcut menus.

❏ Move and copy text by dragging and dropping it.

Recess

You covered a lot of ground in the last handful of pages. You learned how to save and name a file, edit a document, and copy and move text. You deserve a break. In fact, if anyone deserves a break, it's you. Take the rest of the day off. Take a hot bath. Then rent an old Clark Gable movie and marvel at how dashing people were in the old days.

Lesson 2-5

Deleting Text

Notes:

Back in Lesson 2-2, you learned how to delete a character at a time by pressing the Del or Backspace key. What if you're in a hurry and want to delete a bunch of text? This lesson explains how.

And if you diligently learned all you needed to learn from Lesson 2-3 about selecting text, you are going to find this lesson very easy. Because all you have to do to delete text after you have selected it is press the Del key.

on the CD

To learn how to delete sentences, whole paragraphs, and even an entire document with the wave of a hand, open the Delete Me file in the Office 101 folder and follow these steps:

1 **Select a word in the middle of the first paragraph and press the Del key.**

To select a word, double-click it. After you press the Del key, the word disappears.

2 **Press F8, press End to select everything from the cursor to the end of the line of text, and press Del.**

Now that text is gone, too.

3 **Select what's left of the first paragraph and the entire second paragraph and then press Del.**

Remember that you can select lines of text by clicking the left margin and dragging the cursor downward or upward. The next step teaches you a shortcut for deleting text and entering text at the same time.

4 **Select the next paragraph and type** Gotcha!

The paragraph disappears and you are left with the word you typed. You just killed two birds with one stone. One way to delete text is to select the text and simply type what you want to appear in its place.

5 **Choose** <u>E</u>dit⇨Select A<u>l</u>l **and press the Del key.**

Now you're left with a blank screen. Suppose that you regret deleting this text? How can you get it back? Good question. Better leave the Delete Me file open and read "Undoing a mistake."

extra credit

Undoing a mistake

Everybody makes mistakes, so Word 97 offers a means of reversing errors. By clicking the Undo button, by making choices from the Undo drop-down list, and by choosing Edit⇨Undo, you can return a document to the pristine state it was in before you made an error. Follow these steps to "undelete" the text you deleted at the start of this lesson:

1. **Click the Undo button.**

   The paragraphs you last deleted return to the document. By clicking Undo, you can delete your most recent action.

2. **Click the down-arrow beside the Undo button to open the Undo drop-down list.**

   On this list are the last 99 things you did to your document — if, of course, you did as many as 99 things. In the case of the Delete Me file, Typing "Gotcha!" appears at the top of the list. If this list were long, you'd need to scroll to get to the bottom.

3. **Click Typing "Gotcha!" on the drop-down list.**

   "Gotcha!" is removed from the document, and the paragraph you typed over when you typed "Gotcha!" is revived.

4. **Choose Edit⇨Undo Clear.**

   Now you get the second paragraph and half of the first paragraph back. The Edit⇨Undo command works like the Undo button. It reverses the change you most recently made.

5. **Click the Undo drop-down list and click the second Clear on the list.**

   Notice that, after you move the cursor over the second Clear, the bottom of the drop-down list reads Undo Two Actions. By clicking the second, third, fourth, or whatever action on the list, you can undo two, three, four, or however many actions.

6. **Click the Redo button five times to delete the parts of the document again.**

   Redo is the button to the right of Undo. The Redo button "redoes" what you "undid." The button works the same as the Undo button and has its own drop-down list. Click Redo if you "undo" something and decide you didn't want it undone. You can also choose Edit⇨Redo to redo an undid, if you'll pardon my French.

With the Undo and Redo commands, you can fix most of the mistakes you make in documents.

☑ Progress Check

If you can perform the following tasks, you've mastered this lesson:

❑ Delete text by using the Del key.

❑ Delete text by selecting and typing.

Changing Fonts and Character Styles

Lesson 2-6

So far in this unit you've learned the basic editing techniques you need to write the first draft of a document. But man does not live by bread alone, and neither does woman, so this lesson explains how to dress up a document. After

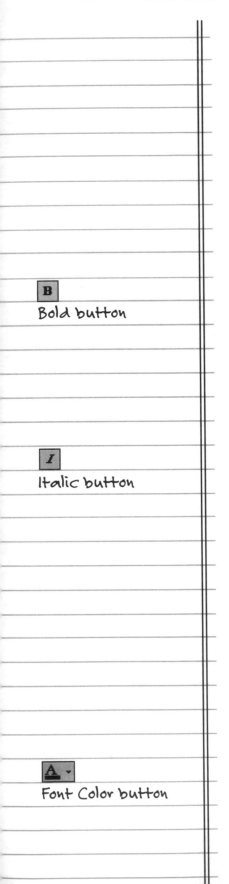

B

Bold button

I

Italic button

A ▾

Font Color button

you write your important words, you can give them even more power by changing their appearance on the page. This lesson explains how to use fonts and character styles to attract your readers' attention and make them want to read your documents first.

A *font* is a typeface design of a particular style and format. For example, it might interest you to know that the main text in this book is laid out in Berkely font. Besides choosing a font for text, you can change its size, as well as **boldface it**, *italicize it,* or <u>underline it</u>. You can also choose what Word 97 calls *text effects,* including embossing and engraving. You have a lot to learn here. Better get going.

To learn about fonts and character styles, open the Fonts and Things file in the Office 101 folder and do the following:

1 Select line 1 (not the title at the top of the page) and click the Bold button on the toolbar.

The text is boldfaced. Boldfaced text is heavier than regular text. It is almost always used in headings, including the headings in this book. Use it when you want text to stand out on the page. You can also press Ctrl+B to apply boldface to text.

By the way, you don't have to select text to change its appearance. For example, you could click the Bold button and then start typing to boldface text. But I think it is better to write the first draft in plain text and then agonize over fonts, character styles, and text effects.

2 Select line 2 and press Ctrl+I.

This line is italicized. You can also click the Italic button to italicize text. By convention, italics show emphasis, but don't go overboard with italics or else *readers may think that you're screaming at them!* Foreign words are always set in italics, *n'est-ce pas?*

3 Select line 3, click the down arrow beside the Font drop-down list on the Formatting toolbar, scroll to the bottom of the list, if necessary, and find and click Times New Roman.

Times New Roman is a font. Notice how the characters in line 3 have changed. All the fonts that are available on your computer system can be found on the Font drop-down list. Word 97 puts the fonts you have used so far in the document at the top of the list so you can get to them faster.

4 Select line 4, choose Arial from the Font drop-down list on the Formatting toolbar, click the down arrow next to the Font Size drop-down list on the Standard toolbar, and choose 16 from the list.

The text is now laid out in the Arial font and is now 16 *points* high. The larger the point size, the taller and wider the text. To change the size of text, use the Font Size drop-down list.

5 Select line 5, click the down arrow beside the Font Color button on the Formatting toolbar to open the drop-down list, and click the Blue square.

The Font Color button is the rightmost button on the Formatting toolbar. By clicking a button from the drop-down list, you can change the color of characters. As you slide the pointer across the squares, a yellow box identifies the different colors. To go back to plain text after you choose a color, choose Automatic on the drop-down list.

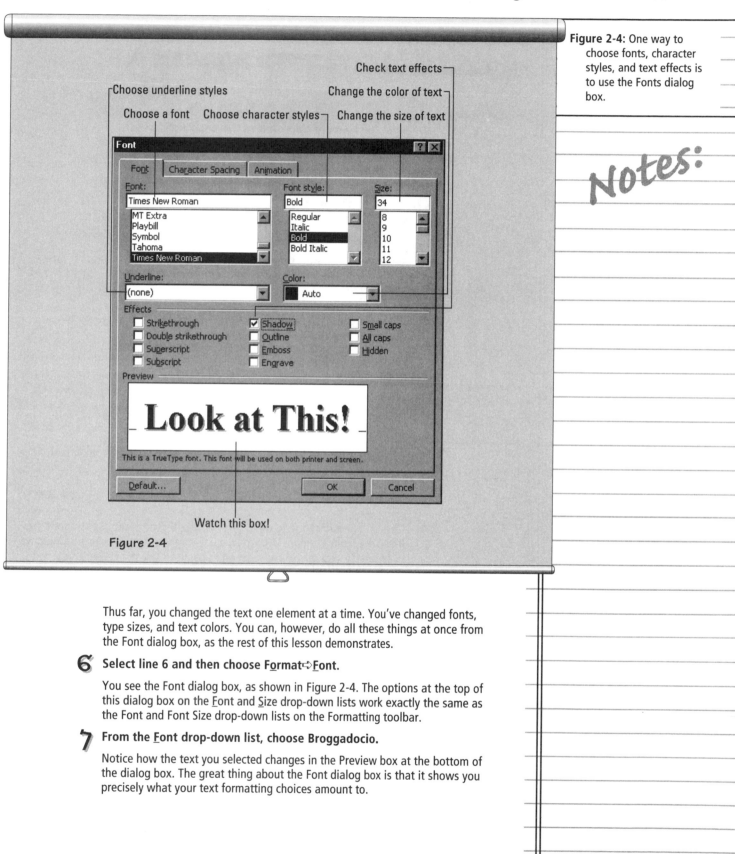

Figure 2-4: One way to choose fonts, character styles, and text effects is to use the Fonts dialog box.

Notes:

Check text effects
Change the color of text
Choose underline styles
Choose a font   Choose character styles   Change the size of text

Watch this box!

Figure 2-4

Thus far, you changed the text one element at a time. You've changed fonts, type sizes, and text colors. You can, however, do all these things at once from the Font dialog box, as the rest of this lesson demonstrates.

6 **Select line 6 and then choose Format⇨Font.**

You see the Font dialog box, as shown in Figure 2-4. The options at the top of this dialog box on the <u>F</u>ont and <u>S</u>ize drop-down lists work exactly the same as the Font and Font Size drop-down lists on the Formatting toolbar.

7 **From the <u>F</u>ont drop-down list, choose Broggadocio.**

Notice how the text you selected changes in the Preview box at the bottom of the dialog box. The great thing about the Font dialog box is that it shows you precisely what your text formatting choices amount to.

Notes:

☑ **Progress Check**

If you can perform the following tasks, you've mastered this long lesson:

❏ Boldface, italicize, and underline text.

❏ Choose a new font.

❏ Change the size of text.

❏ Choose a text effect.

❏ Set your default font and type size.

8 Click the Size drop-down list and type the following: 32.

I want you to type **32** because 32 isn't a choice in the Size drop-down list and I want you to know how to choose point sizes that aren't on the list. Notice again what happens to the text in the Preview box.

9 From the Font style drop-down list, choose Bold Italic.

Of course, you can boldface and italicize text at the same time without going to the Font dialog box, but doing it here is easier. Instead of selecting the text and pressing Ctrl+B and Ctrl+I, you just click one option.

10 Click the Color drop-down list, choose Pink, glance at the Preview box, and click OK.

You can even change text colors in the Font dialog box.

11 Select line 7, choose Format⇨Font, and make the following selections in the Font dialog box: the Matura MT Script Capitals font at 24-points high.

Now you experiment with text effects.

12 Click different Effects check boxes.

As you click the check boxes, watch the Preview box. The choices are many and all present interesting ways to embellish text.

13 Uncheck all the Effects check boxes except Shadow and then click OK.

Shadow text looks pretty cool, I think, especially if you use it on an unusual font such as Matura MT Script Capitals.

As the final exercise in this lesson, I want you to do something important. After you create a new document and start typing, Word 97 gives you the default font. The default font is the one that appears automatically. What is your favorite font? You can make it the default font by completing Steps 14 and 15.

14 Choose Format⇨Font to open the Font dialog box, choose the font you like best from the Font drop-down list, choose from the Size drop-down list the size you prefer for reading text, and click the Default button in the lower-left corner of the dialog box.

A dialog box asks if you want to change the default font.

15 Click Yes.

Now, whenever you create a new document and start typing, you see your favorite font.

Unit 2 Quiz

For the following questions, circle the letter of the correct answer or answers. This short quiz is designed to help you remember what you learned in Unit 2. Each question may have more than one right answer.

1. **Click the button shown here to accomplish which of the following tasks:**

    A. Insert a CD in the computer.

    B. Open a new document.

    C. Save a document.

    D. Play the air guitar.

    E. Exit Word 97.

2. **To break a line and start a new paragraph, you perform the following action:**

    A. Press Ctrl+Enter.

    B. Press Enter.

    C. Keep typing until you get to the next line.

    D. Click the Show/Hide ¶ button.

    E. Choose Insert⇨Break.

3. **In word processing, *drag* refers to which of the following actions:**

    A. To race sleek, souped-up cars.

    B. To dress in women's clothing (if you're man enough).

    C. Click the down arrow on a scroll bar.

    D. Click, hold the mouse button, and move the cursor across the screen.

    E. Copy text to a new place.

4. **If you needed a title for a techno-thriller spy novel about a mad nuclear submarine captain and the rugged naval cadet who thwarts his evil intentions, which of the following titles would serve you best?**

    A. *Far, Far from Where Love Is*

    B. *The Night Is for Lovers*

    C. *Destination Zero: The Brink of Doom*

    D. *Caressed by the Love of Angels*

    E. *All the Lovely Women*

5. **To copy text, you select the text and then perform the following action:**

   A. Press Ctrl+C to copy the text to the Clipboard and then press Ctrl+V to paste the text in the document.

   B. Click the Copy button to copy the text and then click the Paste button.

   C. Choose Edit⇨Copy and then choose Edit⇨Paste.

   D. Right-click the text, choose Copy from the shortcut menu that appears, and then right-click again and choose Paste from the shortcut menu.

   E. Press and hold the Ctrl key and drag the text to a new place.

6. **To delete text, you perform the following action:**

   A. Press the Backspace key.

   B. Press the Del key.

   C. Select the text and press the Del key.

   D. Select the text and start typing.

   E. Select the text and choose Edit⇨Clear All.

7. **What is a font?**

   A. A small fountain.

   B. A typeface design.

   C. Times New Roman.

   D. A place where you can get sodas and milkshakes.

   E. A town in France.

Unit 2 Exercise

on the CD

1. Open the Quiz 2 file in the Office 101 folder.

2. Delete the question marks in the first paragraph by pressing Del or the Backspace key.

3. The second paragraph, which falls under the heading `Beautiful Oaxaca`, is too long. Place the cursor before `Little has changed` and start a new paragraph there.

4. Select the first paragraph under the heading `Beautiful Oaxaca`.

5. Move the first paragraph to a location below the second paragraph.

6. Cut the last paragraph of the document but don't delete the paragraph.

7. Change the fonts and font sizes in this document. (Choose decorative fonts of your own.)

Polishing and Printing Your Document

Objectives for This Unit

- ✓ Laying out the margins of a page
- ✓ Indenting text from the margin
- ✓ Left-aligning, right-aligning, justifying, and centering text
- ✓ Changing line spacing
- ✓ Correcting spelling errors
- ✓ Printing a document

After you finish Unit 3, you will no longer be a novice word processor. You will have achieved intermediate status. You will be awarded a yellow belt in an elaborate ceremony, after which you will break this book in half with a single karate chop.

In Units 1 and 2, you learned basic editing techniques and how to create, open, and close documents. In Unit 3, you back away from the text a little and start to look at the page itself. This unit deals with page layouts, including margins and indentations. It shows how to align text on the page. It also describes how to use one of the greatest inventions of the Twentieth Century, the spell-checker. By following the techniques in this unit, you learn to create polished documents that will impress your impressionable friends. And, last but not least, you learn how to print those documents.

Lesson 3-1   # Laying Out Margins

Margins are the empty white spaces on the top, bottom, and left and right sides of the page. In new documents, Word 97 automatically makes the top and bottom margins 1 inch high and the left and right margins 1.25 inches wide.

I can think of many reasons to change the size of the margins. If you want a lot of white space to the left or right side of the text so that readers can jot down notes there, you can widen the margins. In this book, you might notice, the left and right margins are wide for that very purpose.

To get practice with margin settings, create a new document and follow these steps:

1   Choose File➪Page Setup.

You see the Page Setup dialog box shown in Figure 3-1. Notice the settings for the top, bottom, left, and right margins. As you change these settings in the following steps, keep your eye on the Preview box. It shows precisely what will happen to page margins as you change them.

2   Click the Top box, delete the number that appears there, and type 2.

Now the top margin is 2 inches high instead of 1.25 inches high in the Preview box.

3   Click 10 times on the upward-pointing arrow on the right side of the Bottom box.

Now the bottom margin is also 2 inches high. Besides entering numbers directly in the boxes, you can click the up or down arrows.

4   Change the Left and Right settings.

As you do so, notice what happens to the page in the Preview box.

5   Click OK or press Enter to close the Page Setup dialog box.

heads up

Changing the margins in a document is pretty simple. However, as the next lesson explains, the best way to change how much white space lies to the left and right of text is to indent the text. Word 97 is kind of touchy about when it lets you change margins. You can't change margin settings in the middle of a document unless you create a new section (with the Insert➪Break command). Better read on to find out about indenting, and while you're at it, you might as well read "Putting headers and footers on pages" about creating headers and footers.

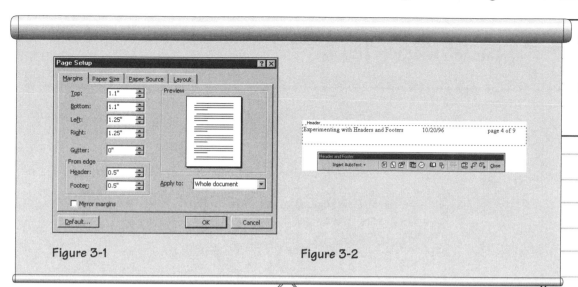

Figure 3-1

Figure 3-2

Figure 3-1: Telling Word 97 how big to make the margins.

Figure 3-2: Entering a header on the top of the page.

extra credit

Putting headers and footers on pages

A *header* is a little description that appears along the top of a page so the reader knows what's what. Headers usually include the page number, the title, and other descriptive information. A *footer* is the same thing as a header, except a footer appears along the bottom of the page, as befits its name. To create a header or footer, follow these steps:

1. **Choose View⇨Header and Footer.**

   As shown in Figure 3-2, Word 97 switches to Page Layout View, if you weren't already there, and you see a box at the top of your screen along with the word `Header`. You also see the Header and Footer toolbar.

2. **Type the header in the box (if a header and not a footer is what you want).**

   As you type, you can call on all the formatting commands in Word 97. For example, you can choose a font for the header, boldface the header text, or change its color, if that's your cup of tea.

3. **Click the Switch Between Header and Footer button.**

   This button takes you from the Header box at the top of the page to the Footer box at the bottom. (To find out the name of a button on the Header and Footer toolbar, gently slide the pointer over the button. You see a box with the button's name in it.)

4. **Enter the footer, if you want to, and click the Close button on the toolbar after you finish.**

On the Header and Footer toolbar you see a handful of useful buttons. Click the Insert Date button, as I did in the example header in Figure 3-2, to make today's date appear in the header of footer. I also typed the word **page**, entered a blank space, clicked the Insert Page Number button, entered a space and the word **of**, and then entered another blank space and clicked the Insert Number of Pages button. My header tells the reader which page he or she is on and how many total pages are in the document.

☑ Progress Check

If you can perform the following tasks, you've mastered this lesson:

❑ Change or set up the margins in a document.

❑ Enter a header and footer.

Lesson 3-2

Indenting Text

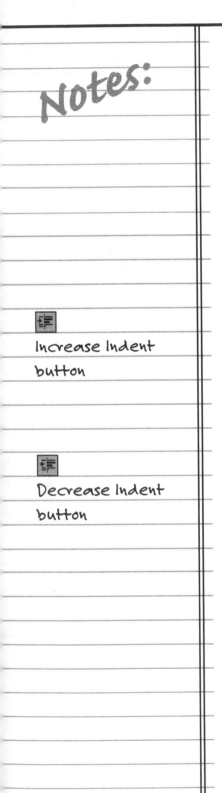

Notes:

Increase Indent button

Decrease Indent button

One way to make items in your text stand out is to indent them. For example, if your document includes a lengthy quote from a book, you can indent the quote so readers know it was borrowed from another source.

heads up

Text is indented with respect to the margins, not the edge of the page. For example, to move a long quotation to the middle of the page to make it stand out from the rest of the text, indent the text; don't change the margins on its left and right side. Margin settings are meant to create a uniform white space around the text on all the pages or on certain pages of a document. If you want to push text farther away from the margin, indent it.

on the CD

To find out about indenting, open the Indenting file in the Office 101 folder and then follow these steps:

1 Click anywhere in the second paragraph.

This paragraph is a quoted passage that needs to be indented.

2 Click the Increase Indent button.

The Increase Indent button is on the right side of the Formatting toolbar. After you click it, Word 97 indents the paragraph a half-inch from the left margin. If you click the button again, the text is indented by another half-inch.

Notice the indent markers on the left side of the ruler along the top of the document window. These markers always show you precisely how the paragraph the cursor is in has been indented. As you carry out the following step, watch the indent markers.

3 Click the Decrease Indent button.

Now the indent has been decreased by a half-inch and you are back where you started. Did you notice what happened to the indent markers? In the following three steps, you change indentations by dragging these markers on the ruler. The Increase Indent and Decrease Indent buttons are fine for changing left indents, but suppose you want to change right indents, as you need to do to the passage in the sample document.

4 Drag the *right-indent marker* — the triangle on the right side of the ruler — to the left by a half-inch.

Now Word 97 indents the paragraph from the right margin.

5 Drag the square on the left side of the ruler to the right by a half-inch.

Dragging the square, called *the left indent marker,* moves the entire paragraph. In the next step, you learn how to indent only the first line of a paragraph.

6 Click anywhere in the first paragraph and drag the first-line indent marker to the right by a half-inch.

The *first-line indent marker* is the downward-pointing triangle on the left side of the ruler. When you drag it, you indent the first line only.

Besides changing indents with the ruler, you can change them with the Format⇨Paragraph command.

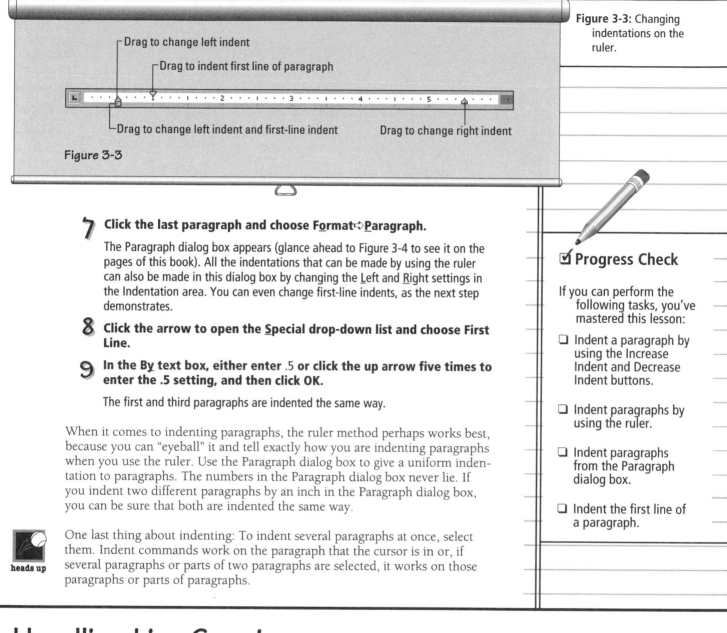

Drag to change left indent

Drag to indent first line of paragraph

Drag to change left indent and first-line indent   Drag to change right indent

Figure 3-3

Figure 3-3: Changing indentations on the ruler.

7 **Click the last paragraph and choose Format⇨Paragraph.**

The Paragraph dialog box appears (glance ahead to Figure 3-4 to see it on the pages of this book). All the indentations that can be made by using the ruler can also be made in this dialog box by changing the Left and Right settings in the Indentation area. You can even change first-line indents, as the next step demonstrates.

8 **Click the arrow to open the Special drop-down list and choose First Line.**

9 **In the By text box, either enter .5 or click the up arrow five times to enter the .5 setting, and then click OK.**

The first and third paragraphs are indented the same way.

When it comes to indenting paragraphs, the ruler method perhaps works best, because you can "eyeball" it and tell exactly how you are indenting paragraphs when you use the ruler. Use the Paragraph dialog box to give a uniform indentation to paragraphs. The numbers in the Paragraph dialog box never lie. If you indent two different paragraphs by an inch in the Paragraph dialog box, you can be sure that both are indented the same way.

heads up

One last thing about indenting: To indent several paragraphs at once, select them. Indent commands work on the paragraph that the cursor is in or, if several paragraphs or parts of two paragraphs are selected, it works on those paragraphs or parts of paragraphs.

☑ **Progress Check**

If you can perform the following tasks, you've mastered this lesson:

❑ Indent a paragraph by using the Increase Indent and Decrease Indent buttons.

❑ Indent paragraphs by using the ruler.

❑ Indent paragraphs from the Paragraph dialog box.

❑ Indent the first line of a paragraph.

Handling Line Spacing   Lesson 3-3

At some point or another in your storied word-processing career, you're sure to be asked to change the line spacing of a document. Your boss will ask you to double-space a document so he or she can read it more easily, and then your boss will have a change of heart and ask you to single-space the lines to make the annual report shorter than it is. You get the idea.

Figure 3-4: Choosing a line-spacing option in the Paragraph dialog box.

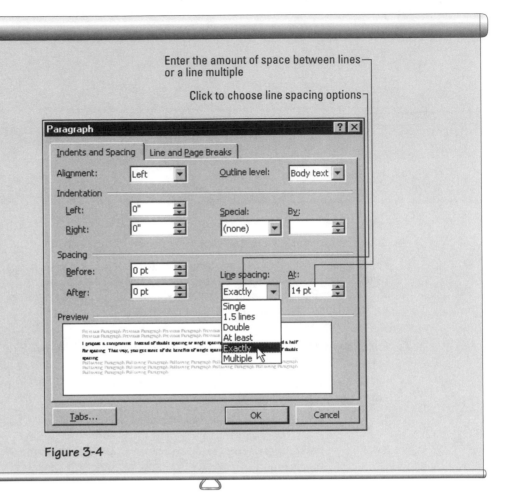

Enter the amount of space between lines or a line multiple

Click to choose line spacing options

Figure 3-4

Notes:

Line spacing determines how much white space appears between lines of text. Fortunately, changing line spacing is as easy as pie.

To explore the Word 97 line spacing commands, open the Line Spacing file in the Office 101 folder and follow these steps:

1   Click the first paragraph and then press Ctrl+1.

Instead of being double spaced, the paragraph is single spaced.

2   Click the second paragraph and then press Ctrl+2.

You get a double-spaced paragraph.

3   Click the third paragraph and press Ctrl+5.

The paragraph gets line-and-a-half spacing.

The following three steps explain how to change line spacing with the Paragraph dialog box.

4   Choose Format⇨Paragraph.

The Paragraph dialog box appears, as shown in Figure 3-4. Besides the Single, Double, and 1.5 Lines settings you just made with shortcut keys, you can make other line-spacing choices in the dialog box.

press Ctrl+1 for single spacing

press Ctrl+2 for double spacing

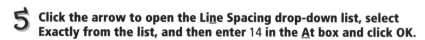

5 **Click the arrow to open the Line Spacing drop-down list, select Exactly from the list, and then enter 14 in the At box and click OK.**

The Exactly option puts an exact amount of space, 14 points in this case, between the baseline of each line of text. (The *baseline* is the imaginary line that the characters rest on. A *point* is a typesetting measurement equal to $1/72$ of an inch.

6 **Select the entire document (press Ctrl+A to do so), choose Format⇨Paragraph to open the Paragraph dialog box, click the arrow to see the Line Spacing drop-down list, choose Multiple from the list, and then enter 4 in the At box and click OK.**

The document is "quadruple-spaced." When you choose the Multiple option, the number you type in the At box determines how many spaces appear between the lines — four in this case.

Close the Line Spacing document without saving it. I hope this lesson has explained line spacing well enough so that you never get spaced out when you have to space the lines in a document.

Recess

Time for a break. It's the seventh inning stretch. Time to stand up, raise your arms over your head, and take a deep breath. And maybe go to the concession stand for a soda and a big bag of popcorn.

☑ **Progress Check**

If you can perform the following tasks, you've mastered this lesson:

❑ Single- and double-space lines by pressing shortcut keys.

❑ Choose line-spacing options in the Paragraph dialog box.

Aligning Text in Documents   Lesson 3-4

By now you must have noticed that the headings in the practice documents you've used thus far have been centered. In other words, the headings appear across the middle of the page. If you envy my ability to center text, you need no longer be envious, because this short lesson describes how to center words on the page. It also explores three other alignment options: left-aligned, right-aligned, and justified.

on the CD

To find out what these options are and how to apply them to text, open the Alignment file in the Office 101 folder and follow these steps:

1 **Click the heading at the top of the page and glance at the alignment buttons on the Formatting toolbar.**

If you notice, the Center button appears to be pressed down. The button looks that way because I clicked the Center button to center the heading. If ever you are not sure how text is aligned, click it and glance at the align buttons.

Center button

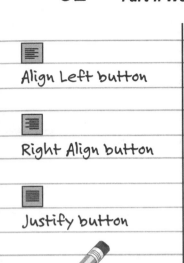

Align Left button

Right Align button

Justify button

☑ **Progress Check**

If you can perform the
following tasks, you've
mastered this lesson:

❑ Center and justify text.

❑ Glance at the align
buttons to see how text
has been aligned.

❑ Right-align and left-align
text.

2 **Click the Align Left button.**

The heading hugs the left margin. Plain text is usually left-aligned, as the text in
this book is.

3 **Click the left-hand column and glance at the align buttons on the
Formatting toolbar.**

As you can see, this column is right-aligned. It clings to, not the right margin in
this case, but the right side of the column. You don't see right-aligned text very
often, but it can be used to elegant effect.

4 **Click the Justify button.**

Justified text does what both left-aligned and right-aligned text does — it
sticks to *both* the left and right margins, or to the left and right sides of the
column. Text is usually justified in formal documents and in columns, where the
words must fit into a narrow space.

5 **Click the right-hand column and, for the fun of it, click the Center
button.**

Text as well as headings can be centered. You can play with the alignment
options to your heart's content until you come up with interesting layouts.

By the way, you can align more than one paragraph at the same time by
selecting more than one paragraph and then clicking the appropriate alignment button.

Lesson 3-5

Checking Your Spelling (And Grammar)

No doubt you've noticed the red squiggly lines that appear from time to under
words in documents. Those words are either misspelled or are proper names
or foreign terms that Word 97 doesn't recognize. In this lesson, you learn how
to correct misspellings, tell Word 97 to ignore what it thinks are misspellings,
and add words to the Word 97 dictionary so that Word 97 understands when
terms are not misspelled. You also get a taste of the Word 97 grammar-
checker so that you can decide for yourself whether it is worthwhile.

on the CD

To try out the many ways to handle red-lined words, open the Miss Spalling
document in the Office 101 folder and follow these steps:

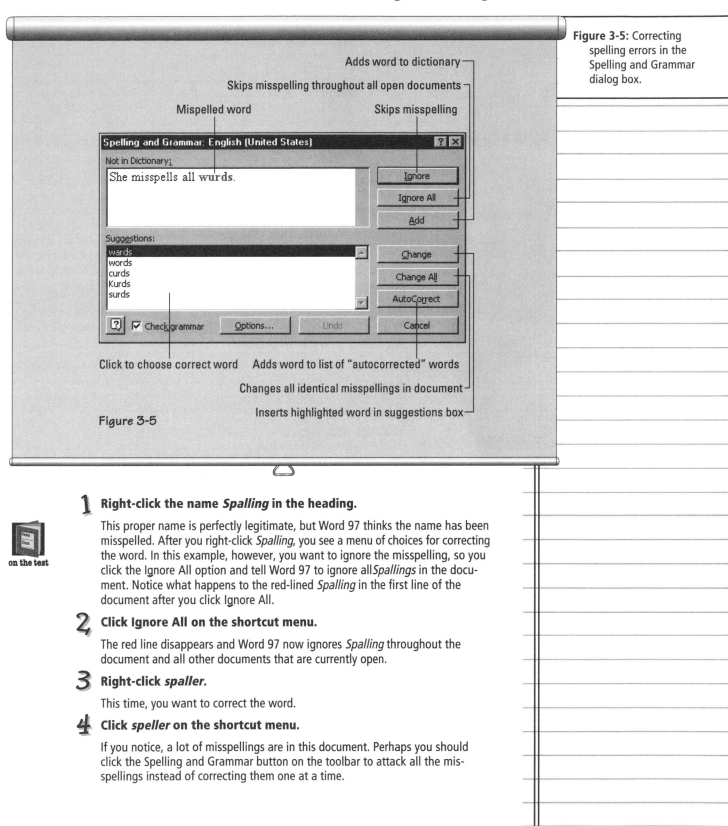

Figure 3-5: Correcting spelling errors in the Spelling and Grammar dialog box.

Adds word to dictionary

Skips misspelling throughout all open documents

Mispelled word

Skips misspelling

Spelling and Grammar: English (United States)

Not in Dictionary:

She misspells all wurds.

Ignore
Ignore All
Add

Suggestions:

wards
words
curds
Kurds
surds

Change
Change All
AutoCorrect

☑ Check grammar   Options...   Undo   Cancel

Click to choose correct word   Adds word to list of "autocorrected" words

Changes all identical misspellings in document

Inserts highlighted word in suggestions box

Figure 3-5

on the test

1 Right-click the name *Spalling* in the heading.

This proper name is perfectly legitimate, but Word 97 thinks the name has been misspelled. After you right-click *Spalling*, you see a menu of choices for correcting the word. In this example, however, you want to ignore the misspelling, so you click the Ignore All option and tell Word 97 to ignore all *Spallings* in the document. Notice what happens to the red-lined *Spalling* in the first line of the document after you click Ignore All.

2 Click Ignore All on the shortcut menu.

The red line disappears and Word 97 now ignores *Spalling* throughout the document and all other documents that are currently open.

3 Right-click *spaller*.

This time, you want to correct the word.

4 Click *speller* on the shortcut menu.

If you notice, a lot of misspellings are in this document. Perhaps you should click the Spelling and Grammar button on the toolbar to attack all the misspellings instead of correcting them one at a time.

Spelling and
Grammar button

Notes:

☑ Progress Check

If you can perform the following tasks, you've mastered this lesson:

❑ Correct a spelling error by right-clicking.

❑ Use the Spelling and Grammar dialog box to fix misspellings and grammar errors.

5 **Click the Spelling and Grammar button.**

As shown in Figure 3-5, the Spelling and Grammar dialog box opens and shows you the next misspelling, which is *wurds.* It appears in red and is shown in context in the Not in Dictionary box. In the Suggestions box, Word 97 offers a bunch of choices for correcting the error.

6 **Click *words* in the Suggestions box and then click the Change button.**

Word 97 finds the next misspelling, *wurds* again. In the next step you tell the program to correct all *wurds* in the document so that you don't have to keep correcting this error.

7 **Click the Change All button.**

In the document are two more *wurds,* but they've now been corrected. Next the spell-checker lands on *she she.* Besides looking for misspellings, Word 97 looks for instances of two words in a row.

8 **Click the Delete button.**

This button appears where the Change button normally stands when the same words have been entered in a row.

Next the spell-checker stops on *Anza.* I happen to know that Anza is a charming cowtown in Southern California. For the next step, suppose that you live in Anza and you want to add this word to the dictionary to prevent the spell-checker from ever stopping on the town's name again.

9 **Click the Add button.**

De Anza, the courageous Spanish explorer, camped in Anza in 1755, but the Word 97 spell-checker will never get the chance to camp there now that *Anza* has been added to your dictionary.

Next the spell-checker stops on *Anywy.* In the Suggestions box is the correct spelling, *Anyway.* Suppose that you misspell this word often. You can tell Word 97 to keep its eye open for *Anywy* and enter *Anyway* in its place whenever you type the misspelling.

10 **Click the AutoCorrect button.**

Now, whenever you type the letters *anywy,* Word 97 inserts the missing *a* automatically.

The next error Word 97 finds is not a spelling error but a grammar error. Or is it? The sentence, displayed in green, reads, "Teenage girls are flattered by his attention and matrons blush." Notice the suggestion Word 97 makes for correcting this so-called error. Where I come from, "His attention and matrons blush flatters teenage girls" is no substitute for the original.

11 **Click the Ignore button.**

If you want to accept the substitute that Word 97 suggests, click the Change button instead. Next Word 97 suggests putting a semicolon where a comma is.

12 **Click Ignore again.**

The Word 97 grammar-checker is a nit-picker and is often wrong. If the grammar-checker annoys you, you can turn it off by clicking the Check grammar check box in the Spelling and Grammar dialog box.

heads up

The Word 97 smell-checker can't catch all misspellings. For example, the following sentence includes a misspelling, but Word 97 can't catch it because the misspelled word is in the dictionary: Nero diddled while Rome burned. "Diddle" is a legitimate word, so Word 97 doesn't catch the error. The moral is: Don't expect the spell-checker to catch all your smelling errors.

Printing a File

Lesson 3-6

This short lesson explains how to print the masterpieces that you create in Word 97. As the following steps show, nothing is easier than printing a document — provided your printer is hooked up correctly and Word 97 understands where to send the printing instructions. Besides explaining how to print a document, this lesson tells how to preview what you print so that you can catch errors before you commit them to paper.

on the CD

Open the Print Me document and follow these steps to learn about printing:

1 **Click the Print Preview button.**

You see the first page of the document. Now is your chance to find errors on this page.

(Print Preview button icon)
Print Preview button

2 **Click the Multiple Pages button and drag the cursor across the page icons until the bottom of the menu reads** 2 x 2 page.

The Multiple Pages button is the fourth from the left on the toolbar. You now see four pages. Are the pages laid out correctly? Getting a bird's-eye view of pages in this manner gives you an excellent opportunity to find errors.

3 **Click the Close button to leave the Print Preview screen.**

Assuming that this document is ready for printing (it is), you can actually give the Print command. If you had spotted an error on the Print Preview window, you could correct the error now.

4 **Click the Print button on the Standard toolbar.**

Clicking the Print button prints the entire document from start to finish. Suppose, however, that you just want to print part of a document.

(Print button icon)
Print button

5 **Choose File⇨Print or press Ctrl+P.**

The Print dialog box appears, as shown in Figure 3-6. The All option is selected by default in the Page Range area. If you click OK now, you print the entire document.

6 **Click the Pages radio button and then type the following:** 1,3-4.

These instructions tell Word 97 to print pages 1, 3, and 4. By entering commas and hyphens between page numbers, you can tell Word 97 to print specific pages and page ranges. Don't enter blank spaces in the text box.

7 **Click the Number of Copies box and type** 2.

You just told Word 97 to print two copies of the document.

Figure 3-6: Printing a document.

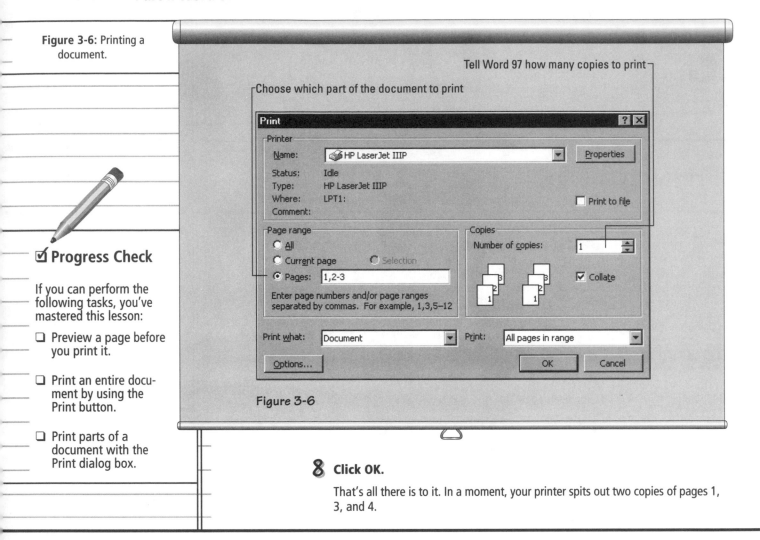

Choose which part of the document to print

Tell Word 97 how many copies to print

Figure 3-6

8   **Click OK.**

That's all there is to it. In a moment, your printer spits out two copies of pages 1, 3, and 4.

Unit 3 Quiz

For the following questions, circle the letter of the correct answer or answers. This short quiz is designed to help you remember what you learned in Unit 3. Each question may have more than one right answer. (The right answer to question 5, for example, is C.)

1. **To set up or change the margins, choose which of the following commands:**

   A. File⇨Page Setup.

   B. Insert⇨Break.

   C. View⇨Header and Footer.

   D. Edit⇨Margins.

   E. Format⇨Page.

2. **Which of the following methods work for changing the left indentation of a paragraph?**

   A. Choose Format⇨Paragraph and change the Left setting in the paragraph dialog box.

   B. Drag the left-indent marker on the ruler.

   C. How am I supposed to know?

   D. Press the Tab key.

   E. Click the Increase Indent button.

3. **To double space text in a document, perform the following action:**

   A. Press Enter twice after each line.

   B. Use the Zoom box to make the letters bigger.

   C. Press Ctrl+1.

   D. Press Ctrl+2.

   E. Choose Format⇨Paragraph to open the Paragraph dialog box, choose Double in the Line Spacing drop-down list, and then click OK.

 4. **Click this button to perform which of the following tasks:**

   A. Close a document.

   B. Center text on the page.

   C. Put text in columns.

   D. Left-align text.

   E. Print a document.

5. **Volvo, also the name of an automobile manufacturer, means which of the following in Latin?**

   A. Swedish meatball

   B. Ford

   C. I roll.

   D. Alphabet soup

   E. Car

6. **When a word is underlined with a red squiggly line, it means which of the following:**

   A. The word is misspelled.

   B. You've committed a grammatical error.

   C. The Word 97 dictionary does not recognize the word.

   D. An insurance company has redlined your neighborhood.

   E. All is not well in Cleveland.

7. **If you click the button shown here, which part of a document do you print:**

   A. The page the cursor is on

   B. The first page

   C. The text you selected

   D. The title page

   E. All of it

Unit 3 Exercise

on the CD

1. Open the Quiz 3 file in the Office 101 folder.

2. Preview this document by clicking the Print Preview button.

3. The margins are too narrow. Make the margins wider.

4. In the middle of the letter are three short sentences. Indent them.

5. Change the line spacing of the body of this letter to one and a half lines.

6. The body of the letter is justified. Left-align the body of the letter.

7. Fix the spelling errors in this document.

8. Print the letter.

Part I Review

Unit 1 Summary

▶ **Starting a program:** Click the Start button on the taskbar, choose <u>P</u>rograms, and then choose an Office 97 program from the menu.

▶ **Opening and closing files:** Choose <u>F</u>ile⇨<u>O</u>pen, click the Open button, or press Ctrl+O. In the Open dialog box that appears, click the Up One Level button and double-click folders until you reach the folder with the file you want to open. Then either double-click the file or click it and then click the <u>O</u>pen button.

▶ **Viewing documents:** Click the View buttons in the lower-left corner of the screen to change views. You can also choose options from the <u>V</u>iew menu. Word 97 offers Normal view, Page Layout view, Online Layout view, and others.

▶ **Moving around in a document:** Press shortcut keys or use the scroll bar on the right side of the screen. Press Ctrl+End to get to the end of a document, for example, or Ctrl+Home to get to the top. Click the arrows on the scroll bar to go up or down a line; drag the scroll box to go many pages at once; or click the scroll bar to go up or down a page at a time.

▶ **Getting help:** Choose <u>H</u>elp⇨<u>T</u>his and click the part of the screen you are interested in. You can get help in dialog boxes by clicking the question mark in the upper-right corner and then clicking an option. For in-depth help, choose <u>H</u>elp⇨<u>C</u>ontents and Index. On the Contents tab, double-click book icons and question marks to get to a topic. On the Index tab, type the topic's name and then double-click it in the box in the lower-half of the tab. You can also click the Office Assistant button or press F1, type a question in the box, and click the Search button.

Unit 2 Summary

▶ **Creating and saving files:** Create a document by choosing <u>F</u>ile⇨<u>N</u>ew, pressing Ctrl+N, or clicking the New button. To save a document, press Ctrl+S, click the Save button, or choose <u>F</u>ile⇨<u>S</u>ave. The first time you save the document, the Save As dialog box appears. Click the Up One Level button and double-click folders until you get to the folder in which the file is to be saved. Then enter a name in the File <u>N</u>ame box and click <u>S</u>ave.

▶ **Editing text:** Press Del or the Backspace key to erase characters. Press Enter to start a new line or paragraph. Press Ctrl+Enter to begin a new page.

▶ **Selecting text:** Double-click a word to select it. Drag across text to select it. Double-click in the left margin to select a paragraph. Press Ctrl+A to select an entire document.

▶ **Moving text:** To move text, select the text you want to move and then drag it to a new place. You can also click the Cut button and paste it elsewhere with the Paste button, choose <u>E</u>dit⇨Cu<u>t</u> and then <u>E</u>dit⇨<u>P</u>aste, or press Ctrl+X and then Ctrl+V.

▶ **Copying text:** Select the text and drag it elsewhere while holding down the Ctrl key. You can also click the Copy button and then the Paste button, choose <u>E</u>dit⇨<u>C</u>opy and then <u>E</u>dit⇨<u>P</u>aste, or press Ctrl+C and then Ctrl+V.

▶ **Deleting text:** Select the text and press the Delete key.

▶ **Changing fonts:** Select the text and make choices from the Font and Font Size drop-down lists on the Formatting toolbar. You can also choose F<u>o</u>rmat⇨<u>F</u>ont and make choices in the Font dialog box.

Part I Review

Unit 3 Summary

- **Setting up margins:** Choose File⇨Page Setup. In the Page Setup dialog box, change the Top, Bottom, Left, and Right settings and then click OK.

- **Indenting text:** Click the Increase Indent and Decrease Indent buttons, or else drag indent markers on the ruler. You can also choose Format⇨Paragraph and change indentation settings in the Paragraph dialog box.

- **Changing line spacing:** Press Ctrl+1 to single-space text or Ctrl+2 to double-space it. Otherwise, choose Format⇨Paragraph to open the Paragraph dialog box, choose a Line Spacing setting and, if necessary, make an entry in the At box, and click OK.

- **Aligning text:** Click one of the alignment buttons on the Formatting toolbar: Align Left, Center, Align Right, or Justify.

- **Spell checking:** Right-click a word with a red line underneath it to see and make choices from a shortcut menu with spelling alternatives. Otherwise, click the Spelling and Grammar button and make choices in the Spelling and Grammar dialog box.

- **Printing a file:** Click the Print button to print an entire document. To print part of a document or more than one copy, choose File⇨Print or press Ctrl+P, choose a Page Range option in the Print dialog box, make an entry in the Number of Copies box, and click OK.

Part I Test

This test is hard — hard as nails, in fact. It will make you or it will break you. It will make you sweat bullets. It will determine whether you've been paying attention or sleeping in class. If you've been sleeping, you're going to regret it now. Sweet dreams, baby! Welcome to the nightmare test!

Actually, this simple test is going to help you find out how much you learned in Part I. I designed it as a means for you to review what you learned, not to torture you. The answers to the questions asked here can be found next to the On the Test icons scattered throughout Part I. (The answers can also be found in Appendix A.) If you have trouble with a question, go back to the lesson in Part I that covers the topic you are having trouble with. This test is meant to help you use Word 97 better, not to make you sweat.

True   False

T   F   **1.** Computers are smarter than you are.

T   F   **2.** 🗋 Click this button to start an Office 97 program.

T   F   **3.** To close a file, choose File⇨Exit.

T   F   **4.** Click the arrow that points up on the scroll bar to move up line by line in a document.

Part I Test

T	F	5. You should save files from time to time as you work on them.
T	F	6. Press the ← key to erase characters.
T	F	7. You can select text by dragging the cursor over it.
T	F	8. You can move text by dragging and dropping it to a new place.
T	F	9. In the *Wizard of Oz,* Dorothy was able to get back to Kansas by clicking the heels of the magic slippers and repeating, "There's no place like McDonald's."
T	F	10. If you right-click a word that has a red, squiggly line underneath it, you get a shortcut menu with choices for correcting a misspelling.

Multiple Choice

Circle the correct answer or answers to the following questions. Each question may have more than one right answer.

11. **Why should you save documents every so often as you work on them?**

    A. So you can hear that disk-grinding sound on your computer

    B. To store the changes you've made to the hard disk, where they are stored permanently and won't be lost if there is a power failure or other untoward accident

    C. For the sheer fun of it

    D. So your computer knows you are still awake

    E. To keep all the data on your computer intact

12. **Besides choosing File⇨Open, you can open a document in which of the following ways?**

    A. By clicking the Paste button

    B. By opening up the filing cabinet, taking out a manila folder, and pulling the document out

    C. By eavesdropping on the telephone conversations of the person in the next cubicle

    D. By pulling down the File menu and clicking one of the four file names at the bottom

    E. By choosing the File⇨New command

13. **Can you tell what a button on a toolbar does by doing the following:**

    A. Placing the pointer on the button and reading its name?

    B. Clicking the button to see what happens?

    C. Staring hard at the little picture on the button until you realize what the little picture is supposed to mean?

    D. Placing the mouse pointer on the button and reading the description on the status bar?

    E. Choose Help⇨What's This and then clicking the toolbar button in question?

14. **If you haven't studied adequately for a test and you feel apprehensive or guilty about it, you will have which of the following dreams on the night before the test?**

    A. You are dancing in the sunshine in a meadow of wildflowers.

    B. You are strolling by the peaceful sea under a full moon.

    C. You are walking through the hallways of your old high school and you feel ashamed because you are naked.

    D. You have amazing leaping ability and you are running joyously and speedily across a fantastic desert landscape.

    E. You are in a beautiful garden where butterflies of all shapes and sizes luxuriate on the long petals of exotic, lurid flowers.

Part I Review

15. **Which of the following is *not* a method of selecting text?**

    A. Double-clicking a word

    B. Dragging the mouse cursor down the left margin

    C. Pressing F8 and then pressing arrow keys

    D. Right-clicking in the left margin

    E. Choosing Edit⇨Select All

16. **To copy text by dragging it, which key do you hold down as you drag the text?**

    A. Ctrl

    B. Alt

    C. Shift

    D. F2

    E. None of the above

17. **Where are the View buttons located on the Word 97 screen?**

    A. On the Zoom drop-down list

    B. On the View menu

    C. In the lower-left corner

    D. Where the Undo button is

    E. In an inconvenient, hard-to-find place

18. **Why is there a question mark in the upper-right corner of all dialog boxes?**

    A. It's there to remind you of the universal question, "Why are we here?"

    B. You can click the question mark to close the dialog box.

    C. The question mark is a help button and you can click it and then click an option to see what the option does.

    D. The question mark opens the Help program.

    E. Don't worry about it. It's just there for decoration.

Matching

19. **Match the following buttons with the corresponding commands:**

    A. 💾   1. File⇨Open

    B. 📂   2. Edit⇨Cut

    C. 📋   3. File⇨Save

    D. 📄   4. Edit⇨Copy

    E. ✂   5. File⇨New

20. **Match the following shortcut keys with the corresponding buttons:**

    A. Ctrl+C   1. 📋

    B. Ctrl+O   2. 📄

    C. Ctrl+V   3. 📂

    D. Ctrl+N   4. 📋

    E. Ctrl+X   5. ✂

21. **Match the following song titles with the correct musical genre:**

    A. Country-Western   1. *All Through the Night*

    B. Classical   2. *Tus Locuras Sabrosas*

    C. Jazz   3. *Opus 21: The Galaxies*

    D. Rock and Roll   4. *Yes Darlin', But I Also Love My Truck*

    E. Banda   5. *Twilight in Harlem*

22. **Match the following keyboard shortcuts with their related function:**

    A. Ctrl+X   1. 💾

    B. Ctrl+S   2. ↩

    C. Ctrl+C   3. ✂

    D. Ctrl+V   4. 📋

    E. Ctrl+Z   5. 📋

Part I Lab Assignment

This is the first of the lab assignments you will find at the end of Parts I through V of this book. The object of these assignments is to give you a chance to apply the things you learned in a realistic situation.

In lab assignments, I won't tell you how to do things in a step-by-step fashion as I did in the exercises in the lessons. Instead, these lab assignments give general instructions, the idea being for you to figure out how to do it yourself — or to already know how to do it yourself. By now you are starting to feel like you have command of Word 97. I don't have to tell you to click this or press that anymore because you know how to do it.

For this lab assignment, and the others that follow each part of this book, you are the owner of a small property management company. Your little business has taken off like wildfire. So good are you at managing others' property, everybody in town wants you to manage theirs. However, that poses a problem: So far you have been doing the paperwork by hand. You want the computer to do some of the work for you.

In this lab assignment, you will open and format the standard rental agreement that all tenants under your care are to receive and sign.

Step 1: Opening a document

on the CD

Open the Test 1 file in the Office 101 folder. No doubt you will open this file many times. Maybe you should create a shortcut to it, or a shortcut to the Office 101 folder (the sidebar "Opening documents from the Favorites folder" in Unit 1 explains how to create a shortcut).

Step 2: Looking over the document

When the document opens, it is in Normal view. You can tell it's in Normal view because the graphic in the letterhead doesn't appear. Better switch to Page Layout view. While you're at it, use the scroll bar or press shortcut keys to look over the entire document and get the lay of the land.

Step 3: Moving and deleting text

In case you didn't notice, the last paragraph doesn't belong in this agreement. Better delete it. And, come to think of it, the "Tenant's Responsibilities" stuff should go after the "Manager's Responsibilities" stuff, not before. Move it. Better not come on too strong. You want the tenants to know you are their friend.

Step 4: Changing fonts

The type doesn't look very good in this document. How about choosing new fonts? Remember, you can use more than one font. Give the headings one font and the body text another. You can use different point sizes for the type as well.

Part I Lab Assignment

Step 5: Changing formats

While you're at it, do you like the line spacing in this document? Maybe you should change it. What about text alignment? The body text is justified. It would look better if it was left-aligned. Maybe you should center the headings.

Step 6: Saving and printing

Save your newfangled file and print it.

Excel 97

Part II

In this part...

Part II tackles Microsoft Excel 97, the number cruncher of Microsoft Office 97. Besides teaching you how to enter data into Excel 97, Part II talks about formatting a worksheet so that others can read it and make perfect sense of it. This part also discusses formulas and functions.

After reading Part II, you won't have to do the math yourself — you will be able to let Excel 97 do it for you.

Learning the Ropes

Objectives for This Unit

✓ Creating and moving around in worksheets

✓ Entering and editing the data in cells

✓ Copying, moving, clearing, and deleting cell data

✓ Viewing worksheets in different ways

✓ Printing a worksheet

Prerequisites

▶ Starting an Office 97 program (Lesson 1-1)

▶ Opening a file (Lesson 1-2)

▶ Saving a file (Lesson 2-1)

on the CD

▶ Tour

▶ Cell

▶ Copy Move

▶ View Data

▶ Print Me

▶ Quiz 4

Unit 4 raises the curtain on Microsoft Excel 97, the official bean counter of Office 97. To track, tabulate, manipulate, and manage data in Excel 97, you enter numbers in a worksheet. A *worksheet,* also known as a *spreadsheet,* works like an accountant's ledger — only it's much faster to use. Instead of you crunching the numbers yourself, Excel 97 does the job for you in the twinkling of an eye.

In this unit, you learn how to create a worksheet, enter the data and correct it if you enter numbers incorrectly, move the cursor throughout a worksheet, and view worksheets in different ways. I also show you how to copy, move, and delete data. Last, but not least, you learn how to print the little master-pieces you create with Excel 97.

Creating a Worksheet

In this lesson, you create your first worksheet. Inside a worksheet, information is arranged in columns and rows, very much as it is in a table. You can use worksheets for budgeting, billing, bookkeeping, forecasting, and tracking finances. In the following pages, you try out two techniques for creating a new worksheet. You create your own worksheet from scratch and learn how to take advantage of an Excel 97 template to create a worksheet.

Creating a blank worksheet

After you start Excel 97 (see Lesson 1-1), the program shows you a blank worksheet with the generic title Book 1 in the title bar. Of course, you could start entering data at this point, but suppose that a worksheet is already on-screen and you want to start one of your own. In that case, take one of the following steps:

New button

- Click the New button.
- Press Ctrl+N.

You see an empty worksheet similar to the one in Figure 4-1. If you had the pleasure of slogging through Part I of this book, much of this screen looks familiar to you. Notice the Standard and Formatting toolbars along the top of the screen. On the Standard toolbar, the following buttons work in Excel 97 the same as they do in Word 97: Open (see Lesson 1-2); New and Save (see Lesson 2-1); Cut, Copy, and Paste (see Lesson 2-4); Undo and Redo (see Lesson 2-5); Spelling (see Lesson 3-5); and Print Preview and Print (see Lesson 3-6).

On the Formatting toolbar, the Font drop-down list and Font Size drop-down list (see Lesson 2-6); the Bold, Italic, and Underline buttons (Lesson 2-6); and the alignment buttons (Lesson 3-4) work the same way in Word 97, too. Even the shortcut key equivalents of these buttons are the same. And the menu names, too, are similar. The scroll bar on the right side of the screen and the Zoom menu also should look familiar to you (see Lessons 1-4 and 1-3).

The makers of Office are trying to make it easy for you to use their programs. Read on to find out how to create a fancy worksheet from one of the Excel templates.

Creating a worksheet from a template

on the test

Microsoft includes templates in Excel 97 to help you create good-looking worksheets with practically no effort. A *template* is a preformatted worksheet dressed up to look pretty in public. After you create the worksheet from the template, you plug in your data in place of the placeholder data supplied by Excel 97. Then you have, from the looks of it, a very nice worksheet that appears to have required many hours of your time and work.

Follow these steps to create a worksheet from a template:

1 **Choose File⇨New.**

You see the New dialog box. If you double-clicked the Workbook icon on the General tab, you would create an empty worksheet like the one you just created. But you aren't going to do that.

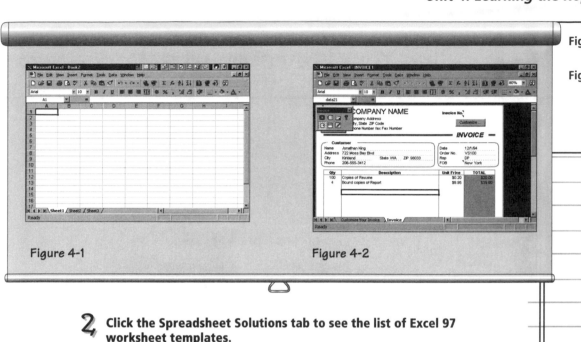

Figure 4-1: An empty worksheet.

Figure 4-2: By creating a worksheet from a template, you leave the formatting work to someone else.

Figure 4-1   Figure 4-2

2 **Click the Spreadsheet Solutions tab to see the list of Excel 97 worksheet templates.**

3 **Click each worksheet template icon and look in the Preview box.**

By clicking the icons and looking in the Preview box, you can get a fair idea of the worksheets that these templates help you create.

4 **Double-click the INVOICE template icon and then click the Enable Macros button to load the macros that come with the INVOICE template.**

After a moment or two, you see a sample invoice. If you examine this worksheet, you see that it, too, is arranged in columns and rows, like the empty worksheet you opened earlier. However, this worksheet is already formatted. Borders appear around some of the columns and rows, the columns and rows are different sizes, and different fonts appear in different parts of the worksheet.

5 **Click the Display Example/Remove Example button on the Invoice toolbar.**

The Invoice toolbar is located in the upper-left corner of the screen. To find the Display Example/Remove Example button, gently slide the mouse pointer over the buttons and read the button names as they appear. The Display Example/Remove Example button is in the lower-left corner of the toolbar.

As shown in Figure 4-2, Excel 97 supplies a sample invoice on the worksheet after you click the Display Example/Remove Example button. Now you can see how you would fill out this worksheet if you were tracking your own expenses.

6 **Choose File➪Close and click No after Excel 97 asks whether you want to save the changes you just made.**

After you finish the lessons in this book about Excel 97 and you know more about entering and editing data, you should be good enough with the program to make use of templates such as this one. Meanwhile, read on to learn about the different parts of a worksheet.

☑ Progress Check

If you can perform the following tasks, you've mastered this lesson:

❑ Create a blank worksheet.

❑ Create a new worksheet from a template.

Lesson 4-2   Finding Your Way around a Worksheet

Notes:

This lesson demystifies some of the clutter that you find on-screen as you run Excel 97. You may, for example, wonder what those numbers along the left side of the screen mean. How about the letters along the top of the screen? Stay tuned to learn the answers to these and other questions.

For this exercise in learning about the different parts of the Excel 97 screen and how they work, follow these steps:

on the CD

1 Open the Tour file in the Office 101 folder.

Lesson 1-2 explains how to open a file if you forget how to do that.

You see the worksheet shown in Figure 4-3. Notice the letters along the top of the screen and the numbers along the left side. The letters are column *headings,* with one letter for each column. The numbers are for rows; each row has its own number. Excel 97 automatically outfits a new worksheet with a grand total of 256 columns and 16,384 rows. The first 26 columns are labeled A to Z; the next 26, AA to AZ; the next 26 BA to BZ; and so on. Rows are numbered 1 to 16,384. I can hardly image anyone who needs a worksheet that big, but a worksheet can be as big as you want.

rectangle around
a cell = active cell

2 Glance at the rectangle in the upper-left corner of the screen and then press the → key.

The rectangle moves one cell to the right. A *cell* is the box that forms where a row and column intersect. Each cell can hold one data item, be it a number, a label, or a formula. By pressing the → key, you moved the *active cell* one cell to the right, from cell A1 to cell B1. If you were to start typing a number or label now, it would appear in the active cell — B1.

Name box lists the
address of the
active cell

3 Move the cursor to cell C7.

To do so, you can either click cell C7 or press → once and then press the ↓ key six times. Look at the column heading letters and row numbers to find cell C7. If you arrive there correctly, you see C7 in the Name box in the upper-left corner of the screen. The *Name box* tells you the address of the active cell.

Formula bar tells
you what is in the
active cell

Notice, in the Formula bar at the top of the screen, the number 13. The Formula bar tells you which number, label, or formula is in the active cell. As the next lesson shows, you can also enter data directly into the Formula bar. Suppose that you weren't sure which formula was used to obtain the numbers in the Totals column in this worksheet. In that case, you would take the following step.

4 Move the cursor to cell G7.

Now the formula bar reads =SUM(C7:F7), which means that the total comes from adding all numbers in between and including the numbers in cells C7 and F7. In other words, cell G7 holds the sum, or total, of the data in cells C7, D7, E7, and F7.

In Lesson 6-1, you discover that constructing simple formulas such as this one is pretty darn simple in Excel. For now, you need to know only that the Formula bar is one place where you can edit or enter data and that the Formula bar explains very clearly what is entered in the active cell.

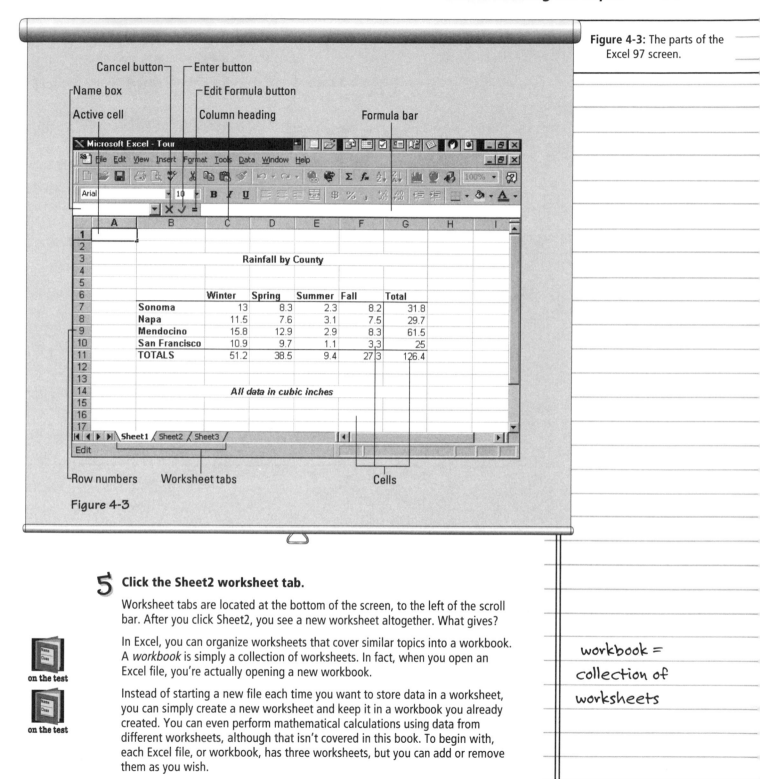

Figure 4-3: The parts of the Excel 97 screen.

Figure 4-3

5 Click the Sheet2 worksheet tab.

Worksheet tabs are located at the bottom of the screen, to the left of the scroll bar. After you click Sheet2, you see a new worksheet altogether. What gives?

In Excel, you can organize worksheets that cover similar topics into a workbook. A *workbook* is simply a collection of worksheets. In fact, when you open an Excel file, you're actually opening a new workbook.

Instead of starting a new file each time you want to store data in a worksheet, you can simply create a new worksheet and keep it in a workbook you already created. You can even perform mathematical calculations using data from different worksheets, although that isn't covered in this book. To begin with, each Excel file, or workbook, has three worksheets, but you can add or remove them as you wish.

By the way, did you notice that Elvis sightings in worksheet 2 correspond nearly one-to-one with inches of rainfall per county in worksheet 1?

on the test

on the test

workbook = collection of worksheets

☑ Progress Check

If you can perform the following tasks, you've mastered this lesson:

❑ Move the cursor from cell address to cell address.

❑ Find information in the Name box and Formula bar.

❑ Move from worksheet to worksheet in a workbook.

6 **Click Sheet1 to get back to the Rainfall by County worksheet.**

See what I mean about Elvis sightings and rainfall. Can we conclude from this data that Elvis is more likely to appear on rainy days, when you can't see well and your head is buried under an umbrella? I think we can.

7 **Close the Tour file.**

Lesson 4-3   Entering and Editing the Data

This short lesson goes into the nitty-gritty of working with Excel 97. It explains how to enter data in a worksheet and how to change data that is already entered in the cells. I also describe tried-and-true techniques for moving the cursor quickly from cell to cell.

on the CD

For this lesson, open the Cell file and follow these steps:

1 **Click cell G4.**

The label in cell G4 reads, "Total," when it should read "Totals." In the next step, you fix this error in the Formula bar.

on the test

2 **Click the Formula bar after the word** Total**, type an** s**, and click the Enter button.**

The Enter button is the green check mark to the left of the Formula bar, between the Cancel button and the Edit Formula button. Besides clicking the Enter button to tell Excel to accept your editorial changes, you can press the Enter key or simply click anywhere on the worksheet.

Click the Cancel button if you start to make a change in the Formula bar but decide that you don't want to make any changes after all.

3 **Move the cursor to cell C6.**

Somebody forgot to make an entry here. After you make an entry in the following step, watch how the totals change.

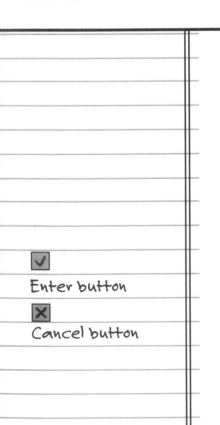

☑
Enter button

☒
Cancel button

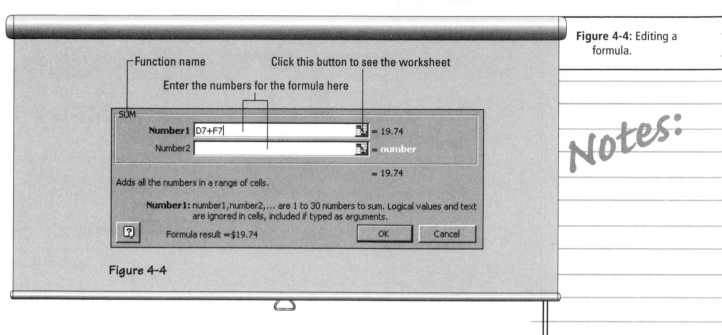

Figure 4-4: Editing a formula.

Figure 4-4

4 **Enter** 6 **and press the Enter key.**

The totals in cells G6 and G10 change instantly. Meanwhile, the cursor moves down the column to cell C7. As a convenience to make data entry easier, Excel moves the cursor down the column after you make an entry directly in a cell and press Enter. This way, you can start entering the next number in the column without having to press keys or click to move the cursor.

5 **Press Ctrl+→ to move the cursor to the last column in the worksheet, cell G7 in this case.**

By pressing Ctrl and an arrow key, you can move the cursor to the edge of the data area of a worksheet. Ctrl+↑ moves the cursor to the first row, for example; Ctrl+↓ moves the cursor to the last rows; and Ctrl+← moves the cursor to the first column.

You might have noticed that the formula in cell G7 is incorrect. Instead of adding the number in cell E7 to the number in F7 to get the total sale, the formula adds D7 to F7. The formula in the Formula bar should read =SUM(E7+F7), not =SUM(D7+F7).

6 **Click the Edit Formula button.**

The Edit Formula dialog box appears, as shown in Figure 4-4. The Number 1 box shows the formula that is currently entered. To fix the formula, you could delete D7 and put E7 in its place, but instead you will enter the cell addresses a box at a time. Entering the numbers a box at a time makes telling Excel 97 exactly what you want to do easier.

7 **Enter** E7 **in the Number 1 box.**

The number in cell E7 is the first of the two numbers you want the SUM function to compute.

Notes:

press Ctrl and an arrow key to move the cursor to the edge of the data area

=

Edit Formula button

Notes:

8 **Click the Number 2 box and enter** F7.

Now Excel 97 knows which two numbers to compute. Moreover, another Number box appears in case you want to include a number in another cell in the formula. If you were confused about which cell addresses you were entering, you could click the button on the right of the Number 1 or 2 box to see your spreadsheet. Check it out.

9 **Click the button to the right of one of the Number boxes.**

You see the worksheet again, with the cell addresses you've entered so far in cell G7 and a blank box below the Formula bar for entering cell addresses directly.

10 **Click the button to the right of the blank box to return to the dialog box, click OK, and then click the Formula bar.**

The new cell address you entered appears in the Formula bar, the formula in cell G7 is correct, and so is the total in cell G7.

Leave the Cell file open if you'd like to read about the AutoFill feature in "Letting AutoFill do the work."

extra credit

Letting AutoFill do the work

Much of the information that you enter in worksheets is *serial information*, or information that follows a pattern, such as the months of the year or the days of the week. Suppose, for example, that you were constructing a worksheet that tracked data by month. In that case, you would enter the twelve months of the year in twelve cells. In its wisdom, Excel recognizes serial entries such as these, and the program can enter them for you with a feature called *AutoFill*. To see how AutoFill works, click cell A12 of the Cell worksheet and follow these steps:

1. **Type** January **in cell A12.**

   Notice that the active cell rectangle — the one around January — now shows a tiny plus sign. That plus sign is a signal that the AutoFill feature may be able to make the next cell entry for you.

2. **Click the tiny plus sign in the lower-right corner of cell A12 and drag it downward over the next cell.**

   The word February appears in a small box. After you release the mouse button, Excel 97 enters the word February in cell A13.

3. **Release the mouse button.**

Besides using AutoFill to enter serial information, you can use the feature to enter the same data in cell after cell. To do so, enter the data you want to enter many times over, click the tiny plus sign, and drag. A box appears with the same data you entered in the previous cell. Release the mouse button if you want to enter the same data a second time.

☑ **Progress Check**

If you can perform the following tasks, you've mastered this lesson:

❏ Enter data in worksheet cells.

❏ Edit a formula in the Formula bar.

❏ Change the data in cells.

Copying, Moving, and Deleting Data

Lesson 4-4

If you worked through Lesson 2-4 about copying and moving data in Word 97, you are going to find this lesson fairly easy. Copying and moving data in Excel 97 is similar to copying and moving data in Word 97. You can cut, copy, and paste, as well as drag and drop data.

heads up

The difference, however, is that you must be careful where you copy and move data in Excel. If you're *not* careful, you may overwrite existing data on the worksheet. What's more, the data being moved or copied must fit in the place to which you want to move or copy it. Fortunately, deleting data is a breeze. All you need to do is select the cells and give the Clear command to empty all the cells of data.

on the CD

To try out the Excel 97 moving, copying, and deleting commands, open the Copy Move file in the Office 101 folder and follow these steps:

1 **Drag the mouse over cells C12 through C15 to select the regions (West, East, North, and South) on the worksheet.**

Dragging is a good way to select cells in Excel 97. To drag, click on a cell, hold down the mouse button, and slide the mouse point over the cells you want to select. You can also click in the first cell, press and hold the Shift key, and click in the last cell.

If you select the cells correctly in Step 1, all cells are highlighted except the first cell, C12, and row numbers 12 through 15 are highlighted on the left side of the screen.

2 **To cut the data from these cells, right-click the highlighted range and choose Cut from the shortcut menu.**

You can also choose Edit⇨Cut, press Ctrl+X, or click the Cut button on the Standard toolbar. After you cut the cells, flashing lights, much like those on a Las Vegas casino marquee, appear around the cells. The marquee lights tell you which cells have been cut. If you copy data (by choosing Edit⇨Copy, pressing Ctrl+C, clicking the Copy button, or right-clicking and choosing Copy), you also see the flashing lights.

3 **Click cell B12, right-click, and choose Paste from the shortcut menu.**

Sorry for being repetitious, but you can also give the Paste command by choosing Edit⇨Paste, pressing Ctrl+V, or clicking the Paste button on the Standard toolbar.

4 **Select cells D11 through E15.**

on the test

To select a block of cells, start in a corner of the cell range and drag across to the other corner. You can also click the first cell, press and hold the Shift key, and click the last cell you want to select. This time, you are going to move the column headings as well as the text underneath.

Cut button

Paste button

Notes:

5 **Choose your favorite Cut command, click cell C11, and choose your favorite means of pasting cell data.**

This block of data moves to a new location. Notice that the percentage figure in cell G12 is still correct. When you move cells, Excel 97 adjusts formulas so that the formulas all remain accurate.

6 **Click anywhere in column E, right-click, and choose <u>D</u>elete from the shortcut menu.**

The Delete dialog box appears. The other way to see this dialog box is to choose <u>E</u>dit⇨<u>D</u>elete. Open this dialog box if you want to delete an entire column or row.

7 **Click the Entire <u>c</u>olumn radio button and then click OK.**

Column E disappears, and the information in columns F, G, and H moves to the left to fill the space. To delete an entire row, click the row you want to delete, open the Delete dialog box, choose the Entire <u>R</u>ow radio button, and click OK. The percentage figure in the last column remains correct, in spite of all the changes you've made to the worksheet.

8 **Click cell F12, the one that reads** 95.7%, **to select that cell.**

In the following step, you see how to copy text by using the drag-and-drop method.

9 **Move the cursor over the lower-right corner of the cell rectangle; after the cursor changes into a black cross, click and drag past cells F13, F14, and F15; then release the mouse button.**

As you drag, you copy the formula from cell to cell. And Excel 97, displaying great foresight and wisdom, adjusts the cell references in the formula as you copy so that the results remain accurate all down the line, from cell F13 to cell F15.

A *cell reference* is the cell address that a formula refers to. For example, the formula in Cell F12 is PRODUCT(E12/D12). In that formula, E12 and D12 are cell references.

10 **Click cell B18.**

Better erase this little piece of sloganeering. Doesn't quite fit the rest of the worksheet.

In Step 11, you do not delete the cell as you did in Steps 6 and 7. You will merely delete the contents of the cell.

11 **Right-click and choose Clear Co<u>n</u>tents from the shortcut menu.**

You can also use this command by choosing <u>E</u>dit⇨Clea<u>r</u>⇨<u>A</u>ll. If you clear the contents of a cell, you delete the data or formula inside it; you don't delete the cell itself. Choose this command to empty cells of their data.

As you can see, Excel 97 offers a bunch of different ways to move, copy, and delete text. Did you notice how similar the cut and copy commands in Excel 97 and Word 97 are? The commands in PowerPoint 97 and Access 97 are similar as well.

☑ Progress Check

If you can perform the following tasks, you've mastered this lesson:

❑ Select data in a worksheet.

❑ Copy data from one block of cells to another.

❑ Move a block of cells to a new place in a worksheet.

Recess

I hear the recess bell. Take a break. Stop by your locker, fish the sandwich out of your lunch bag, and gobble it down before the next class. And while you're standing at your locker, don't peer over the shoulder of other students to read their locker combinations. That would be unethical.

Viewing Worksheets

Lesson 4-5

To help you view and enter data in worksheets, Excel 97 offers different ways of displaying worksheets on-screen. You can see where page breaks fall, remove much of the clutter from the top and bottom of the Excel 97 screen, and "freeze" the heading or row labels so that you always see them, no matter how far you travel on the outskirts of the worksheet.

on the CD

Open the View Data file in the Office 101 folder and follow these steps to learn about worksheet views:

1 **Choose <u>V</u>iew⇨<u>P</u>age Break Preview.**

As shown in Figure 4-5, you see a smaller version of the worksheet. The blue dotted line on the right is where the page "breaks," or gets cut off on the right side, when you print the worksheet. If this spreadsheet were longer, you would see another dotted line along the bottom to show where the page breaks on the bottom.

Handling page breaks is one of the hardest nuts to crack in Excel. One way to handle worksheets that break in the middle is to make the left and right margins narrower. (Lesson 3-1 explains how.) Another way is to print the worksheet in *landscape mode* (you can learn how in "Printing a landscape worksheet," later in this unit). Yet another way is to move the page break in the Page Break Preview window.

2 **Move the pointer over the blue dotted line and, after the pointer changes into a double arrow, click and drag the dotted line one column to the right.**

Excel 97 shrinks the worksheet to make it fit on one page. If this worksheet had one or two more columns, or if the right margin was wider, you may not have been able to drag the dotted line to the right. You would have what is known in Excel 97 circles as a "page break problem." You would need to make the worksheet's margins narrower, make the columns in the worksheet narrower, or print in landscape mode to fit the worksheet on a single page.

3 **Choose <u>V</u>iew⇨<u>N</u>ormal to return to Normal view.**

As you know already, Normal view is the view for entering and editing data in cells. Does Excel 97 offer views for making editing and entering data easier?

Figure 4-5: On the Page Break Preview screen, you can see where pages break in a worksheet.

Figure 4-6: By "freezing panes," you can make sure that you enter data in the right cells.

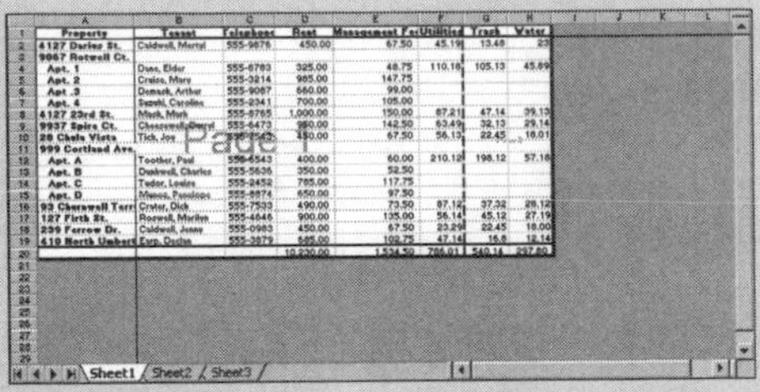

Figure 4-5 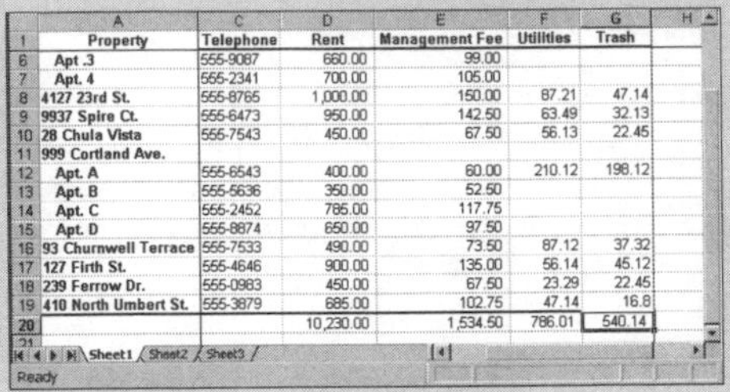   Figure 4-6

4 **Move the cursor to cell G20.**

To get there quickly, press Ctrl+End to get to the last cell in the worksheet.

Suppose that you wanted to change the formula in this cell. How would you know what you're changing? You can't tell which column or row you're working with because you can't see the column headings or row labels.

5 **Press Ctrl+Home to move to the first cell in the worksheet.**

In the next step, you "freeze the panes" of the worksheet so that, wherever you go, you always see the column headings in row 1 and the row labels in column A. Before you freeze the panes, however, you must tell Excel 97 which rows and columns to freeze.

6 **Click cell B2.**

To tell Excel which rows and columns to freeze, put the cursor in the row *below* the row you want to freeze (row 2 in this case, because you want to freeze row 1) and in the column to the right of the column you want to freeze (column B in this case, because you want to freeze column A).

7 **Choose Window⇨Freeze Panes and then press Ctrl+End.**

Your screen looks like Figure 4-6. Even though the cursor is in the last row of the worksheet, you can still see the column headings and row labels. Obviously, being able to see headings and labels is a great advantage when you are working on a long spreadsheet with many columns and rows.

8 **Choose View⇨Full Screen.**

Full Screen view presents another way to focus on data entry. In Full Screen view, the toolbars, Formula bar, and so on disappear, and more cells appear onscreen. What's more, Full Screen view gives you a better picture of what the worksheet will look like after you print it, because this view removes most of the clutter from the screen.

9 **Click the Close Full Screen button to leave Full Screen view.**

10 **Choose Window⇨Unfreeze Panes to end the "freeze pane" arrangement.**

I hope your point of view concerning ways to view Excel 97 worksheets was the same as my point of view. At any rate, leave the View Data file open if you want to learn about printing a landscape-format worksheet in "Printing a landscape worksheet."

Ctrl+End takes you to the last cell in the worksheet

Ctrl+Home takes you to the first cell in the worksheet

☑ **Progress Check**

If you can perform the following tasks, you've mastered this lesson:

❑ View and make adjustments on the Page Break Preview screen.

❑ Freeze the panes in a worksheet.

❑ Switch to Full Screen view.

Printing a Worksheet

Unless you print a worksheet, how can you show others what an expert you are in using Excel 97? In this lesson, you learn how to print part of a worksheet, how to print an entire worksheet, and how to print an entire workbook. So that you don't embarrass yourself, this lesson also explains how to get a sneak preview of what you are about to print before you actually print it.

on the CD

To learn about the Excel 97 printing options, open the Print Me file and follow these steps:

1 Click the Print Preview button.

The Preview screen appears and you get a bird's-eye view of the worksheet. Print Me fits on the page, but was the data entered correctly?

2 Click the Zoom button.

Now you can see the data a little better. If this were a long worksheet, you would use the scroll bars to slide the data around on-screen and look at it more closely.

3 Click the Close button to get out of the Preview screen.

You can print the worksheet on-screen, print parts of the worksheet, or print an entire workbook, as the following steps demonstrate.

4 Click the Print button.

After you click the Print button, Excel prints the worksheet on-screen in its entirety. Suppose, however, that you want to print only part of a worksheet or an entire workbook?

5 Choose File⇨Print or press Ctrl+P.

The Print dialog box appears, as shown in Figure 4-7.

6 Enter a 2 in the Number of copies text box.

To enter a **2**, you can either type the number yourself or click the up arrow at the side of the text box.

7 Glance at the Print range area of the dialog box and make sure that the All radio button is selected.

The All setting prints whatever you choose in the Print what area in its entirety. Print Me is only one page long, but if the worksheet were three or four pages long, you could make entries in the Page(s) From and To text boxes to tell Excel which pages to print.

8 In the Print what area, click the Entire workbook radio button.

By clicking this button, you tell Excel to print all the worksheets in the workbook. The Selection radio button is for printing cells that you select before opening the Print dialog box.

9 Click OK.

As long as your printer is turned on, you get two copies of all the worksheets in the workbook, a total of four pages altogether.

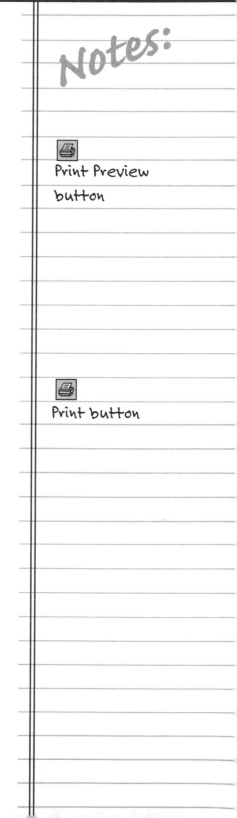

Notes:

Print Preview button

Print button

Figure 4-7: Printing a worksheet.

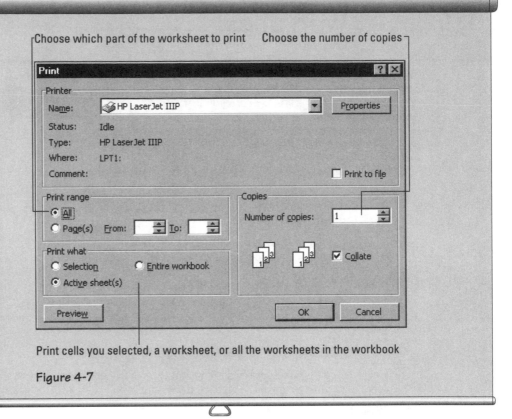

Choose which part of the worksheet to print   Choose the number of copies

Print cells you selected, a worksheet, or all the worksheets in the workbook

Figure 4-7

Ctrl+P opens the
Print dialog box

✓ Progress Check

If you can perform the following tasks, you're ready to move on to the Unit 4 quiz:

❏ Preview a worksheet before you print it.

❏ Print an entire worksheet.

❏ Print an entire workbook.

Printing a landscape worksheet

Maybe the best way to get around the problem of not being able to fit a worksheet on the page is to print the worksheet in *landscape mode*. In landscape mode, the page is "turned on its side" and is wider than it is tall so that you can fit more columns on the page. To print a landscape page, follow these steps:

1. **Choose File➪Page Setup.**

   You see the Page tab of the Page Setup dialog box.

2. **Click the Landscape radio button.**

3. **Click the Print Preview button.**

   Excel 97 shows you how the page is to appear after you print it. Notice how this page is wider than it is long. Do all the columns fit?

4. **Click the Close button.**

Unit 4 Quiz

For the following questions, circle the letter of the correct answer or answers. This short quiz is designed to help you remember what you learned in Unit 4. Each question may have more than one right answer.

1. **The active cell is which of the following?**

    A. The one on which you're performing math.

    B. A revolutionary group bent on usurping the central government.

    C. The one with a rectangle around it.

    D. The one whose label, number, or formula appears in the Formula bar.

    E. None of the above.

2. **If the cursor is in cell address C4, where is the cursor located in the worksheet?**

    A. Row C, column 4.

    B. Column C, row 4.

    C. The third column and the fourth row.

    D. The high-rent district.

    E. Near the top.

3. **If you have any doubts about how Excel 97 arrived at a number in a cell, you can perform which of the following actions to determine which formula Excel used to produce the number?**

    A. Look in the Formula bar.

    B. Change the numbers around and see what happens.

    C. Click the cell where the number is and look in the Formula bar.

    D. Throw up your hands in dismay.

    E. Choose Help➪What's This and click the number in question.

4. **To erase the data in a bunch of cells and empty them out, you must perform which of the following actions?**

    A. Click each one and delete the words or letters in the Formula bar.

    B. Select the cells and choose Edit➪Clear➪Contents.

    C. Select the cells, right-click, and choose Clear Contents from the shortcut menu.

    D. Select the cells one at a time and press the Del key.

    E. All of the above.

Notes:

5.   **To find out whether a worksheet fits on the page, you can perform which of the following actions?**

A. Click the Print Preview button and have a look-see.

B. Choose View⇨Full Screen.

C. Choose View⇨Page Break Preview.

D. Print the worksheet and find out.

E. Choose View⇨Normal.

6.   **To print an entire workbook, you can perform which of the following actions?**

A. Click the Print button.

B. Press Ctrl+P to open the Print dialog box and then click OK.

C. Open the Print dialog box, choose the All radio button, and click OK.

D. Open the Print dialog box, click the Entire Workbook radio button, and then click OK.

E. Click the worksheet tabs one at a time to see each worksheet in the workbook and click the Print button as you do so.

Unit 4 Exercise

on the CD

1.   Open the Quiz 4 file in the Office101 folder.

2.   Enter **March** and **April** in cell D5 and D6 by using AutoFill.

3.   Go to worksheet 2 and then come back to worksheet 1.

4.   Click cell F8 and edit the formula. (The formula is incorrect; it should sum cells B8 through E8.)

5.   Delete column E.

6.   Switch to the Page Break Preview screen to see whether this worksheet fits on a single page. Switch back.

7.   Print both worksheets in this workbook.

Making a Worksheet Look Just Right

Prerequisites
- Opening a file (Lesson 1-2)
- Moving around the Excel 97 screen (Lesson 4-2)
- Selecting cells (Lesson 4-4)

on the CD

- Formatting
- Columns and Rows
- Align
- Borders and Colors
- Quiz 5

Objectives for This Unit

✓ Formattng the numbers and text in cells

✓ Adjusting column widths and row heights

✓ Deleting columns and rows

✓ Aligning numbers and text in columns

✓ Including borders, patterns, and colors in worksheets

So far in Part II, you have learned how to enter and edit raw data in an Excel 97 worksheet. Raw data, however, is not pretty to look at. Studies show that nine out of ten people yawn when presented with row after row of numbers. You can, however, prevent people from yawning by taking advantage of the techniques presented in Unit 5.

This unit explains how to format numbers and text so that others can more easily understand what you are trying to communicate. Unit 5 tells how to make columns wider or more narrow, make rows taller or shorter, and delete rows and columns. In this unit, you also learn how to align numbers and text in columns, and how to change the appearance of text and numbers. Finally, this unit describes how to dress up a worksheet by putting borders around cells and by applying color.

You may not be a snappy dresser, but at least your worksheets will be well dressed after you finish the exercises in Unit 5.

Lesson 5-1

Formatting Numbers and Text

Notes:

When others first see your worksheets, they should be able to tell right away what the numbers mean and where the column headings and row labels are. To that end, Excel 97 lets you format numbers in different ways and change the font of column headings and row labels. If you completed Lesson 2-6 about applying fonts and character styles in Word 97, you may find this lesson particularly easy, because the techniques for handling fonts and character styles in Excel 97 are nearly the same as in Word 97.

on the CD

To practice formatting numbers and text, follow these steps:

1 **Open the Formatting file in the Office 101 folder.**

As soon as you open this file, a swarm of numbers leaps into your face and you flinch in terror. Can you make this worksheet easier to read and understand? Of course you can — by formatting it. By the end of this lesson, you should have this worksheet looking as clear and readable as the worksheet in Figure 5-1.

2 **Click in cell A1, if that cell is not already the active cell.**

Now that cell A1 is the active cell, the words *Book Sales* are selected and ready to be formatted.

3 **Click the Font drop-down list and choose Arial Black and then click the Font Size drop-down list and choose 12 to make the text 12 points high; then click the Italic button.**

In case you didn't do Lesson 2-6, the Font drop-down list and Font Size drop-down list are on the left side of the Formatting toolbar. Click the downward pointing arrows to open the drop-down lists.

Changing fonts and font sizes in a worksheet is the surest way to grab readers' attention. Now that the title is larger and in boldface type, everybody knows that the numbers on the worksheet represent book sales.

4 **Select cells A3 to G3, the column headings on the worksheet, and click the Bold button in the Standard toolbar; then select cells A4 to A8 and click the Bold button to boldface those cells as well.**

By boldfacing the labels in a worksheet, you let readers know what the numbers themselves represent. Speaking of numbers, you would do your readers a favor by formatting them, too. Some of the numbers on this worksheet represent dollar figures, others represent percentages, and others represent quantities. And come to think of it, some of the monetary figures display far too many numbers to the right of the decimal point. You fix that problem in the following step.

5 **Click cell F4 and drag to cell G9 to select the monetary figures in columns F and G and then click the Decrease Decimal button.**

All the numbers now have only two decimal places.

heads up

Clicking the Decrease Decimal button or the Increase Decimal button means nothing to the actual figures in a worksheet — these buttons only affect the display of decimal places. If the numbers in a worksheet appear not to add up or compute correctly, try clicking the Increase Decimal button to see what the numbers in the worksheet really are.

I

Italic button

B

Bold button

.00
+.0

Decrease Decimal button

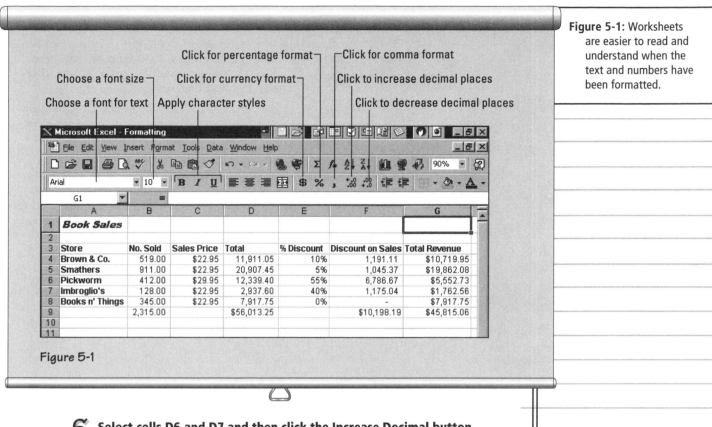

Click for percentage format ─┐   ┌─ Click for comma format

Choose a font size ─┐   Click for currency format ─┐   Click to increase decimal places

Choose a font for text   Apply character styles   Click to decrease decimal places

Figure 5-1

Figure 5-1: Worksheets are easier to read and understand when the text and numbers have been formatted.

6 **Select cells D6 and D7 and then click the Increase Decimal button.**

As monetary figures, the numbers in these cells should go to two decimal places.

What else could you do to improve the appearance of this worksheet? I think putting commas in the numbers would help a lot.

7 **Click cell B4 and drag to cell G9 to select all the numbers in the worksheet; then click the Comma Style button.**

With commas, it's easier to make sense of these numbers. Notice what the Comma Style button did to cells E8 and F8. Previously, these cells contained zeroes, but now hyphens appear in E8 and F8.

In the following two steps, you will experiment with the program's two options for putting dollar signs on figures. If you noticed, many figures in the worksheet represent dollar figures. However, rather than put dollar signs on all the monetary figures, I think a worksheet is easier to read if you put dollar signs only on the monetary figures in the Totals columns and rows. A lot of dollar signs in a worksheet makes the worksheet look crowded and renders it harder to read. In the next two steps, you will put dollar signs in column C (so readers know what the sales price of the books are); in cells D9 and F9; and in column G, the Total Revenue column.

8 **Select cells C4 to C8 and click the Currency Style button (which has a dollar sign on it); then select D9 and F9 and click the Currency Style button; finally, select G4 to G9 and click the Currency Style button again.**

Dollar signs appear at the left sides of the cells you selected. But Excel 97 offers another option for attaching dollar signs to figures. If you use this second option, the dollar sign appears right next to the figure. You try out this method in the following step.

Increase Decimal button

Comma Style button

☑ Progress Check

If you can perform the following tasks, you've mastered this lesson:

❑ Format text by changing its font and its font size or by choosing a character style.

❑ Apply comma, percentage, and currency formats.

❑ Display fewer or more numbers to the right of the decimal point.

9 Select the same cells you selected in Step 8, but this time right-click after you select the cells, choose Format Cells from the shortcut menu to see the Number tab of the Format Cells dialog box, click Currency in the Category list, and click OK.

Now the dollar signs appear directly to the left of the numbers. Besides right-clicking and choosing Format Cells from the shortcut menu, you can also choose Format⇨Cells to open the Format Cells dialog box. The Number tab in this dialog box offers many ways to format cells.

Steps 5 and 6 in this lesson explained how to click the Increase Decimal and Decrease Decimal buttons to tell Excel 97 how many decimal places to display. However, you don't have to concern yourself with decimals when you choose a currency format for numbers, because Excel 97 displays all monetary figures to two decimal places.

The figures in column E represent percentages. Readers would understand that better if these figures were assigned the Percentage format.

10 Select cell E4 to E8 and click the Percent Style button.

The Percent Style button has a percent symbol on it. Your worksheet should look like the one in Figure 5-1. You can close the Formatting file now. You've come a long way since Step 1 in this lesson. Keep reading Unit 5 to learn other ways to dress up a worksheet.

Lesson 5-2

Changing the Width and Height of Columns and Rows

To make all the labels and numbers fit in the columns and rows on a worksheet, you often need to make columns wider and rows taller. That task is the subject of this important lesson. Readers have been known to get claustrophobia when words and numbers are packed too tightly in a worksheet.

To find out how to adjust columns and rows, follow these steps:

1 Open the Columns and Rows file in the Office 101 folder.

When Excel 97 can't fit text in a column, it lets the text spill into the following column — unless something happens to be in that column as well. In Figure 5-2, you can see that Excel 97 has let "McCullom Tool & Die" spread its wings all the way from column B to column F. The column labels in cell B10 and D10, however, are too wide, and Excel 97 has cut those labels off in favor of the column labels in cell C10 and E10. Several numbers in this worksheet are cut off, too. If Excel 97 can't display a number in its entirety, the program shows you a bunch of number signs (####).

What a mess this worksheet is. How can you fix it?

in a cell means that the number is too wide for the column

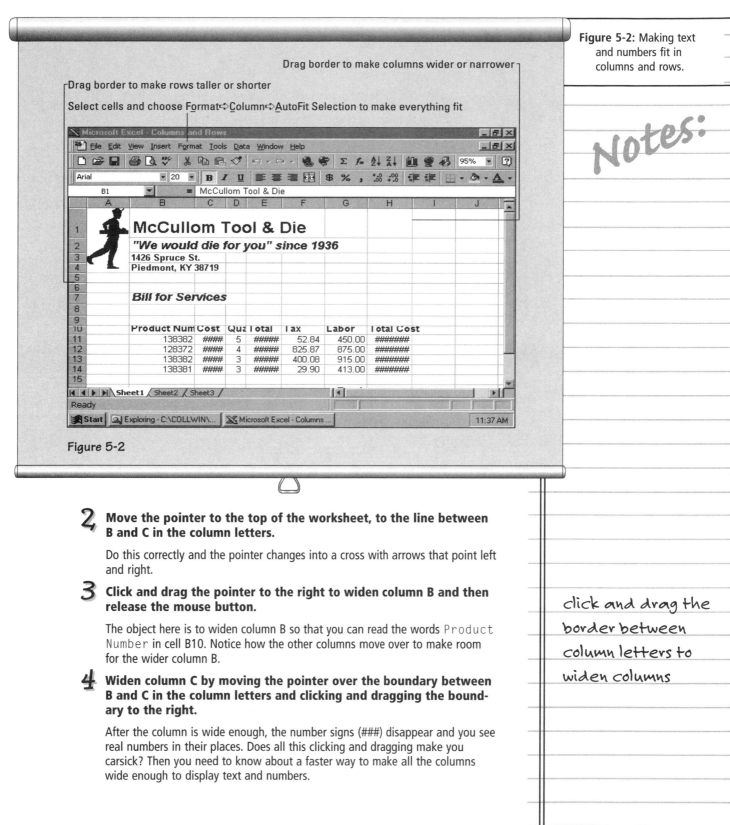

Figure 5-2: Making text and numbers fit in columns and rows.

Figure 5-2

Drag border to make columns wider or narrower

Drag border to make rows taller or shorter

Select cells and choose Format⇨Column⇨AutoFit Selection to make everything fit

Notes:

2 **Move the pointer to the top of the worksheet, to the line between B and C in the column letters.**

Do this correctly and the pointer changes into a cross with arrows that point left and right.

3 **Click and drag the pointer to the right to widen column B and then release the mouse button.**

The object here is to widen column B so that you can read the words Product Number in cell B10. Notice how the other columns move over to make room for the wider column B.

4 **Widen column C by moving the pointer over the boundary between B and C in the column letters and clicking and dragging the boundary to the right.**

After the column is wide enough, the number signs (###) disappear and you see real numbers in their places. Does all this clicking and dragging make you carsick? Then you need to know about a faster way to make all the columns wide enough to display text and numbers.

click and drag the border between column letters to widen columns

☑ Progress Check

If you can perform the following tasks, you've mastered this lesson:

❑ Drag a column border at the top of the screen to change column widths.

❑ Drag a row border on the left side of the screen to make rows taller or shorter.

❑ Choose Format⇨Column and Format⇨Row commands to adjust columns and rows.

5 **Select all the cells in the invoice (cells B10 to H16) and then choose Format⇨Column⇨AutoFit Selection.**

This command makes each column wide enough to accommodate its largest cell. Also on the Format⇨Column menu is a command called Standard Width. Choose this command to make all columns the same width, no matter how narrow or wide their numbers or words are.

Bill for Services in cell B7 looks a little cramped. As the next three steps demonstrate, you can change the height of rows as easily as you can change the width of columns.

6 **Gently place the cursor on the borderline between the 7 and 8 in the row numbers on the left side of the screen and then click and drag the border downward and release the mouse button.**

To make a row taller, go to the row numbers on the left side of the screen, click the borderline *below* the row whose height you want to change, and start dragging. To make a row shorter, drag up instead of down.

Wouldn't you know, but the Format menu also offers commands for changing the height of rows.

7 **Click the 10 in the row numbers and drag to the 16 to select all the rows in the invoice.**

8 **Choose Format⇨Row⇨AutoFit.**

Excel 97 makes each row tall enough to accommodate its tallest character.

By dragging column and row borders along the top or side of the screen and by choosing commands from the Format menu, you can tug and pull the columns and rows of a worksheet until they look just right.

Leave the Columns and Rows file open if you care or dare to try the next lesson, which explains how to insert and delete columns and rows.

Lesson 5-3

Inserting and Deleting Columns and Rows

In the previous lesson, I explained how to prevent claustrophobia in worksheets by making rows taller and columns wider. Worksheets can also suffer from agoraphobia, the unsettling feeling that arises when one is surrounded by too much open space. To prevent agoraphobia in a worksheet, you can delete unnecessary columns and rows. This lesson explains how to to do that. The lesson also explains how to insert columns and rows in case, like me, you enjoy the wide open spaces.

To learn how to delete columns and rows, you need the Columns and Rows file (if you closed the file at the end of the last lesson, open it) and follow these steps:

1 **Click and drag the pointer across row numbers 5 and 6 on the left side of the screen to select rows 5 and 6.**

To tell Excel 97 how many rows to insert, select that many rows. Because you selected two, you can insert two new rows below rows 5 and 6.

2 **Right-click and choose Insert from the shortcut menu.**

Two new rows appear below row 5 and 6. Notice that the numbers in the worksheet are still accurate — Excel 97 has adjusted the cell references in formulas for you.

You can also insert rows by selecting a row or rows and then choosing Insert⇨Rows.

3 **Select the two rows you just inserted and choose Edit⇨Delete.**

on the test

You can also delete rows by right-clicking and choosing Delete from the shortcut menu. I bet you knew that already, but you may not know that selecting a row and pressing the Del key *does not* delete a row. If you select a row and press Del, you delete all the numbers and text in the row, but *not* the row itself.

4 **Click the G column heading at the top of the screen to select the column and then right-click and choose Delete.**

Do you notice a theme here? The shortcut menu and Edit menu commands for inserting and deleting rows are very similar.

5 **Click the Undo button.**

Lesson 2-5 explained how to undo mistakes by using the magical Undo button. I mention Undo here, too, because the Undo button comes in very handy when you are inserting and deleting rows and columns.

6 **With column G still selected, right-click and choose Insert from the shortcut menu.**

Two new columns appear to the right of column G. If you had selected two columns before you chose Insert, two columns instead of one would be inserted in the document.

Excel 97 makes inserting and deleting columns and rows easy. You don't need to worry about formulas going haywire, because the program adjusts cell references in formulas after you delete or insert rows and columns. And if you delete or insert something and live to regret it, you can always click the Undo button to get back to where you started.

drag across the row numbers to select rows

Notes:

click column letters or drag across them to select rows

☑ **Progress Check**

If you can perform the following tasks, you've mastered this lesson:

❑ Insert one or more columns.

❑ Insert one or more rows.

Aligning Numbers and Text   Lesson 5-4

In this lesson, you learn a very important beauty secret — how to lay out text and numbers in a worksheet. How a worksheet is laid out says a lot about how much thought and effort went into it. I want your friends and coworkers to think that you spend hours laying out your worksheets, even if you do the job in five minutes while you chat on the phone with an aluminum-siding salesperson.

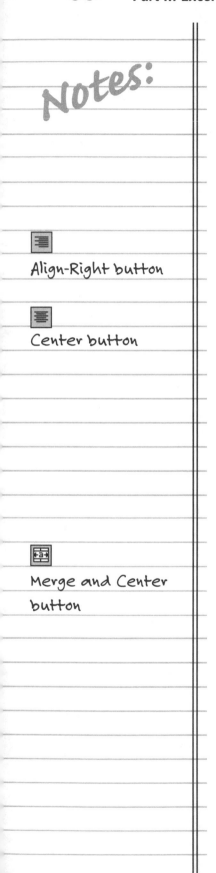

Notes:

on the CD

This lesson explains how to center, right-align, and and left-align text and numbers. It also describes how to merge cells and even offers a tricky technique for turning letters sideways.

To try your hand at aligning text and numbers in a worksheet, follow these steps:

1   **Open the Align file in the Office 101 folder.**

Unless you change alignment settings yourself, words are left-aligned in the cells and numbers are right-aligned so that the hundreds, tens, ones, and so on line up underneath each other. In the following three steps, you try out basic alignment techniques.

2   **Select all the column headings and click the Align-Right button.**

The column headings were left-aligned, but now they hug the right side of the cells, as do the numbers below the headings.

3   **Select all the text and numbers in cell A7 to F11 and click the Center button.**

The data now lines up smack-dab in the middle of the columns where everyone can see it. In wide columns such as these, data can get lost on the left or right side of cells, but centering data is a good way to flush it out and make it stand in the open.

Now look at cells A2 and A4 at the top of the screen. In Figure 5-3, the words in these cells (`The number of mergers has increased steadily in the past half decade`) are centered across the entire table. To format words in that manner, you must merge cells and center the data across the cells. The following two steps explain how.

4   **Select cells A2 to F2.**

You merge these cells in the next step and center the title of the worksheet as well.

5   **Click the Merge and Center button.**

Your worksheet looks like Figure 5-3. Try merging and centering the sentence in cell A4.

6   **Select Cells A4 to F4 and click the Merge and Center button.**

These cells are merged and centered as well.

As for that vertical `Ouch!` in cell F6, the following steps show you how to make text of your own stand on its ear.

7   **Click cell F6 and then choose Format⇨Cells or press Ctrl+1.**

The Format Cells dialog box appears.

8   **Click the Alignment tab.**

In the Orientation area, you can see that I swung the text in cell F6 to 90 degrees. Try moving the text to a 45-degree angle.

9   **Either type 45 in the Degrees box or click the red diamond and drag it clockwise until the Degrees box says 45 and then click OK.**

There you have it — a 45-degree "Ouch!"

on the test

Align-Right button

Center button

Merge and Center button

heads up

Turning text on its ear is a great way to get around page break problems. Instead of letting a column head take up valuable space, you can turn it on its side.

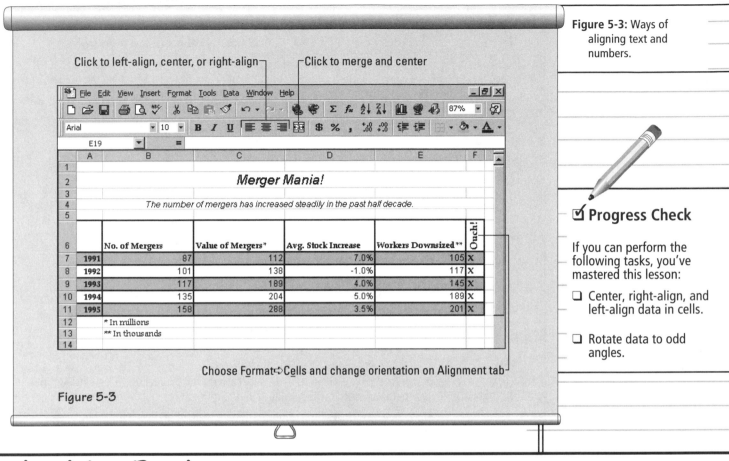

Click to left-align, center, or right-align

Click to merge and center

Merger Mania!

The number of mergers has increased steadily in the past half decade.

	No. of Mergers	Value of Mergers*	Avg. Stock Increase	Workers Downsized**	Ouch!
1991	87	112	7.0%	105	X
1992	101	138	-1.0%	117	X
1993	117	189	4.0%	145	X
1994	135	204	5.0%	189	X
1995	158	288	3.5%	201	X

* In millions
** In thousands

Choose Format⇨Cells and change orientation on Alignment tab

Figure 5-3

Figure 5-3: Ways of aligning text and numbers.

☑ Progress Check

If you can perform the following tasks, you've mastered this lesson:

❑ Center, right-align, and left-align data in cells.

❑ Rotate data to odd angles.

Applying Borders, Patterns, and Colors

No worksheet is complete without borders. Borders steer the reader's eye to the totals column, column headings, row labels, and other important parts of a worksheet. You could say that a worksheet is naked until you give the poor thing borders — and you don't want a worksheet walking around naked, do you? And if you want a jazzy worksheet, you may also consider dressing its rows and columns in different colors, gray shades, or patterns. This lesson explains how.

on the CD

To try your hand at drawing borders and working with colors and gray shades, open the Borders and Colors file in the Office 101 folder and read on.

Putting borders on a worksheet

on the CD

In Lesson 5-2, you formatted the numbers in this worksheet. Now you are going to add borders. Excel 97 offers two ways to put borders on a worksheet, so follow these steps:

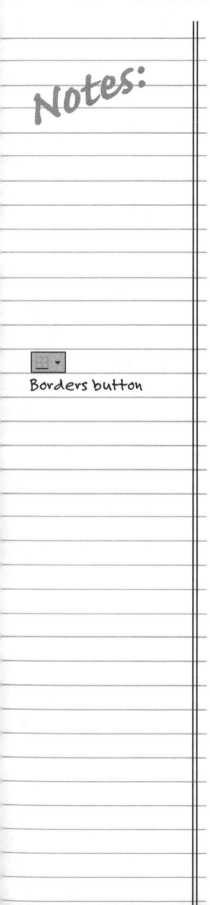

Borders button

1 **Select cells A3 to G3, the column headings in the worksheet.**

To add borders to parts of a worksheet, you start by selecting the parts of the worksheet around which, or inside of which, you want to draw the borders.

2 **Click the arrow beside the Borders button to see the Borders drop-down list, and then click the second button in the middle row — the one that shows a thick line under the square.**

As soon as you click the button, a thick line appears under cells A3 to G3, the cells you selected in Step 1.

Notice that the Borders button now shows a thick line instead of a thin one. Excel 97 puts your last choice from the Borders drop-down list on the button in case you want to use the same borders command again.

3 **Select cells A8 through G8 and click the Borders button.**

A border identical to the one you drew in Step 2 appears beneath these cells, too. Suppose that you want to draw a border on the top, right side, or left side of some cells. In that case, you must go back to the Borders drop-down list.

4 **Select cells G3 through G9, the `Total Revenue` column and then click the arrow beside the Borders button.**

As shown in Figure 5-4, the drop-down list offers 11 border choices, plus the one in the upper-left corner, which removes borders. Which choice you make from the drop-down list determines where the borders go — on all sides, in between, or to the left, right, top, or bottom of the cells you selected.

5 **Click the dark square in the lower-right corner of the drop-down list to place a dark border around all the cells in G3 through G9.**

The worksheet is starting to take shape. Everybody who sees it will know precisely where the Total column is, where the column headings are, and where the Totals row is at the bottom. What do you want to do about cells A4 to G8, the raw data that the total calculations are made from? To put borders around those cells, you try out the program's second way to draw borders.

6 **Select cells B4 to F8, right-click and choose Format Cells from the shortcut menu, and then click the Border tab in the Format Cells dialog box.**

You now see the Border tab of the Format Cells dialog box, as shown in Figure 5-5. From here, you can apply different kinds of borders to different parts of a worksheet. Notice that the borders you drew already — the thick lines on the outside of the cells you selected — appear in the dialog box. In the following three steps, you tell Excel 97 to keep the borders you drew already and apply borders to the cells on the inside of cell block B4 to F8.

7 **Under Style, click the bottom-most line in the left-hand column.**

The Style menu offers many more line choices than does the Borders drop-down list. You can apply thick lines, double lines, and dotted lines of various widths.

8 **In the Presets area, click the Inside button.**

Your dialog box should look like the one in Figure 5-5. To choose a border on the Border tab, choose a line in the Style menu and then click a Preset button or one of the Border buttons. These eight buttons place borderlines on the top, middle, and sides of the cells you selected. You can even draw diagonal lines through the cells.

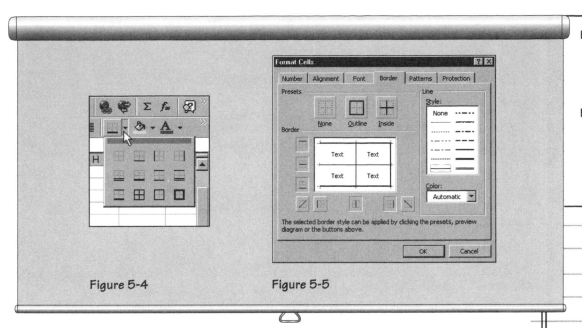

Figure 5-4

Figure 5-5

Figure 5-4: To draw
borders, select the
cells and click a
button on the Borders
drop-down list.

Figure 5-5: You can
choose an assortment
of borderlines from
the Borders tab of the
Format Cells dialog
box.

9 **Click OK to close the Format Cells dialog box.**

Borderlines appear around the interior cells of the worksheet. Something is
wrong, however: When you draw borders around these cells, you lose the thick
line on the left side of column G.

10 **Repeat Step 3: Select A8 through G8 and click the Borders button.**

Drawing handsome borders on the first attempt can be difficult, but by
tinkering with the Borders button and the Border tab in the Format Cells
dialog box, you can make the borders in a worksheet look just right. Read on
to discover how to apply colors and patterns to worksheets.

Applying colors and patterns

To experiment with colors and patterns, open the Borders and Colors file in
the Office 101 folder, if you haven't already done so, and follow these steps:

1 **Select cells A4 through A8, the row labels in the worksheet.**

Before applying a color or pattern, you select the cells you want to dress up.

2 **Choose Format⇨Cells and click the Patterns tab in the Format Cells
dialog box after the dialog box appears.**

You can also right-click and choose Format Cells or press Ctrl+1 to open the
Format Cells dialog box. It is shown in Figure 5-6.

3 **Under Color, click the box with your favorite color in it.**

The color you choose appears in the Sample box so that you can get a good
look at it. The two rows of squares at the bottom of the Color menu offer
"grainy" colors for people who are used to seeing grainy color on their TV sets.

Figure 5-6: Applying colors and patterns to parts of a worksheet.

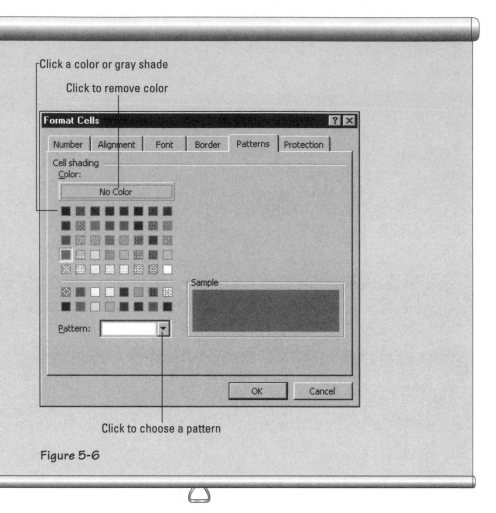

Figure 5-6

4 **Click OK.**

Cells A4 through A8 are "colorized." Try the following shortcut for bringing color to cells C4 through C8.

5 **Select cells C4 through C8 and then press F4.**

Pressing F4 (or choosing Edit⇨Repeat or pressing Ctrl+Y) repeats the last command you made. You can use this excellent shortcut not only in Excel 97, but also in all the Office 97 programs.

6 **Select cells E4 through E8 and then press Ctrl+1.**

Excel 97 takes you straight to the Patterns tab of the Format Cells dialog box. You've been second-guessed.

7 **Click the Pattern drop-down list and select a pattern from the top of the list.**

The Sample box shows the pattern you chose. If you choose a color before you chose a pattern, you get a pattern and a color.

8 **Click OK.**

pressing F4 repeats the last command

on the test

☑ Progress Check

If you can perform the following tasks, you've mastered this lesson:

❑ Put borders around or inside parts of a worksheet.

❑ Apply color and patterns to parts of a worksheet.

In my opinion, patterns don't look good in worksheets, but I leave you to be the judge of what looks good and what doesn't. If you don't have a color printer, you don't necessarily need to resort to patterns to highlight columns and rows. You can choose gray shades instead. The Color menu on the Patterns tab offers four shades of gray.

Unit 5 Quiz

For the following questions, circle the letter of the correct answer or answers. This short quiz is designed to help you remember what you learned in Unit 5. Each question may have more than one right answer.

1. **To change the formatting of text, you perform which of the following actions?**

   A. Click the Bold button.

   B. Choose a Font from the Font drop-down list.

   C. Click the Italic button.

   D. Choose a point size from the Font Size drop-down list.

   E. All of the above.

2. **These buttons do which of the following?**

   A. Round up the number.

   B. Increase the indent.

   C. Decrease or increase the number of decimal places in a number.

   D. Merge and center the number in a cell.

   E. Change the numbers to Currency format.

3. **To change the width of a column, you perform which of the following actions?**

   A. Drag the line between the letters at the top of the worksheet.

   B. Select the cells and choose Format⇨Column⇨AutoFit Selection.

   C. Start all over.

   D. Drag the border of a cell.

   E. Merge the cells in the columns.

4. **To delete a row, you perform which of the following actions?**

   A. Select the row and click the Del key.

   B. Select the row and choose Edit⇨Delete.

Notes:

C. Click the row number.

D. Select the row, right-click, and choose <u>D</u>elete from the shortcut menu.

E. Select the row and click the Undo button.

5. **This button does which of the following?**

A. Moves numbers to the left side of the cells.

B. Moves numbers to the right side of the cells.

C. Centers numbers in the cells.

D. Increases the number of decimal places displayed.

E. Saves the file.

6. **To apply borders to cells, you perform which of the following actions?**

A. Click the Borders button and make a choice from the drop-down list.

B. Select the cells, click the Borders button, and make a choice from the drop-down list.

C. Select the cells, press Ctrl+1, click the Border tab of the Format Cells dialog box, and make choices.

D. I never need to do that.

E. Select the cells and click the button with a B on it in the Formatting toolbar.

Unit 5 Exercise

on the CD

1. Open the Quiz 5 file in the Office 101 folder.

2. Switch to worksheet 2 and switch back again.

3. Boldface the title, column headings, and row labels. Make the title bigger.

4. Decrease the number of decimal places shown in column E.

5. Widen the columns so you can read them better.

6. Delete rows 1 and 3.

7. Center, right-align, or left-align the numbers and text in the cells to improve the worksheet's appearance.

8. Apply borders to the appropriate parts of the worksheet.

Generating Numbers and Results

Objectives for This Unit

✓ Creating formulas from worksheet data

✓ Copying formulas from cell to cell

✓ Using functions in formulas

✓ Using range names in formulas

✓ Creating charts from worksheet data

Prerequisites

▶ Opening and closing a file (Lesson 1-2)

▶ Finding your way around a worksheet (Lesson 4-2)

▶ Entering and editing worksheet data (Lesson 4-3)

▶ Copying, moving, and deleting data (Lesson 4-4)

on the CD

▶ Formula
▶ Function
▶ Range
▶ Chart
▶ Quiz 6

Unit 6 gets to the heart of Excel 97 — it explains how to write formulas that compute the numbers in worksheets. In the previous two units, you saw how Excel 97 computes new results instantaneously each time you change a number. For Excel 97 to do that accurately, you must construct the formulas correctly, which you learn to do in this unit. Unit 6 also explains how to create a glorious chart from the data you so laboriously assembled, entered, and computed.

The unit starts with a lesson about computing simple formulas and copying these formulas from cell to cell. Then you discover how to take advantage of *functions* — the predefined formulas that come with Excel 97. You can save yourself a lot of time by using functions. You also learn how to use ranges and range names instead of cell references in formulas. Charts, you will be glad to know, are easy to create. I show you just how easy in this unit.

Lesson 6-1   # Constructing and Copying Formulas

To construct a simple formula in a worksheet, all you need to do is revisit the math concepts that you learned in grade school: addition, division, exponentiation, multiplication, percentages, and subtraction. By entering arithmetic operators in formulas, you can add (+), divide (/), exponentiate (^), multiply (*), get the percentage of (%), and subtract (–) the values in cells. For example, the formula =F6+F7 totals the numbers in those cells. The formula =F6*F7 mutliplies the figures.

By copying formulas from cell to cell, you save yourself the trouble of entering cell references in formulas over and over. For example, in Figure 6-1, rather than enter a new formula in the Total row to obtain the income totals for each month, you can enter a formula in cell C8 and copy that formula to D8, E8, F8, and G8.

on the CD

To learn how to create simple formulas and copy them from cell to cell, open the Formula file in the Office 101 folder and follow these steps:

1 Click cell C8 and look in the Formula bar.

The formula in cell C8 adds cells C5, C6, and C7 to get the total income for the month of January. In the next step, you enter a formula that calculates February's income.

2 Click cell D8, click the Formula bar, type =D5+D6+D7, and then press the Enter key.

Don't enter spaces between the elements in a formula — in this case, the cell references, equal sign, and plus signs. If you enter the formula correctly, the Formula bar on your screen looks like the one in Figure 6-1.

heads up

Before you enter a formula in the Formula bar or directly in a cell, type an equal sign (=). If you don't, Excel 97 thinks you're entering text, not a formula.

By the way, you could enter the formula as follows: **=d5+d6+d7**. Excel 97 doesn't care whether you enter upper- or lowercase letters in cell references. After you press the Enter key or click the Enter button to submit the formula, the program changes all letters in cell references to uppercase.

If you're a poor typist, entering cell references in the Formula bar isn't easy, so Excel 97 offers another way to enter cell references. The next step demonstrates it.

3 Click cell E8, click the Formula bar, type =, and click cell E5.

You see E5 in the Formula bar after the equal sign. What's more, marquee lights (flashing dashes) appear around cell E5 in the worksheet.

4 Type + in the Formula bar and click cell E6; type + in the Formula bar and click cell E7; then click the Enter button.

Besides entering cell references by typing them, you can click the cells themselves. If you look in the Formula bar, you see the formula you entered by clicking cells.

You now know how to enter formulas by typing them and by clicking cells. Does Excel 97 offer other ways to enter formulas? Indeed it does.

type the equal sign (=) before entering a formula

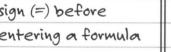

click cells to enter cell references in formulas

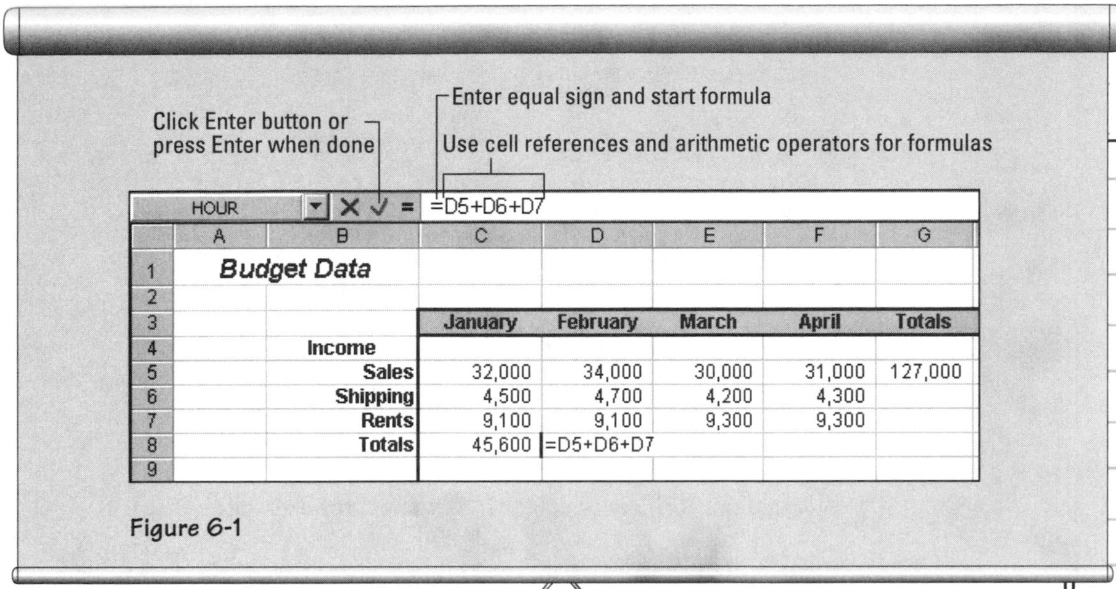

Figure 6-1: Entering a formula in the Formula bar.

Click Enter button or press Enter when done

Enter equal sign and start formula

Use cell references and arithmetic operators for formulas

HOUR	▼ X √ =	=D5+D6+D7				
	A	B	C	D	E	F	G
1		*Budget Data*					
2							
3			January	February	March	April	Totals
4		Income					
5		Sales	32,000	34,000	30,000	31,000	127,000
6		Shipping	4,500	4,700	4,200	4,300	
7		Rents	9,100	9,100	9,300	9,300	
8		Totals	45,600	=D5+D6+D7			
9							

Figure 6-1

5 **Right-click cell E8 and choose <u>C</u>opy from the shortcut menu; right-click cell F8 and then choose <u>P</u>aste from the menu.**

Excel 97 does not copy the result of the formula from E8 to F8; the program copies the formula itself. And after it copies the formula, Excel 97 adjusts the cell references so that the formula works in the cell to which it has been copied. Notice that the marquee lights continue to shine around cell E8. Those lights tell you which formula is on the Clipboard, in case you want to copy and paste the formula to another cell.

6 **Click cell G5.**

The formula in G5 totals cells C5, D5, E5, and F5. In the following step, you learn a way to copy a formula from one cell to several cells at once.

7 **Press Ctrl+C to copy the formula in cell G5 and then drag the pointer across cells G6 to G8 to select those cells; then press Ctrl+V to paste the formula in all three cells.**

Again, Excel 97 adjusts cell references so that these formulas are accurate, too.

8 **Click cell H6, type =G6/4, and click the Enter button.**

By using the division operator (/), you divide the total in G6 by 4 (the number of months) to obtain the average monthly revenue from shipping. The following step describes yet another technique for copying formulas.

9 **Click in Cell H6, move the pointer to the lower-right corner of cell H6, and, after the pointer changes into a black cross, click and gently slide the cursor across cells H7 and H8; then release the mouse button.**

So you can also copy a formula from cell to cell by dragging. Amazing!

on the test

10 **Click cell C15.**

The formula in this cell, =C5*5%, includes the multiplication operator. This formula multiplies the sales figure in cell C5 by 5 percent, the sales tax rate. Rather than enter **=C5*.05**, you can simply put the percentage operator (%)

Notes:

behind a number — 5, in this case — to tell Excel 97 that the number is a percentage.

11 **Click in cell D15, enter =D5*5% in the Formula bar, press Enter, and then copy the formula across cells E13 to F13 by dragging it there (Step 9 explains how).**

That takes care of sales tax expenses.

12 **Copy the formula in C17 to cells D17 to F17.**

What's your favorite copying method? Whatever it is, use that method.

13 **Copy the formula in cell G13 to cells G14 through G17 and then copy the formula in cell H13 to cells H14 through H16.**

Now you're ready to find out the net profit in the budget projection.

14 **Click cell D21, enter =D8-D17, and press the Enter key.**

This formula uses the subtraction operator to subtract the total expenses in cell D17 from the total income in cell D8 to arrive at a profit projection. In formulas, you can refer to cells anywhere in a worksheet. You don't need to stay with cell references directly above or directly below the cell into which you enter the formula.

15 **Close the Formula file without saving your changes.**

on the test

You can use simple formulas such as these to compute the data in worksheets. By the way, combining formulas in cells also is possible. To do that, enclose parts of the formula in parentheses. The formula =D7+(D8*6%), for example, adds the amount in cell D7 to the result of multiplying the amount in D8 by .06, or 6 percent. The formula =(E2+E3+E4)+(E6+E7+E8) adds the total of the first three cells to the total of the second three cells.

☑ Progress Check

If you can perform the following tasks, you've mastered this lesson:

❑ Construct a formula by using arithmetic operators.

❑ Copy a formula to another cell.

Lesson 6-2   # Using Functions in Formulas

Functions are canned formulas that come with Excel 97. Instead of laboriously constructing a formula, you can rely on a function to do the work for you. Excel 97 offers hundreds of functions, some of which are very obscure and are fit only for use by rocket scientists. In this lesson, you test-drive common functions that you can use in just about any worksheet. And you find out how using functions makes entering cell references easier.

When it comes to using functions, you can click the AutoSum button, type function names yourself, or use the Excel 97 Paste Function and Function Wizard. Read on, my friend.

Using AutoSum to add numbers in cells

This part of the lesson explains how to use the SUM function. The SUM function totals the numbers in a row or column of a worksheet. Of all the functions, SUM is probably the one that you use most often in Excel 97, so the program offers the AutoSum button for entering the SUM function automatically. Follow these steps to learn about the SUM function:

on the CD

1 **Open the Function file in the Office 101 folder and click cell D8.**

This worksheet looks familiar, because you saw one very much like it in the last lesson. In this lesson, you make similar computations to those you made in Lesson 6-1, but this time you use functions instead of constructing formulas.

Last time around, you entered the formula **=D5+D6+D7** in cell D8 to get the total income projection for the month of February. You can do that a lot faster by using the SUM function, as the following step demonstrates.

2 **Click the AutoSum button on the Standard toolbar and then click the Enter button.**

If you click back in cell D8, you see that Excel 97 entered the following formula in that cell: =SUM(D5:D7). Use the SUM function to add the cells in a range — in this case, the range D5:D7. Because adding cells is such a common task in worksheets, Excel 97 offers the AutoSum button for entering a SUM function formula. Use this button often. You can even use AutoSum to enter more than one formula at the same time, as the following two steps demonstrate.

3 **Select cells E8 and F8 and click the AutoSum button.**

After you click the AutoSum button, Excel 97 makes an educated guess as to which cells you want to add up. In this case, it knows to add the cells directly above E8 and F8. But sometimes the program guesses wrong. If that happens, you must tell Excel 97 which cells to compute.

4 **Select cell G6 and click the AutoSum button.**

What happened here? The formula =SUM(G5) appears on the Formula bar and in cell G6, and the marquee lights surround cell G5. If you press the Enter key now, Excel 97 will enter 127,000, the total in cell G5. That's not what you want.

5 **Select cells C6 through F6 and press the Enter key.**

After you select these cells, the marquee lights appear around them so that you know which cells the SUM function formula is computing. After you press the Enter key, you add up the cells in C6 through F6, and the following formula appears in cell G6: =SUM(C6:F6).

The cells in parentheses at the end of a function are called the function's *argument.* The argument determines which cells the function computes. Some functions require more than one argument, as you see shortly.

Cell G7 is now the active cell. Watch what happens after you click the AutoSum button this time.

Notes:

Σ

AutoSum button

put function
arguments in the
parentheses

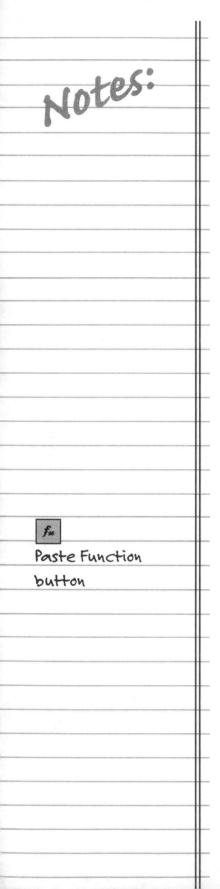

Notes:

f_x

Paste Function

button

6 **Click the AutoSum button, glance at the marquee lights and Formula bar, and click the Enter button.**

This time, Excel 97 knows that you want to add the cells to the left of the active cell, and the program enters the right arguments for the SUM function formula (cells C7:F7). But suppose that you want to use the SUM function to add cells that aren't directly beside the active cell.

7 **Click cell G8, the Subtotal cell, and then click the AutoSum button and glance at the marquee lights; select cells G5 through G7 to make those cells the argument for SUM function and press Enter.**

So far you've used the all-important SUM function, but Excel 97 offers other functions, too. In the following step, you find out how to obtain the average of a range of cells by using the AVERAGE function.

8 **Click cell H6, type** =average(C6:F6), **and click the Enter button.**

The AVERAGE function returns the average amount in the cells named in the argument, in this case cells C6:F6. It doesn't matter whether you enter function names in upper- or lowercase letters, because Excel 97 changes them to uppercase after you enter the formula.

You could simply copy the formula in cell H6 to H7 and H8, as you learned to do in the last lesson, but I want you to check out the Excel 97 Paste Function dialog box and its Function Wizard next. Better leave the Function file open.

Using the Paste function and Function Wizard

Excel 97 offers a whole library of functions for making computations in worksheets. In this part of Lesson 6-2, you learn about a few of them.

on the test

1 **Click cell H7 and click the Paste Function button.**

The Paste Function dialog box appears, as shown in Figure 6-2. Functions in this dialog box are arranged by category in the Function category list. The list includes an All category, which lists all the functions in alphabetical order, and a Most Recently Used category, which lists the functions you used since you began running Excel 97.

2 **Click Statistical in the Function category list and then click AVERAGE in the Function name list.**

To find the function you need, click a category, click a function name, and then read the description in the bottom of the dialog box. You now see a description of the AVERAGE function and the arguments that it requires. These descriptions are worth reading, because they tell you how to use the functions wisely.

3 **Click OK.**

The Function Wizard appears, as shown in Figure 6-3. Take a moment to look at the explanations of how to use the AVERAGE function in this Wizard. These descriptions are also very useful. Did you notice that Excel 97 guessed incorrectly about which cells to use as an argument for the AVERAGE function? Excel 97 wants to use cell H6. How can you fix that?

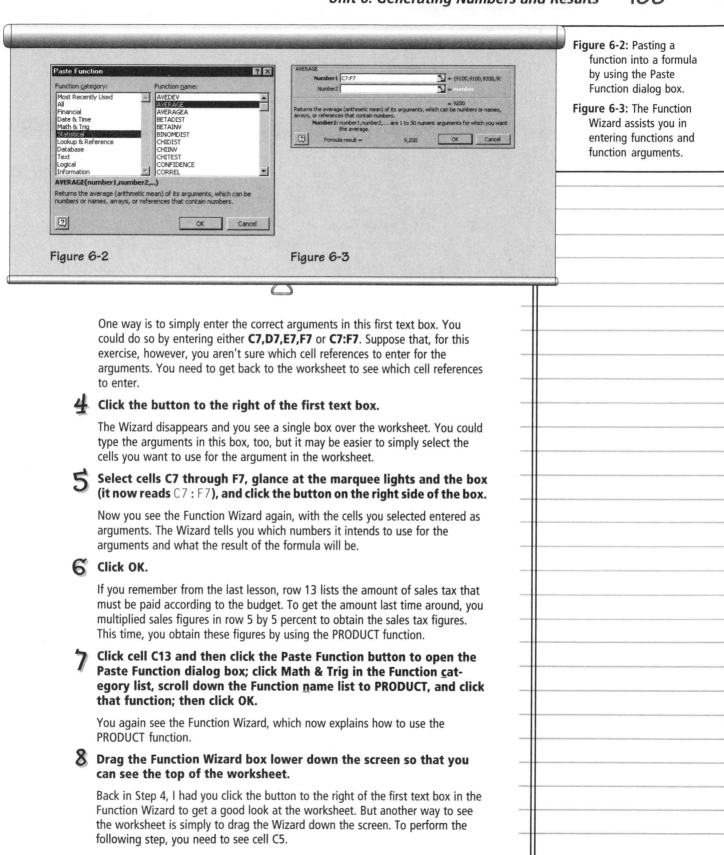

Figure 6-2: Pasting a function into a formula by using the Paste Function dialog box.

Figure 6-3: The Function Wizard assists you in entering functions and function arguments.

One way is to simply enter the correct arguments in this first text box. You could do so by entering either **C7,D7,E7,F7** or **C7:F7**. Suppose that, for this exercise, however, you aren't sure which cell references to enter for the arguments. You need to get back to the worksheet to see which cell references to enter.

4 Click the button to the right of the first text box.

The Wizard disappears and you see a single box over the worksheet. You could type the arguments in this box, too, but it may be easier to simply select the cells you want to use for the argument in the worksheet.

5 Select cells C7 through F7, glance at the marquee lights and the box (it now reads C7 : F7**), and click the button on the right side of the box.**

Now you see the Function Wizard again, with the cells you selected entered as arguments. The Wizard tells you which numbers it intends to use for the arguments and what the result of the formula will be.

6 Click OK.

If you remember from the last lesson, row 13 lists the amount of sales tax that must be paid according to the budget. To get the amount last time around, you multiplied sales figures in row 5 by 5 percent to obtain the sales tax figures. This time, you obtain these figures by using the PRODUCT function.

7 Click cell C13 and then click the Paste Function button to open the Paste Function dialog box; click Math & Trig in the Function category list, scroll down the Function name list to PRODUCT, and click that function; then click OK.

You again see the Function Wizard, which now explains how to use the PRODUCT function.

8 Drag the Function Wizard box lower down the screen so that you can see the top of the worksheet.

Back in Step 4, I had you click the button to the right of the first text box in the Function Wizard to get a good look at the worksheet. But another way to see the worksheet is simply to drag the Wizard down the screen. To perform the following step, you need to see cell C5.

9 **Click cell C5 in the worksheet.**

The marquee lights start flashing, and C5 appears in text box Number 1. To enter the second argument for the PRODUCT function, you now must make an entry in text box Number 2.

10 **Click text box Number 2, type 6%, and click OK.**

After you click text box Number 2, the Wizard adds another text box, in case you want to enter a third argument for the PRODUCT function, but you don't need to do that for this formula.

Now the amount of tax for the February budget projection appears in cell C13 and the formula bar reads =PRODUCT(C5,6%). You've done it — you've used the PRODUCT function successfully.

Excel 97 offers many, many functions, some of them very esoteric. By reading function descriptions in the Paste Function dialog box and by having the Function Wizard help you enter arguments and functions correctly, you can take advantage of the numerous functions that Excel 97 offers.

Recess

I just put you through the wringer, didn't I? Sorry about that. Learning about functions is not easy, but after a while, you discover three or four especially useful ones and apply them with ease.

Meantime, go to recess. Take a break. You've been through the wringer, after all. (The wringer, by the way, was a device used long before the invention of the computer or the dryer to dry clothes. You squeezed clothes through the wringer, a dual set of rolling-pinlike devices. And you did it on Blue Monday, which was considered a "blue" day because, well, that was the day when everyone washed their clothes by hand.)

Lesson 6-3

Using Range Names in Formulas

Use range names to enter cell references

In the last two lessons, you discovered that entering all those cell references can be a chore. Not everyone has the nimble fingers of an expert typist. Typing =C1+C2+C3+C4+C5, for example, can cause a finger cramp. In this short lesson, you learn a fast way to enter cell references. You learn how to name cell ranges and use those names in formulas. You also discover that including range names in formulas makes it easier for others to understand what your formulas are meant to calculate.

To learn the ins and outs of range names, follow these steps:

1 **Open the Range file in the Office 101 folder and click cell G5.**

Here it is again — the budget worksheet. Something, however, is amiss in this worksheet. If you look at the Formula bar, you see that the formula for

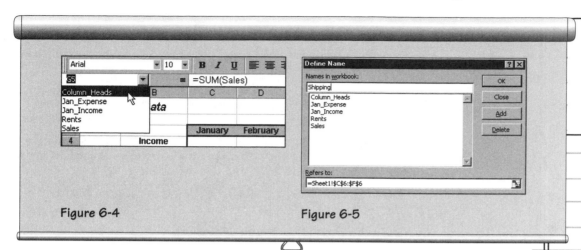

Figure 6-4

Figure 6-5

Figure 6-4: Choosing a range name from the Name drop-down list box.

Figure 6-5: Defining a range name.

projecting January sales reads =SUM(Sales), not =C5+D5+E5+F5 or =SUM(C5:F5). How can that be? You find out in the following step.

2 **Click the down arrow in the Name drop-down list box to see the list of range names that have been defined for this worksheet.**

As shown in Figure 6-4, the Name box is to the left of the Formula bar. Five range names, including Sales, have been defined in this worksheet. In the next step, you define a new range name.

3 **Select cells C6 through F6 (the Shipping income figures) and choose Insert⇨Name⇨Define.**

You see the Define Name dialog box shown in Figure 6-5. Excel 97 has already entered the name Shipping in the Names in workbook text box in case you want to use that name. To enter a name of your own in the box, type it. Range names cannot include blank spaces. To get around that problem, enter an underscore character as I've done in the first three range names in the worksheet.

4 **Click OK to accept the range name Excel 97 suggests.**

Next, you see how to use a range name in a formula.

5 **Click cell G6; then click the Formula bar and type the following: =SUM(.**

In the following step, you paste in the range name as the argument.

6 **Choose Insert⇨Name⇨Paste; click Shipping in the Paste Name dialog box and click OK; type) and press the Enter key.**

If you click cell G6, you see the formula =SUM(Shipping). A stranger who clicked cell G6 would know right away what this formula meant, but he or she would need to ponder over a formula like =C5+D5+E5+F5 or =SUM(C5:F5).

heads up

However, there is one disadvantage to using range names in formulas: A range name always refers to a specific set of cells. Unlike conventional formulas that include cell references, you can't copy and paste or drag to copy formulas that include range names. For instance, if you tried dragging the formula in cell G6 to cell G7, you would get the same result, 17,700. Nevertheless, you can copy formulas with range names from one place to another and then edit them, as the next step demonstrates.

Notes:

Name drop-down list box is at the left side of the Formula bar

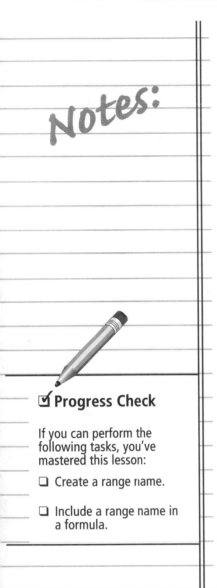

Notes:

☑ Progress Check

If you can perform the following tasks, you've mastered this lesson:

❑ Create a range name.

❑ Include a range name in a formula.

heads up

7 **Copy the formula in cell G6 to cell H6, erase** SUM **in the Formula bar, enter** AVERAGE **in its place, and then click the Enter button.**

Instead of =SUM(Shipping), cell H6 now reads =AVERAGE(Shipping), and the formula correctly produces the average income from shipping in the four-month period.

8 **Copy the formula in cell H6 to cell H7, click the Formula bar, delete the word** Shipping **and either type the word** Rents **or paste it in as you learned to do in Step 6, and then press Enter.**

The new formula, =AVERAGE(Rents), correctly produces the average income from rents.

9 **Click cell C17 and type the equal sign (=).**

In the next step, you subtract the total January income projections from the total January expense projections to get the projected net income. The range names you need have already been created.

10 **Choose** Insert⇨Name⇨Paste, **click** Jan_Income **in the Paste name dialog box, and then click OK.**

So far, the formula reads =Jan_Income.

11 **Enter a minus sign (–), choose** Insert⇨Name⇨Paste, **click** Jan_Expense **in the Paste Name list box, click OK, and then click the Enter button.**

The formula in cell C17 is =Jan_Income-Jan_Expense, and you learn the projected net profit for January.

12 **Click the down arrow in the Name text box and select Column_Heads.**

The column heads in the worksheet are selected instantaneously. Besides using range names in formulas, you can use them to mark the parts of a worksheet that you want to get to quickly. In a long worksheet with many rows, you would be grateful to have the Column_Heads range name, because all you would have to do is choose it in the Name box to get to the top of the worksheet.

Lesson 6-4 Building a Chart from Your Data

One of the fastest ways to impress impressionable people is to create a chart from worksheet data. Computers have made it very, very easy to create charts. Before computers, preparing a chart took hours and hours, but now all you need to do to create a chart with Excel 97 is to click a few menu commands. And if you're fickle and don't like the chart you create, you can simply choose another type of chart.

To create a chart from the data in a spreadsheet, follow these steps:

on the CD

1 Open the Chart file in the Office 101 folder.

To create a chart, Excel 97 needs the raw data. To provide the data, you select the cells whose data is to be included in the chart. You can select all the data or some of the data in the chart. For this chart, you plot all the data.

2 Select cells B2 to F7 (the entire chart) and click the Chart Wizard button.

You can also choose Insert⇔Chart to see the Chart Wizard's first dialog box as shown in Figure 6-6.

This dialog box offers 14 kinds of charts. By clicking a chart in the Chart type list, viewing the Chart sub-types, and reading the descriptions below the Chart sub-type area, you can find the kind of chart that is best for presenting your data. Try clicking a few names in the Chart type list to see what these charts look like.

3 Click Bar in the Chart type list and then click the Next button.

The second Chart Wizard dialog box appears. This dialog box wants to know which data series — the car model names or quarter totals — to use for the legend and for the bars in the chart. You can see a preview of the chart in the dialog box. If you were to click Next now, Excel 97 would use the quarter totals in the legend, as the dialog box shows.

Don't concern yourself with what series are and a legend is. All you need to do in this lesson is experiment with the buttons in this dialog box to see how they affect the sample chart.

4 Click the Rows radio button to put the car model names in the legend and then click Next.

The third Chart Wizard dialog box appears, as shown in Figure 6-7. This one wants to know the title of the chart and how to label the X-axis and Y-axis of the chart. (The *X-axis* is the horizontal side of the chart and the *Y-axis* is the vertical side.)

5 In the Chart title box, enter Car Sales; in the Category (X) axis box, enter Sales by Quarter; in the Value (Y) axis box, enter Units Sold.

Notice where these labels appear in the dialog box. You're starting to see what your chart is going to look like after you finish it. If you're particular about the chart's appearance, you can click the other tabs in this dialog box and make entries or choices. For each option you click, the dialog box provides a preview of how the finished chart will look.

6 Click the Next button.

The fourth and final dialog box appears. This one wants to know where to put the finished chart. If you click the Add new sheet radio button, Excel 97 puts the chart on a new worksheet in the workbook, and you're invited to type a name for the new worksheet in the text box.

7 Leave the As object in radio button selected to place the chart in the worksheet beside the data from whence it originated and then click the Finish button.

The new chart appears over the data in the worksheet, but you can drag it to a new place.

Chart Wizard button

Figure 6-6: Creating a chart from the data in a worksheet.

Figure 6-7: Providing a title and labels for the chart.

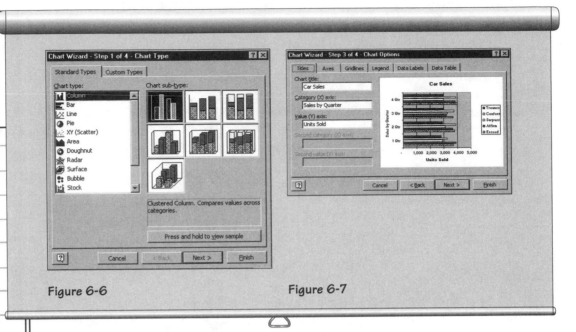

Figure 6-6   Figure 6-7

Notes:

click and drag the black squares to resize the chart

Chart Type button

❏ **Progress Check**

If you can perform the following tasks, you're ready to move on to the Unit 6 quiz:

❏ Fill in the Chart Wizard dialog boxes to create a chart.

❏ Reposition a chart on a worksheet.

❏ Change the size of a chart.

❏ Change chart types.

8 **Click the chart, press and hold the mouse button until you see the pointer become a four-headed arrow, and then drag the chart to a new position on the worksheet.**

Besides changing the chart's position, you can change its size. To do so, drag one of the black squares at the corner or side of the chart. Dragging a square on the corner makes the chart larger or smaller but keeps its proportions; dragging a square on the side makes the chart taller, shorter, wider, or narrower.

9 **Drag the squares to tug and pull, tug and pull until the chart looks just right.**

If a bar chart doesn't suit you, you can even reverse your decision and choose a different kind of chart by using the Chart toolbar. This toolbar appeared on-screen after you created the chart. If you don't see the Chart toolbar, choose View⇨Toolbars⇨Chart.

on the test

10 **Click near the perimeter of the chart to make the black squares appear around the outside of the chart, not around the gray plot area; then click the down arrow beside the Chart Type button to open the drop-down list and click Column Chart in the list.**

The bar chart flips on its side and becomes a column chart.

If you want to tinker with the chart at this point, you can choose commands on the Chart menu. These commands take you back to the same Chart Wizard dialog boxes you used in the first place to create your chart. Happy sailing. I hope your course is well charted.

After you finish playing with charts, close the Chart file and prepare yourself for the fun and always exciting end-of-the-unit quiz and exercise.

Unit 6 Quiz

For the following questions, circle the letter of the correct answer or answers. I designed this short quiz to help you remember what you learned in Unit 6. Each question may have more than one right answer.

1. **The formula =H8-H14 performs which of the following tasks?**

   A. Adds the amount in cell H8 to the amount in cell H14.

   B. Creates a cell range encompassing cells H8 to H14.

   C. Subtracts the amount in cell H14 from the amount in H8.

   D. Multiplies the amount in cell H8 and cell H14.

   E. Sorry, math is not my forte.

2. **What is wrong with the formula SUM(C7:C10)?**

   A. It doesn't have enough arguments.

   B. The cell range is invalid.

   C. It doesn't start with an equal sign.

   D. SUMthing's wrong is all I know.

   E. The parentheses should be around SUM.

3. **You should use which of the following techniques to copy a formula from one cell to another?**

   A. Select the cell containing the formula, right-click, and choose Copy; then right-click where the formula is to go and choose Paste.

   B. Select the cell containing the formula, choose Edit⇨Copy, click where you want to copy the formula, and then choose Edit⇨Paste.

   C. Select the cell containing the formula, press Ctrl+C, click where you want to copy the formula, and press Ctrl+V.

   D. Click the cell containing the formula, move the pointer to the lower-left corner of the cell, and, after you see the pointer become a cross, drag over the cells to which you want to copy the formula.

   E. Select the cell containing the formula, press Ctrl+C, click where you want the formula copied, and then right-click and choose Paste.

4. **Clicking the AutoSum button enters which of the following functions?**

   A. AUTO

   B. AUTOSUM

   C. AVERAGE

   D. PRODUCT

   E. SUM

Notes:

5. **The formula =AVERAGE(A1:A5) obtains the average amount in which of these cells?**

   A. A1 through A5.

   B. Row 5.

   C. A1, A2, A3, A4, and A5.

   D. Column A.

   E. Cell block A.

6. **After you select a range name from the Name text box, Excel 97 performs which of the following actions?**

   A. Inserts the range name in a formula.

   B. Adds the amounts in the cell range named in the Name text box.

   C. Deletes the cells in the range.

   D. Names the cells in the range.

   E. Selects the cells in the range.

Unit 6 Exercise

on the CD

1. Open the Quiz 6 file in the Office 101 folder.

2. In cell E5, enter a simple formula by using the multiplication operator (*) that obtains the result of multiplying the price in cell C5 by the quantity in cell D5.

3. Copy the formula to cells E6, E7, and E8 by cutting and pasting.

4. Using the PRODUCT function in cell C5, determine the tax for the items sold.

5. Copy the formula you just entered to cells F6:F8 by dragging the formula in cell F5 to those cells.

6. Click cell G5, click the Formula bar, and enter a SUM function formula for determining the total price of the items listed in row 5. Then copy the formula to cell G6:G8.

7. Use the AutoSum button to enter the subtotal for all items sold in cell G9.

8. Open the Name drop-down list box and choose Total_Bill.

9. To get the total bill in cell G13, enter a formula that totals the subtotal and installation costs.

Unit 4 Summary

♦ **Creating a worksheet:** Click the New button or press Ctrl+N to open a new worksheet. To create one from a template, choose File⇨New, click the Spreadsheet Solutions tab, and double-click a template icon.

♦ **Parts of a worksheet:** Data is entered in cells, the boxes that are formed where columns and rows intersect. To find out the address of the active cell where the cursor is, look in the Name box. To see what has been entered in the active cell, look in the Formula bar. Click a Sheet tab at the bottom of the screen to see another worksheet.

♦ **Entering and editing data:** To enter data, type the data in a cell and press the Enter key or click elsewhere. You can also type entries in the Formula bar and press Enter or click the Enter button. To edit what is in a cell, click the cell and make your changes in the Formula bar. To edit a formula, click the Edit Formula button and use the dialog box to change cell addresses.

♦ **Copying, moving, and deleting data:** Drag over cells to select them. To select a block of cells, click one corner and drag to the other. Use the standard Cut, Copy, and Paste commands that work in all the Office 97 programs. You can get these commands on the Edit menu; by right-clicking; by pressing Ctrl+X, Ctrl+C, or Ctrl+V; or by clicking the Cut, Copy, and Paste buttons. To delete an entire row or column, click in the row or column, choose Edit⇨Delete, choose Entire Row or Entire Column in the Delete dialog box, and click OK.

♦ **Viewing data:** Choose View⇨Page Break Preview to see where pages break in a worksheet and then adjust the page breaks if necessary. To freeze the panes in a worksheet and always see row and column labels on-screen, place the cursor directly below the row you want to freeze and directly to the right of the column you want to freeze and then choose Window⇨Freeze Panes. Choose View⇨Full Screen to switch to Full Screen view.

♦ **Printing:** Click the Print button to print a worksheet on-screen in its entirety. To print part of a worksheet or an entire workbook, press Ctrl+P or choose File⇨Print and choose options in the Print dialog box.

Unit 5 Summary

♦ **Formatting text and numbers:** To format text, select the cells that contain the text and then click the Bold, Italic, or Underline button on the Formatting toolbar. You can also choose a new font from the Font drop-down list or change the size of characters by making a choice from the Font Size drop-down list. To format numbers, select the cells and click the Currency Style, Percent Style, or Comma Style button. To get more choices, choose Format⇨Cells to open the Format Cells dialog box. The Number tab in this dialog box offers many ways to format cells.

♦ **Adjusting columns and rows:** To widen a column, click and drag the line beside its letter along the top of the screen. Make a row taller or shorter by dragging the line below its number in the row numbers on the left side of the screen. You can also select the column or rows the size of which you want to change, by choosing Format⇨Row or Format⇨Column, and by choosing an option from the submenu.

♦ **Inserting and deleting columns and rows:** To insert a column or row, select the number of columns or rows you want to insert and then right-click and choose Insert or choose Insert⇨Columns or Insert⇨Rows. To delete columns or rows, select the columns or rows and choose Edit⇨Delete or right-click and choose Delete.

♦ **Aligning numbers and text:** Select cells and click an alignment button to change the way in which the numbers or text in cells align. Excel 97 offers three alignment buttons: Align-Left, Center, and Align-Right. To merge cells

Part II Review

and center text across the cells that are being merged, select the cells and click the Merge and Center button.

▶ **Applying borders, colors, and patterns:** To apply borders, select the parts of the worksheet around which or inside of which you want to draw borders, open the Borders drop-down list on the Formatting toolbar, and click a button. You can also select the cells, right-click, choose Format Cells from the shortcut menu to open the Format Cells dialog box, click the Border tab, make a selection from the Style menu, and click one or more of the border buttons. To apply colors, select the cells, choose Format⇨ Cells to open the Format Cells dialog box, click the Pattern tab, click one of the boxes under Color, and click OK.

Unit 6 Summary

▶ **Writing and copying formulas:** To write a formula, click the cell that is to hold the formula, click the Formula bar, type an equal sign (=), and write the formula. To construct the formula itself, enter cell references and arithmetic operators. To copy a formula, select the cell with the formula you want to copy and either drag across nearby cells or choose a Copy command and then move to another cell and paste the formula there.

▶ **Using functions in formulas:** Click the AutoSum button to add the numbers in cells directly to the left or directly above the active cell. To use one of the Excel 97 formulas, click the Paste Formula button, and, in the Paste Function dialog box, click a function category, and then a function name. When you click OK, you see the Function Wizard, where you can enter arguments for the function. After you have done so, click OK again.

▶ **Using range names in formulas:** To create a range name, select the cells in the range, choose Insert⇨Name⇨Define to open the Define Name dialog box, either accept the name Excel 97 suggests in the Names in Workbook box or enter a name of your own, and then click OK. Enter a range name in a formula by choosing Insert⇨Name⇨Paste, clicking the name in the Paste Name box, and clicking OK. You can click a range name in the Name Box to go immediately to the range in a worksheet.

▶ **Creating a chart:** Select the parts of the worksheet whose data you want to plot in the chart and click the Chart Wizard button. You see the first of four Chart Wizard dialog boxes. Fill in each dialog box, clicking Next as you go, and when you've filled in the last dialog box, click the Finish button. To change the position of the chart, click and drag it to a new place. Change the size of the chart by tugging the black squares on the corners and sides. To change the chart type, click the down arrow beside the Chart Type button on the Chart toolbar and make a choice from the drop-down list.

Part II Test

The Part II test is a backbreaker. It will make you regret what a stumblebum you are around computers. This test is certain to make you want to give up and take a nap. It is guaranteed to hurt your pride and ruin your self-esteem.

Actually, this simple test will prove how well you are getting along with the Office 97 programs. If you completed Part I as well as Part II, you are well on your way to becoming one of those people whom others seek out when they want computer advice. Believe me, computers are just dumb machines. Never let all the buttons, commands, arrows, and menu names on a computer screen intimidate you.

The answers to the questions asked here can be found next to the On the Test icons scattered throughout Part II. (The answers can also be found in Appendix A.) If you have trouble with a question, go back to the lesson in Part II that covers that topic.

True False

T F 1. A template is a sophisticated, preformatted file that you can use to create files of your own.

T F 2. The active cell is the one with the boldface rectangle around it.

T F 3. To delete a row, select that row and press the Del key.

T F 4. To select several rows, click their numbers on the right side of the screen.

T F 5. Pressing F4 repeats the last command you made.

T F 6. #### in a cell means that the number is too big to be displayed.

T F 7. This button merges cells and centers the text in the cells across the new, wider cell.

T F 8. The formula =D7+(D8*6%) adds the amount in cell D7 to the result of multiplying the amount in cell D8 by .06.

T F 9. Σ You click this button to gain entrance to a fraternity party.

T F 10. f_* You click this button to enter a function in a formula.

Multiple choice

Circle the correct answer or answers to the following questions. Each question may have more than one right answer.

11. **Why is keeping similar worksheets in a workbook preferable to creating lots of different worksheets?**

    A. Because you can perform calculations with data in the different worksheets.

    B. Because keeping worksheets together saves you the trouble of opening and working with individual worksheets.

    C. Because copying and moving data between the worksheets is easier.

    D. Because you can compare and contrast data more easily.

    E. All of the above.

Part II Test

12. **To select a block of cells in a worksheet, you perform which of the following actions?**

    A. Right-click and choose Select.

    B. Drag from one corner of the cell block to another.

    C. Wag the mouse pointer back and forth.

    D. Choose Edit⇨Clear⇨All.

    E. Drag the cursor down the row numbers on the left side of the screen.

13. **To move to the last cell in a worksheet, you perform which of the following actions?**

    A. Press Ctrl+Home.

    B. Press Ctrl+↓.

    C. Press Ctrl+End.

    D. Choose File⇨End.

    E. Press the ↓ key over and over.

14. **Worksheet is to workbook as what is to what in the following list?**

    A. Peas are to a pod.

    B. Grain elevators are to astronauts.

    C. Turkeys are to billiard balls.

    D. Rain is to spittle.

    E. Baseball is to tropical fish.

15. **Click which of these buttons to display numbers to two decimal places?**

    A. The Increase Decimal button.

    B. The Decrease Decimal button.

    C. The Currency Style button.

    D. The Comma Style button.

    E. The Percent Style button.

16. **Click a cell containing a formula and use which of the following methods to copy the formula to other cells?**

    A. Choose Edit⇨Copy, select the cells you want to copy the formula to, and choose Edit⇨Paste.

    B. Right-click and choose Copy; then select the cells that you want to receive the formula, right-click, and choose Paste.

    C. Press Ctrl+C, select the cells to which you want to copy the formula, and then press Ctrl+V.

    D. Move the pointer to the lower-right corner of the cell containing the formula you want to copy; after the pointer changes into a black cross, click and gently slide the cursor across the cells to which you want to copy the formula.

    E. All of the above.

17. **The formula =PRODUCT(F8,F9) performs which of the following functions?**

    A. Adds the amount in cell F8 to the amount in cell F9.

    B. Multiplies the amount in cell F8 by the amount in cell F9.

    C. Produces something.

    D. Divides cell F8 by cell F9.

    E. Multiplies the arguments in the parentheses.

18. **This button, located on the Chart toolbar, performs which of the following functions?**

    A. Creates a new chart.

    B. Displays a topographical map.

    C. Creates an area chart.

    D. Enables you to change chart types.

    E. Creates a surface chart.

Part II Test

Matching

19. Match the following buttons with the corresponding button names:

    A. ☒   1. Save
    B. ☑   2. Cancel
    C. 💾   3. Enter
    D. =   4. Paste
    E. 📋   5. Edit formula

20. Match the following button names with the right buttons:

    A. Comma Style   1. %
    B. Currency Style   2. ,

    C. Decrease Decimal   3. .00
    D. Percent Style   4. .00
    E. Increase Decimal   5. $

21. Match the following formulas with their function equivalents.

    A. =F6+F7+F8   1. =PRODUCT(F7,8)
    B. =F6*F7   2. =SUM(F6:F8)
    C. =F6+F7+F10+F11   3. =PRODUCT(F6,F7)
    D. =F7*8   4. =(SUM(F6:F7))+
                           (SUM(F10:F11))
    E. =(F6+F7+F8)/3   5. =AVERAGE(F6:F8)

Part II Lab Assignment

If you did the lab assignment at the end of Part I, you already know lab assignments are meant to give you practice in real-life situations. Instead of telling you in a step-by-step fashion how to do a task, I give you general instructions in a lab assignment. The idea is for you to use your newfound skills to do the job without me peering over your shoulder. If you have questions about how to do the tasks I am about to set before you, review the lessons in Part II. Or, easier yet, look at the summary reviews at the start of this test.

In the lab assignment in Part I, you edited and formatted a rental agreement for the exciting new company of which you are the president and sole employee, Pierspont Property Management at 122 Pier Street in Pierspoint, Pennsylvania. In this lab assignment, you will fiddle with a worksheet to find out how much you are receiving in rents, what the maintenance costs of your small business are, and what your profits are.

on the CD

To take the test, open the Test II file in the Office 101 folder and go to it.

Part II Lab Assignment

Step 1: Entering and viewing data

Delete the data in cells I10 through I18, in the Miscellaneous column, and enter new data (make it up yourself, but you are responsible for covering miscellaneous expenses, so you might go easy on the numbers here). If this were a real worksheet and you knew these properties well, you would have a hard time telling which property is which, because you can't see column A when the cursor is in column I. You better freeze the panes on this worksheet so you can see columns A and I at the same time.

Step 2: Formatting and aligning the numbers and text

Obviously, some of the columns are too narrow. Fix that. And the column headings in this worksheet need to be in boldface. How about the property names? Maybe they need to be boldface, too. And you may want to increase the font of the text in cells B1, B2, and B3 so that you can read the name and address of the company better. While you're at it, do you want to format the numbers in this worksheet in a different way? Most of the numbers represent monetary figures. You may also try aligning the text in the columns in different ways to make this worksheet easier to read.

Step 3: Putting borders on columns and rows

No worksheet is complete without borders of some kind. Try to draw borders that direct attention to the most important parts of the worksheet. Use borders that make the heading rows and the Totals columns and rows stand out.

Step 4: Crunching the numbers

Enter formulas that compute your management fee in cells D10 through D18. As property manager, you get 10 percent of the total rent you collect on each property. You're also responsible for covering site upkeep on the properties, however, as well as for miscellaneous expenses. To determine your total profit on each property, therefore, you must deduct figures in column E and I from figures in column D; to do so, you must create somewhat complicated formulas for column J, the Profits column. *Hint:* The subtraction formula you create requires putting the total expenses in column E and I in parentheses (E10+I10).

After you calculate the total profit on each property, use the SUM function to determine the totals for each column except the Property column.

Step 5: Seeing the final results

Print the worksheet. Can you fit the entire worksheet on one page? You may need to readjust column widths, or maybe you can print the worksheet in landscape mode (the sidebar in Lesson 4-5 explains how). Finally, build a chart from the data in the worksheet. If I were you, I wouldn't include the Totals columns in the chart, because that would throw the thing way out of whack, and besides, the object of a chart is to compare data, not to see the sum of its parts. Experiment with chart types in the Chart Wizard and use the Chart Type button on the Chart toolbar to find the right chart for presenting this data.

PowerPoint 97

Part III

In this part...

Part III takes on Microsoft PowerPoint 97, one of my favorite Office 97 programs. I guess I like PowerPoint 97 so much because the program lets me put on airs. I'm not much of an artist or presenter, but that doesn't matter to PowerPoint 97. The program gives me many, many tools with which to hide my shortcomings. I could take a PowerPoint 97 presentation to the Annual Brooklyn Bridge Sales Conference and succeed in selling that renowned bridge, if I wanted to.

You can use PowerPoint 97 to put together presentations for seminars, business meetings, sales conferences — you name it. Part III explains how to create a slide presentation, enter the text, change the look of the slides, and give the presentation.

Laying the Groundwork

Prerequisites

▶ Starting an Office 97 program (Lesson 1-1)

▶ Opening a file (Lesson 1-2)

▶ Moving around on-screen (Lesson 1-4)

▶ Selecting text (Lesson 2-3)

Objectives for This Unit

✓ Creating a presentation with the AutoContent Wizard, from a template, or from scratch

✓ Viewing slides so that you can move and edit them

✓ Rearranging the slides

✓ Importing clip art images into slides

on the CD

▶ View

▶ Format

▶ Design

▶ Clip Art

If your boss just asked you to give the presentations at your company's next meeting, and you have no idea where to start, this part of the book is just for you. Unit 7 lays the groundwork for the presentations that Unit 8 teaches you how to give. This unit explains how to create a presentation and dress the presentation in its Sunday best. It offers techniques for viewing PowerPoint 97 slides so that you can manipulate, rearrange, shift, and relocate them. It shows you how to change character fonts, prepare the notes you read from during a presentation, and import clip art to hypnotize or dazzle viewers.

By the way, you don't need a slide projector or other fancy gadget to complete the exercises in this unit. *Slide* is the PowerPoint term for the images that you create in this program, but that doesn't mean you need a slide projector to create or show images, because you can also show PowerPoint 97 presentations on computer screens. In fact, it might interest you to know that slide projectors, overhead projectors, and the like are becoming obsolete. Soon, instead of carrying a film camera, you will carry a digital camera to far-flung places, and to bore your friends and relatives with the images you captured, you will show those images on a computer screen. But I'm getting ahead of myself. This is supposed to be a computer book, not a science fiction novel.

Lesson 7-1   Creating a Presentation

PowerPoint 97 offers three ways to create new presentations: with the AutoContent Wizard, with a template, or from scratch. I describe each technique in this lesson. Lesson 7-1 also explains how to insert a new slide in a presentation you're working on.

Each time you start the program, you see the PowerPoint dialog box shown in Figure 7-1. Where you go from this dialog box is the subject of this lesson.

Creating a presentation by using the AutoContent Wizard

The AutoContent Wizard presents five dialog boxes, each of which asks you questions about the kind of presentation you want to create. After you're done, you end up with a presentation that you can modify to suit your tastes. To find out how the AutoContent Wizard works, start PowerPoint 97 if you've not already done so, and then follow these steps:

1 **In the PowerPoint dialog box, click the AutoContent wizard option button to talk to the AutoContent Wizard and then click OK.**

If the PowerPoint dialog box isn't on-screen to begin with, you can still use the AutoContent Wizard by choosing File⇨New, clicking the Presentations tab in the New Presentation dialog box, and double-clicking the AutoContent Wizard icon.

The first AutoContent Wizard dialog box appears and simply tells you what the AutoContent Wizard does.

2 **Speed-read the message in this dialog box and then click Next.**

The next AutoContent Wizard dialog box asks what kind of presentation you want to create. Notice that the presentations are organized into categories. You may click the buttons to see all the generic presentations you can create with the AutoContent Wizard. In this lesson, you create a presentation for selling the Brooklyn Bridge.

3 **In the dialog box, click the Sales/Marketing button, click Product/ Services Overview in the box on the right, and click the Next button.**

The Wizard's next dialog box wants to know whether the presentation is for a meeting or for general consumption on a kiosk or the Internet.

4 **Click Next, since the Presentations, Informal Meetings, Handouts radio button is selected already.**

The Wizard's fourth dialog box appears. From here, you tell PowerPoint 97 how you intend to deliver the presentation and whether you want to hand out materials to complement the presentation. In the following step, you answer yes to both questions by clicking the Next button.

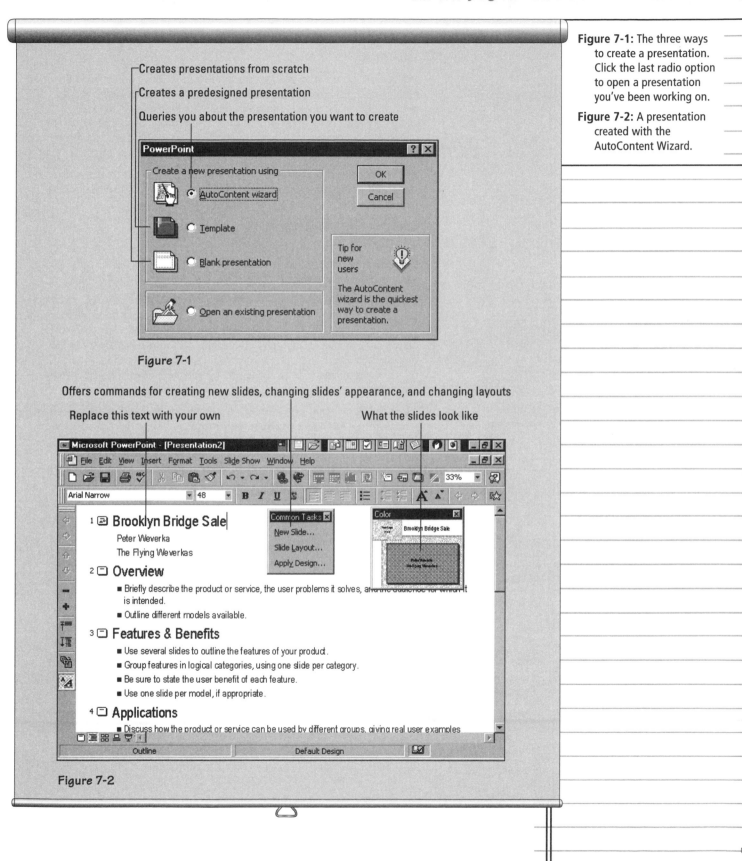

Figure 7-1: The three ways to create a presentation. Click the last radio option to open a presentation you've been working on.

Figure 7-2: A presentation created with the AutoContent Wizard.

Creates presentations from scratch

Creates a predesigned presentation

Queries you about the presentation you want to create

Figure 7-1

Offers commands for creating new slides, changing slides' appearance, and changing layouts

Replace this text with your own

What the slides look like

Figure 7-2

title bar = stripe at the top of the dialog box

5 **Click Next.**

The Wizard's next dialog box asks for a title for the presentation. The title you enter in the Presentation Title text box will appear in tall, boldface print in the first slide in the presentation. Very likely, your name and the title of the company you work for appear in the other two boxes. PowerPoint 97 got this information when you installed Office 97. What is in these two boxes also appears on the first slide but in smaller print.

6 **In the Presentation Title text box, delete the text that is there and enter** Brooklyn Bridge Sale**, correct the information in the other two boxes, if necessary, and then click Next.**

7 **Click the Finish button in the last dialog box.**

Your screen now looks like the one in Figure 7-2. (You may need to drag the Common Tasks toolbar and Color dialog box to the side to see the presentation you created. To do so, click the dialog box's title bar and drag it aside.)

The AutoContent Wizard provides generic text and titles for the presentation. At this point, you can delete the text in the generic presentation and enter text of your own in its place. I show you how to do that throughout this unit. For now, all you need to know is that the Color dialog box shows what the slides are going to look like as you present them and that the Common Tasks toolbar offers means of creating new slides, changing their appearance, and changing their layout.

8 **Choose File⇨Close, and click No after PowerPoint 97 asks whether you want to save the changes you made.**

Creating a presentation from a template

Another way to create a presentation is to use a generic template. As the following steps show, you can get the very same presentations from templates as you can get from the AutoContent Wizard. Follow these steps to see what I mean:

1 **If you are starting from the PowerPoint dialog box (refer to Figure 7-1), click the Template radio button and then click OK. Otherwise, choose File⇨New.**

You see the New Presentation dialog box.

2 **Click the Presentations tab.**

To find out what these presentations look like, you can click a template icon and look in the Preview box. Try clicking a few icons now to see the many slide designs that PowerPoint 97 offers.

3 **Find and click the Product Overview (Standard) icon and then click OK.**

You see a slide that bids you to insert a product photo and your company's logo. Never mind that now. You don't know it yet, but the presentation you just created is not new.

4 Choose <u>View</u>⇨<u>O</u>utline or click the Outline View button in the lower-left corner of the screen to see this presentation in Outline view.

There — does that look familiar? Except for the title, "Brooklyn Bridge Sale," and your name and company's name, this presentation is the same one you created by using the AutoContent Wizard (refer to Figure 7-2).

5 Choose <u>F</u>ile⇨<u>C</u>lose to toss the file off-screen (and answer <u>N</u>o when PowerPoint 97 asks whether you want to save your changes).

Creating a presentation by inserting slides

The third and final way to create a presentation is to do it yourself from scratch. If you go this route, PowerPoint 97 gives you the opportunity to create a slide by using a predefined layout or by using no layout whatsoever. Use the techniques described here to build a slide presentation one slide at a time.

To insert slides one at a time for a presentation, follow these steps:

1 Click <u>B</u>lank Presentation and then click OK if you are starting from the PowerPoint dialog box (refer to Figure 7-1). If you are not starting there, click the New button.

The New Slide dialog box appears, as shown in Figure 7-3. Each slide, or *autolayout*, in this dialog box creates a different kind of slide. Click a slide layout in the dialog box and read its description in the lower-right corner of the New Slide dialog box to find out precisely what these layouts are meant for.

2 Click Title Slide, the first slide, and then click OK.

You see a generic title slide on-screen. The two "click here" boxes invite you to click and enter a title and subtitle.

3 Click the first box in the title slide and type Brooklyn Bridge Sale; then click the second box and type Offered by Me!

heads up

Notice how PowerPoint 97 formats the text as you enter it. You can save yourself a lot of trouble by choosing predesigned slides and slide presentations. These designs were invented by pros. I don't mean to sound snooty, but professional artists are a lot better than you and I at designing presentations.

4 Choose Insert⇨New Slide.

You see the New Slide dialog box all over again. From here, you can choose yet another slide for your presentation.

Besides choosing Insert⇨New Slide, you can press Ctrl+M or click the New Slide button on the Standard toolbar to create a new slide.

5 Click the blank slide, the last one in the dialog box, and click OK.

The slide you insert appears after the other one in the presentation.

Notes:

New button

press Ctrl+M or choose Insert→ New Slide to enter a new slide

New Slide butt'

Save butt'

Figure 7-3: Use the New Slide dialog box to insert slides one by one in presentations.

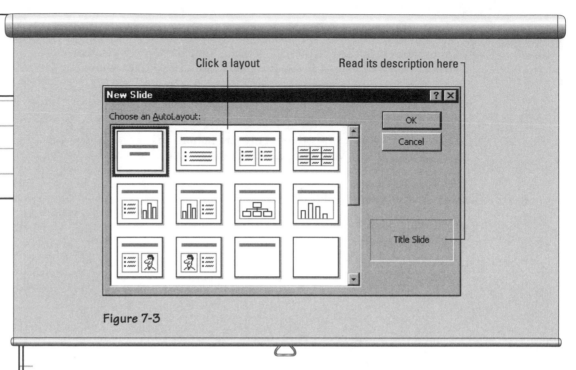

Click a layout   Read its description here

Figure 7-3

☑ Progress Check

If you can perform the following tasks, you've mastered this lesson:

❑ Create a presentation with the AutoContent Wizard.

❑ Create a presentation from a template.

❑ Create a presentation from scratch.

6 **Click the Save button and save this file in the Office 101 folder under the name** First Try**.**

Lesson 2-1 explains how to save a file if you need a refresher course. The techniques for saving a file are the same in all the Office 97 programs.

Lesson 7-2   Four Ways to View and Work on Slides

As you put together a presentation, one of the hardest things to do is get a fix on how the presentation is taking shape. If you focus on the text, you lose sight of what the slides actually look like. If you focus on the slides' appearance, you can overlook a spelling error. And unless you can see all or most of the slides at once, you may have a hard time telling whether slides are in the right order. To help you see your slide show from the correct vantage point, PowerPoint 97 offers four ways to view presentations.

To explore the four ways of viewing a presentation, follow these steps:

on the CD

1 **Open the View file in the Office 101 folder.**

The presentation appears in Outline view. Outline view is good for focusing on the text in a presentation. In this view, you can tell whether words are mis-spelled, and you can see the actual content of the presentation.

use the Outline
iew to focus on
ntent

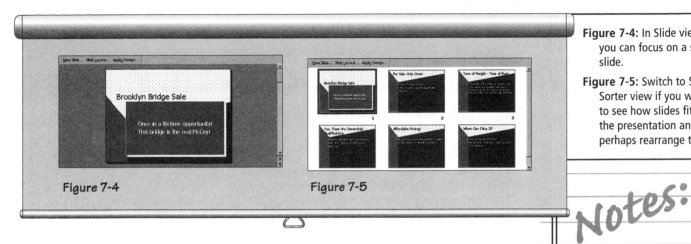

Figure 7-4

Figure 7-5

Figure 7-4: In Slide view, you can focus on a single slide.

Figure 7-5: Switch to Slide Sorter view if you want to see how slides fit in the presentation and perhaps rearrange them.

Notes:

2 Click the Slide View button.

The Slide View button, along with the other View buttons, is located in the lower-left corner of the screen. You can also access Slide view by choosing View⇨Slide. As Figure 7-4 demonstrates, Slide view shows very clearly what individual slides look like. On-screen, you can see the lovely greens and bright reds.

Slide View button

3 Click the down arrow on the vertical scroll bar two or three times.

To see the next or previous slide in a presentation in Slide view, click the arrows on the scroll bar.

4 Click the Slide Sorter View button.

Now you're in Slide Sorter view. The other way to get to Slide Sorter view is to choose View⇨Slide Sorter. From this view, you get a clear picture of how the slides follow one another in a presentation, as Figure 7-5 shows. If a slide is out of order, you can "slide" it to a new location, as you do in the following step.

Slide Sorter View button

on the test

5 Click slide 3, press and hold the mouse button, drag slide 3 across slide 2, and release the mouse button.

A vertical line appears to show where you're dragging the slide. If a slide in this view needs closer attention, double-click it. You will see the slide in Slide view.

6 Click slide 1 and then click the Notes Page View button.

Sorry for repeating myself like Flaubert's parrot, but you can also get to this view by choosing View⇨Notes Page. In "Creating and printing presentation notes" you learn how to write notes on slides. The audience doesn't see these notes. You can refer to these notes as you give a presentation. In any case, it's hard to read the notes on-screen, so you likely have to choose a Zoom command to make the text large enough to read.

Notes Page View button

7 Click the down arrow on the Zoom drop-down list and select 100% from the list.

Now you can see the notes. Click the down arrow on the vertical scroll bar to read all of them.

8 Click the Outline View button or choose View⇨Outline.

Now you're back where you started — in Outline view.

Outline View button

This lesson described four views. Actually, there is a fifth view, but I'm saving Slide Show view for Unit 8, when you concentrate on actually giving a presentation.

Progress Check

If you can perform the following tasks, you've mastered this lesson:

❑ Switch to Slide view.

❑ Switch to and move a slide in Slide Sorter view.

❑ Switch to Notes Pages view.

❑ Switch to Outline view.

extra credit

Creating and printing presentation notes

Sometimes you may want to have notes on your slides to give you cues on what to say while you're giving a presentation. You can see these notes (in Notes Page View), but your audience can't — they just think you are a really good public speaker. To create notes on your slides, follow these steps:

1. **In Slide Sorter View, click the slide to which you want to add notes.**

2. **Click the Notes Page View button.**

3. **Click the box below the slide and start typing.**

   You may need to zoom in to see the letters as you type them. (Step 7 in the Lesson 7-2 explains how.)

4. **Click a View button other than Notes Page View after you finish.**

To print notes, choose File➪Print, choose Notes Page from the Print what drop-down list, and click OK.

Lesson 7-3

Entering and Formatting Text

If you happened to have graduated from Lesson 2-5, which explains formatting text in Word 97, you may find this lesson downright repetitious. The same formatting techniques for changing fonts and character styles in Word 97 also work in PowerPoint 97. So you don't bored, this lesson does offer something that Lesson 2-5 didn't offer: bulleted and numbered lists. During a slide presentation, when you want to hit the high points or most important aspects of a topic, bulleted and numbered lists can come in very handy.

on the CD

To practice formatting text in PowerPoint 97, open the Format document and follow these steps:

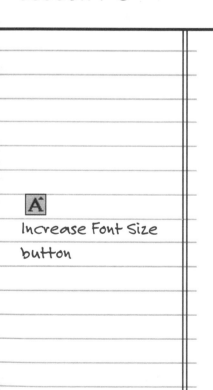

A⃗

Increase Font Size button

1 **Click the title of the slide, select the text, type in a new name for the slide, and then click the Bold button.**

Go ahead. Get creative and rename this slide anything you want to call it. The point is that after you create a slide, entering text on the slide is as easy as clicking the slide and typing.

Boldfacing the headings in slides is never a bad idea. Bold text makes the headings stand out. You can format text in other ways as well.

2 **Click the Increase Font Size button twice.**

The letters increase in size by 4 points. Rather than rely on the Font Size drop-down list, you can click the Increase Font Size button or click the Decrease Font Size button to change the size of text and immediately see the effects your changes have on the slide.

3 **With the title text still selected, click the Font drop-down list and choose Arial Black from the list.**

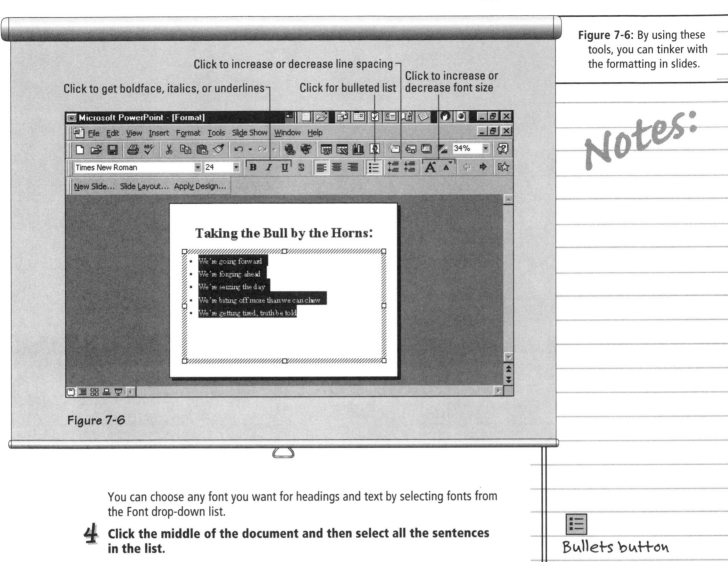

Click to increase or decrease line spacing ⌐

Click to get boldface, italics, or underlines ⌐

Click for bulleted list

Click to increase or decrease font size

Figure 7-6

Figure 7-6: By using these tools, you can tinker with the formatting in slides.

Notes:

You can choose any font you want for headings and text by selecting fonts from the Font drop-down list.

4 Click the middle of the document and then select all the sentences in the list.

You can select the text by dragging over it with the mouse. In the following step, you create a bulleted list.

5 Click the Bullets button.

A bullet appears beside each sentence in the list. As I mentioned earlier, bulleted lists appear often in presentations, where the topic mentioned beside each bullet can be a subject of discussion. While the text is still selected, try the following experiment in changing the amount of space between lines on a slide.

6 Click the Increase Paragraph Spacing button several times.

Now the bulleted items draw farther apart and become easier to read. If you think you clicked the button too many times, click the Decrease Paragraph Spacing button a few times to compensate.

This short lesson explained ways to tinker with the text and text formatting in a slide. Nevertheless, you are better off letting PowerPoint 97 do the work when it comes to formatting. You can create professional-looking presentations that way. Lesson 7-4 describes how to choose one of the PowerPoint 97 designs for a slide presentation.

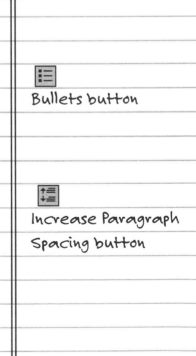

Bullets button

Increase Paragraph Spacing button

☑ Progress Check

If you can perform the following tasks, you've mastered this lesson:

❑ Change the font and font size of text.

❑ Boldface a heading.

❑ Create a bulleted list.

❑ Change the amount of space between lines.

Recess

You've already learned so much in this unit. Pat yourself on the back, go to the refrigerator, pull out your favorite beverage, and give yourself a break.

Or better yet, go to your closet, pull out your smock and beret, and get in the most artistic mood you can achieve: In the next lesson, you get to have a hand at choosing a design for your slides.

Lesson 7-4

Choosing Designs for Slides

Nothing could be easier than choosing a preformatted design for the slides in a presentation. You can do yourself a big favor by choosing a PowerPoint 97 design. You save yourself the trouble of formatting text, and you get a great-looking collection of slides into the bargain.

To try your hand at choosing a PowerPoint 97 design, follow these steps:

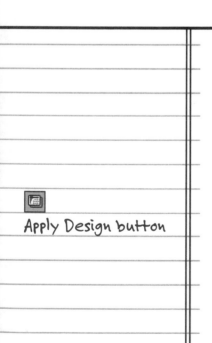

on the CD

Apply Design button

1 **Open the Design file in the Office 101 folder.**

This presentation has been given a design called, believe it or not, Dad's Tie. In the next two steps, you choose a design of your own.

2 **Click the Apply Design button.**

You can also give this command by choosing Format⇨Apply Design or by clicking Apply Design on the Common Tasks toolbar. In any case, the Apply Design dialog box appears, as shown in Figure 7-7.

3 **Click the Fireball design in the Name list box.**

After you click a design name, the box on the right side of the Apply Design dialog box shows you what the design looks like.

4 **Click the Apply button.**

Immediately, the slide presentation turns into a fireball, so to speak.

Feel free to pursue all the designs available in the Apply Design dialog box. Using these designs is an excellent way to make your presentation look professional.

You can return to the Apply Design dialog box and change your mind about designs as many times as you want.

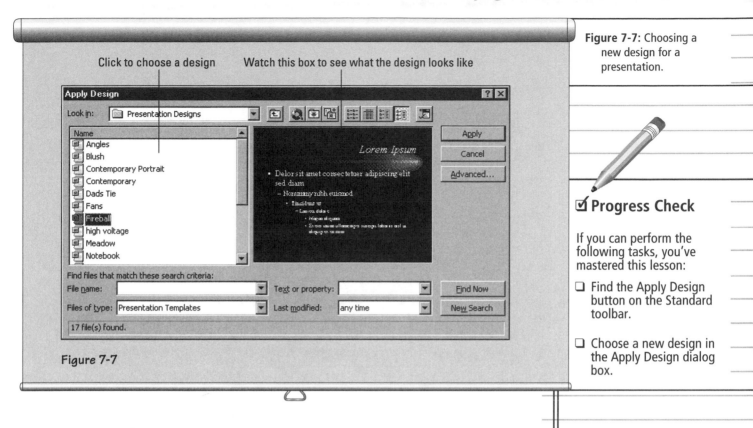

Click to choose a design   Watch this box to see what the design looks like

Figure 7-7

☑ Progress Check

If you can perform the following tasks, you've mastered this lesson:

❑ Find the Apply Design button on the Standard toolbar.

❑ Choose a new design in the Apply Design dialog box.

Dressing Up Slides with Clip Art

Lesson 7-5

This lesson explains how to paste a clip-art image in a slide. When you installed Office 97, you were given the opportunity to install clip-art files. Provided you installed the clip art files, you can put them to work by using clip art to decorate slide-show presentations. (If anybody asks where these images came from, I suppose that you could just lie and say that you created them yourself.)

To try your hand at importing clip art into a slide, follow these steps:

on the CD

1   Open the Clip Art file in the Office 101 folder.

The file you see on-screen is one of two from the New Slide dialog box (refer to Figure 7-3) into which you can import a clip art file merely by double-clicking. (You learned how to create a preformatted slide such as this one in Lesson 7-1.)

2   Double-click the icon that shows a picture of a man with a fat nose.

You may notice that this same big-nosed man appears on the Insert Clip Art button on the Standard toolbar. Later in this lesson, you click the Insert Clip Art button to import a clip-art image into a file that wasn't preformatted for clip art.

After you double-click the icon, the Microsoft Clip Art Gallery dialog box appears, as shown in Figure 7-8.

Figure 7-8: Importing a clip-art image into a slide.

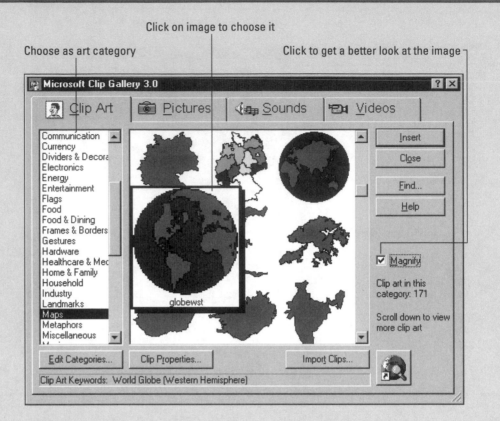

Figure 7-8

Notes:

heads up

3 **Click a category name from the list on the left side of the dialog box.**

How many categories appear and how many clip art images are available to you depends on which clip-art images were loaded on your computer. The Microsoft Office 97 CD holds a number of clip-art images. Insert the CD in your computer and follow the instructions that appear on the screen if you want to access all of the images.

4 **Use the scroll bar on the box in the middle of the screen to scroll downward and view various clip-art images.**

After you spot an image that piques your interest, you can click it and then click the Magnify check box to get a better look at it.

5 **After you find the image you want to import, click the image and then click the Insert button.**

Momentarily, the image arrives and fits snugly in place on the slide. If you try to import a clip art image into a slide that hasn't been formatted for clip art, however, the task is somewhat trickier.

6 **Click the down arrow on the scroll bar to see the next slide in the presentation.**

 Progress Check

If you can perform the following tasks, you're ready to move on to the Unit 7 quiz:

❑ Find and import an image from the Microsoft Clip Art Gallery.

❑ Change the size of an image.

❑ Reposition an image on a slide.

7 **Click the Insert Clip Art button and repeat Steps 3, 4, and 5 to find and import a second image from the Microsoft Clip Art Gallery.**

Because this slide wasn't formatted to receive clip art images, the image doesn't fit correctly after it lands on the slide, so you need to change the image's size and perhaps its dimensions. To do so, drag the squares on the corners and sides of the image. Dragging a square in a corner changes the size of the image but keeps its proportions; dragging a square on the side changes the size of an image as well as its proportions.

8 **Move the pointer over a corner square and, after the pointer turns into a two-headed arrow, click and drag the corner to make the image smaller but keep its proportions.**

You likely have to do this more than once to make the image the right size. Besides changing the image's size, you can also change its position on the slide.

9 **Move the pointer over the middle of the image and, after you see the pointer become a cross with arrows on it, click and drag the image to a new position.**

Use clip art early and often. The Office 97 clip-art files were created by genuine artists. The images make excellent additions to slide presentations.

Insert Clip Art button

Unit 7 Quiz

For the following questions, circle the letter of the correct answer or answers. This short quiz is designed to help you remember what you learned in Unit 7. Each question may have more than one right answer.

1. **To insert a new slide in a presentation, perform the following task:**
   A. Press Ctrl+M.
   B. Choose Insert⇨New Slide.
   C. Click the New Slide button on the Common Tasks toolbar.
   D. Click the New Slide button.
   E. All of the above.

2. **To move a slide in a presentation, you must be in which of the following views?**
   A. Slide view
   B. Outline view
   C. Slide Show view
   D. Slide Sorter view
   E. Any old view

Notes:

A

3. **This button performs which of the following actions?**

   A. Brands you with the scarlet letter A.

   B. Makes the letters smaller.

   C. Inserts a clip-art image.

   D. Makes the letters larger.

   E. Increases the amount of space between lines.

4. **Click this button to perform which of the following tasks?**

   A. Change the slide layout.

   B. Change the design of a presentation.

   C. Insert a new slide.

   D. Create a bulleted list.

   E. Insert a clip-art image.

5. **This button performs which of the following actions?**

   A. Creates a numbered list.

   B. Creates a bulleted list.

   C. Makes a color slide black-and-white.

   D. Boldfaces text.

   E. Inserts a new slide.

6. **To change the position of a clip-art image on a slide, perform which of the following actions?**

   A. Drag a corner of the image.

   B. Click the Insert Clip Art button.

   C. Click and drag the image to a new spot.

   D. Wiggle your finger.

   E. Drag a square on the side of the image.

Unit 7 Exercise

1. Create a presentation by using the AutoContent Wizard.

2. Switch to Outline view and change some of the generic text.

3. Switch to Slide Sorter view and move some of the slides around.

4. Switch to Slide view and choose a new design for the presentation.

5. Boldface the title of slide 1 and make the text in the title larger as well.

6. Add a blank slide and import a clip art image into it.

Show Time!

Objectives for This Unit

✓ Dress-rehearsing a presentation

✓ Showing a presentation

✓ Giving a timed presentation that "shows itself"

✓ Printing a handout of a presentation

Prerequisites

▶ Opening a file
  (Lesson 1-2)

▶ Viewing slides
  (Lesson 7-2)

on the CD

▶ Rehearse
▶ Big Show
▶ Automatic
▶ Handout
▶ Quiz 8

After you prepare and arrange the slides in a presentation, the fun begins. Now you can show off your masterpiece to the world. Unit 8 explains how.

Hearing the audience twitter at an embarrassing gaffe that you failed to detect can be disconcerting, so this unit starts by showing you how to preview a presentation so that you catch errors in the rehearsal stage. In this unit, you also learn how to give a slide presentation. I even show you a couple of techniques for making presentations livelier. Instead of a head-on presentation, for example, you can tell PowerPoint 97 to give a timed, automatic presentation that runs on its own. This unit explains how to accomplish that feat, too. It also tells you how to print a presentation so that you can hand out paper copies of the slides you create.

Figure 8-1: In Slide Show view, you can see exactly how the slides are going to look as you make a presentation.

Figure 8-1

Lesson 8-1

Previewing a Presentation

Before the big day arrives for an all-important presentation, preview your work. Preview the presentation two or three times, in fact. Make sure that the presentation doesn't include any snafus that could make your colleagues or audience look at the floor or bow their heads in embarrassment.

To preview a presentation, follow these steps:

on the CD

1 Open the Rehearse file in the Office 101 folder.

The file opens in Slide Sorter view. As you know from Lesson 7-2, this view is good for rearranging slides but doesn't offer an in-depth look at the words and images themselves. For that, you need to switch to Slide Show view.

2 **Click the Slide Show button in the lower-left corner of the screen.**

You can also choose View⇨Slide Show to switch to Slide Show view. As Figure 8-1 shows, Slide Show view enlarges a slide to full-screen size.

3 **Lean toward the computer screen and pretend that you're attending a drive-in movie.**

Do you notice the gaffe in this slide? The text now reads Brooklyn Bride Sale — but it's supposed to read Brooklyn Bridge Sale. Yikes! Better get out of Slide Show view and fix this error.

4 **Either press Esc or right-click and choose End Show from the shortcut menu.**

You land back in the view you started from, Slide Sorter view. Besides right-clicking to open the shortcut menu, you can click the button in the lower-left corner of the screen. The button is difficult to see on dark screens such as the one in this presentation, however, so you may as well learn to right-click instead of relying on the button.

5 **Double-click the first slide to switch to Slide Show view, click between the _d_ and _e_ in Bride, and enter a g to make the word Bridge.**

As is so often the case, fixing one error creates another. Now the heading is too big. The words wrap to the next line.

6 **Select the heading and click the Decrease Font Size button.**

Lesson 7-3 explained how to use this and other formatting buttons. Now the heading fits perfectly. Better start previewing again. That last error was a doozy. I hope you don't run across more errors like that one.

7 **Choose View⇨Slide Show and, after reviewing the first slide again, click anywhere on-screen.**

Clicking the screen in Slide Show view takes you to the next slide in the presentation. You can also press N (for Next) to move forward. Wait! What's this? Another error! The text should read suspension bridge, not sensation bridge. The salesperson got carried away, I guess.

on the test

8 **Right-click and choose End Show to return to Slide Sorter view; then click the Outline View button and correct the error.**

As Lesson 7-2 explained, fixing text errors is easy in Outline view.

9 **Click the Slide Show button and then click on-screen or press N to preview all the slides in the presentation.**

After you review all the slides, PowerPoint 97 takes you out of Slide Show view and puts you back in the view where you started — Outline view in this case.

Besides clicking on-screen or pressing N to move forward through a slide presentation, you can press P to move backward.

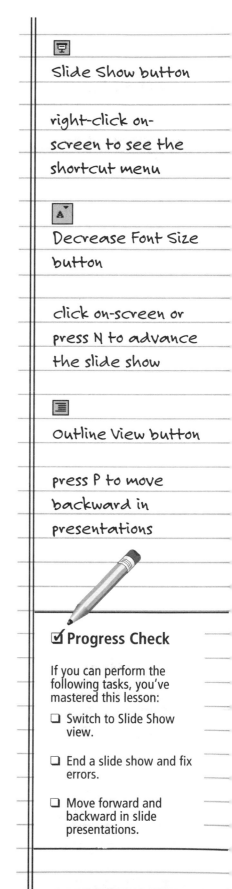

Slide Show button

right-click on-screen to see the shortcut menu

Decrease Font Size button

click on-screen or press N to advance the slide show

Outline View button

press P to move backward in presentations

☑ **Progress Check**

If you can perform the following tasks, you've mastered this lesson:

❑ Switch to Slide Show view.

❑ End a slide show and fix errors.

❑ Move forward and backward in slide presentations.

Lesson 8-2   Giving a Presentation

This lesson is a short one, because previewing slide shows isn't very different from presenting the shows. If you completed Lesson 8-1, you're going to find this lesson easy indeed. It shows you how to present a slide show and also offers one or two techniques for making a show livelier.

on the CD

To learn how to give a presentation, open the Big Show file in the Office 101 folder and follow these steps:

1 **Choose View⇨Slide Show to switch to Slide Show view and then click on-screen three or four times to reach the middle of the show.**

You learned in the last lesson that clicking on-screen or pressing N (for Next) advances the slides.

Suppose, in the middle of the show, that an astute member of the audience asks a question about a slide you presented earlier. You want to go back and show the slide again. As you learned in the last lesson, you can go backward in a slide presentation by pressing P, but a faster way also is available.

2 **Right-click to open the shortcut menu, click Go, click By Title, and select 2 For Sale Only Once! from the drop-down list of slides in the presentation.**

PowerPoint 97 takes you directly to the slide you asked for. By using this technique, you can go anywhere you want in a slide presentation.

on the test

3 **Either press Ctrl+P or right-click and choose Pen from the shortcut menu.**

The pointer changes into a pen.

4 **Click beside the first bulleted item in the bulleted list and, using the pointer like a pen or pencil, click and drag around the bullet to draw a circle around it.**

The pen is a handy instrument. Use it during presentations to underscore, circle, or cross off items on slides as you discuss them. (Or, if the people in the audience start a boring discussion among themselves, use the pen to doodle on a slide.) By the way, pen marks such as the doodles shown in Figure 8-2 appear on-screen only. The next time you view a slide you marked with the pen, the pen marks are gone. I wish that graffiti were as easy to clean off.

5 **Right-click, choose Screen, choose Black Screen, and draw a picture as best you can of the Mona Lisa.**

Well, you can draw a stick figure if you're not artistically inclined. The point of this step is that you can black out the screen and draw away if, for example, you want to spell out an important idea in a presentation. Besides right-clicking, you can press B to blank out the screen.

6 **Either press B or right-click, choose Screen, and choose Unblack Screen to return to the slide.**

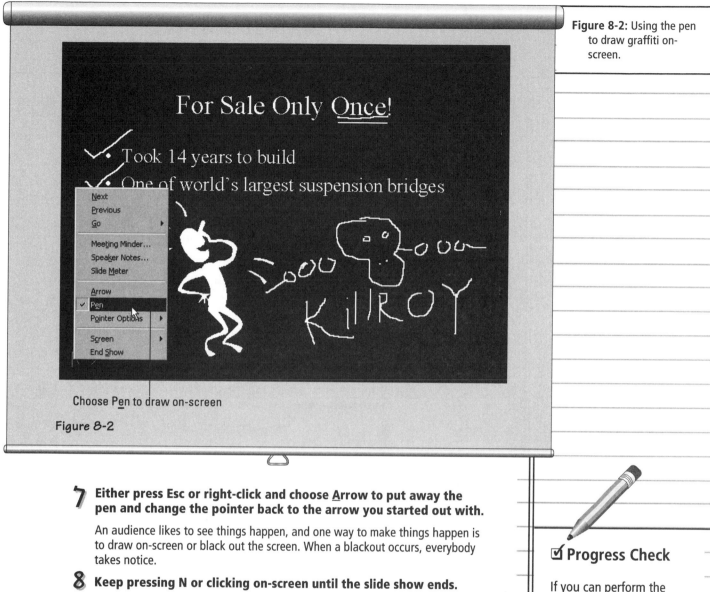

Figure 8-2: Using the pen to draw graffiti on-screen.

Choose P<u>e</u>n to draw on-screen

Figure 8-2

7 **Either press Esc or right-click and choose <u>A</u>rrow to put away the pen and change the pointer back to the arrow you started out with.**

An audience likes to see things happen, and one way to make things happen is to draw on-screen or black out the screen. When a blackout occurs, everybody takes notice.

8 **Keep pressing N or clicking on-screen until the slide show ends.**

As the last lesson explained, you can end a presentation abruptly by pressing Esc or right-clicking and choosing End <u>S</u>how.

Recess

It's time for a recess. Or maybe a better word is "intermission" seeing as this unit is about giving slide presentations. Yes, it's intermission time. Go buy some popcorn. And a theater lobby is one of the best places in the world for flirting, so be sure to do some of that while you are standing in the lobby. Just be sure not to throw popcorn at other theater goers or put gum under the seats when the film starts again.

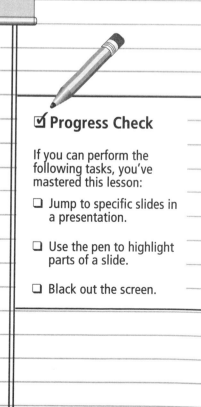

☑ **Progress Check**

If you can perform the following tasks, you've mastered this lesson:

❑ Jump to specific slides in a presentation.

❑ Use the pen to highlight parts of a slide.

❑ Black out the screen.

Lesson 8-3

Giving a Timed, Automatic Presentation

Notes:

At some point or another in your long and storied life, you must have seen a "kiosk" computer presentation — a series of computer images, usually advertisements or notices, that repeats itself on-screen *ad nauseam*. You can create such presentations in PowerPoint 97. To do so, you create a presentation, tell PowerPoint 97 how long to leave each slide on-screen, set the whole works in motion, and go to lunch . . . or Tahiti. After you return, you press the Esc key and the presentation ends.

on the CD

To make a presentation run automatically, without any help from man or beast, follow these steps:

1 Open the Automatic file in the Office 101 folder.

The first thing to do is tell PowerPoint 97 how long to leave each slide on-screen.

2 Right-click the first slide and choose Slide Transition from the shortcut menu.

The Slide Transition dialog box appears, as shown in Figure 8-3.

3 In the Advance area, click the On mouse click check box to remove the check mark.

Now the slide in the presentation doesn't advance after you click the mouse or press N.

on the test

4 Click the Automatically after check box and enter 7 in the seconds text box.

By doing so, you tell PowerPoint 97 to display the slide for 7 seconds.

5 Click the Apply to All button.

As the setting under each slide shows, slides in the presentation stay on-screen for 7 seconds. To give each slide in the presentation a different time setting, select each slide in Slide Sorter view and repeat Steps 2 through 5, but click the Apply button for each slide instead of clicking the Apply to All button.

PowerPoint 97 knows how long to leave each slide on-screen. The next step is to tell the program to display the slides over and over again until you or someone else presses the Esc key.

6 Choose Slide Show⇨Set Up Show.

The Set Up Show dialog box appears, as shown in Figure 8-4.

7 Click to put a check mark in the the Loop continuously until 'Esc' check box and then click OK.

Your loopy slide show is ready to start.

Slide Show button

8 Click the Slide Show button or choose View⇨Slide Show to get the show started.

Each slide appears for 7 seconds.

9 Press Esc after you're thoroughly hypnotized.

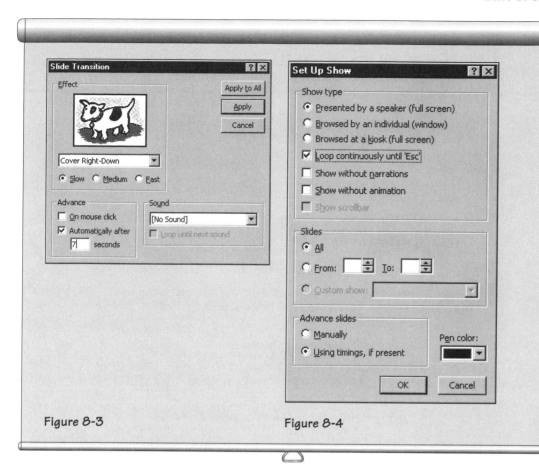

Figure 8-3

Figure 8-4

Figure 8-3:
Telling PowerPoint 97 how long to leave each slide on-screen.

Figure 8-4:
Making a presentation *loop,* or run continuously until someone presses ESC.

If you noticed, slides in the Automatic slide show appear on-screen in unusual ways. You can find out how to make slides do that by reading "Controlling how slides appear on-screen."

extra credit

Controlling how slides appear on-screen

Besides controlling how much time elapses between slides, you can make slides appear on-screen in unusual ways. Follow these steps to learn how:

1. **In Slide Sorter view, right-click a slide and choose Slide Transition.**

   The Slide Transition dialog box appears (refer to Figure 8-3).

2. **From the drop-down list in the Effect area, choose a transition.**

   Transitions have cryptic names, true, but the little doggy in the window demonstrates what the

effect you choose does to the slide. Experiment with the Effect options until you find a good one.

3. **Choose the Slow, Medium, or Fast radio button to determine how fast the slide appears on-screen.**

4. **Click the Apply to All button to make all the slides in the presentation appear on-screen the same way, or click the Apply button and then start all over with the next slide if you want each slide in the presentation to land on-screen in a different manner.**

☑ Progress Check

If you can perform the following tasks, you've mastered this lesson:

❑ Open the Slide Transition dialog box and enter a time setting for slides.

❑ Tell PowerPoint 97 to make the presentation loop continuously.

❑ Start and stop a looping presentation.

Lesson 8-4

Printing a Handout

One way to make sure that your presentations leave a lasting impression on viewers is to print hard copies of the slides and hand them out after you finish the presentation. I'm not saying that viewers are going to remember your presentation long after they see it, but they're more likely to remember your presentation in the days afterward if they see the handouts as they clean out their briefcases and desk drawers.

on the CD

on the test

To learn how to print a handout, open the Handout file in the Office 101 folder and follow these steps:

1 **Choose File⇨Print or press Ctrl+P.**

You see the Print - Handout dialog box. This dialog box doesn't look much different from the Word 97 Print dialog box, does it?

2 **In the Print range area, make sure that the All radio button is selected.**

If you want to print a single slide, you select it in Slide Sorter view and click the Current Slide radio button in the Print - Handout dialog box instead of the All button.

3 **In the Number of copies box, enter 2.**

Now PowerPoint 97 knows how many copies of the presentation you want to print.

4 **Click the down arrow next to Print what to open the drop-down list and then select Handouts (3 slides per page).**

Now PowerPoint 97 knows how many slides to print on each page.

5 **Click OK.**

PowerPoint 97 prints the handouts.

☑ **Progress Check**

If you can perform the following tasks, you're ready to move on to the Unit 8 quiz:

❏ Open the Print - Handout dialog box.

❏ Tell PowerPoint 97 how many slides to print on each page.

❏ Print a PowerPoint 97 presentation.

Unit 8 Quiz

For the following questions, circle the letter of the correct answer or answers. I designed this short quiz to help you remember what you learned in Unit 8. Each question may have more than one right answer.

1. **To move forward in a presentation, you perform which of the following actions?**

    A. Press P.

    B. Click on-screen.

    C. Double-click on-screen.

    D. Press N.

    E. Press M.

2. **To stop running a slide show, you perform which of the following actions?**

   A. Choose File⇨Close.

   B. Choose File⇨Exit.

   C. Turn off the computer (dead wrong answer).

   D. Right-click and choose End Show from the shortcut menu.

   E. Click a View button.

3. **To move to a specific slide in a presentation, you perform which of the following actions?**

   A. Keep pressing N until you get there.

   B. Keep pressing P until you get there.

   C. Switch to Slide Sorter view, click the slide, and start the slide show again.

   D. Right-click, choose Go on the shortcut menu, choose By Title from the submenu, and select the title of the slide you want to go to.

   E. You can't do that. Who would want to do that?

4. **To draw on-screen with the pen, you perform which of the following actions?**

   A. Drag the mouse on-screen.

   B. Right-click and choose Pen from the shortcut menu.

   C. Black out the screen.

   D. Choose Insert⇨Pen.

   E. Choose Slide Show⇨Pen.

5. **To print handouts of a presentation, you perform which of the following actions?**

   A. Press Ctrl+P to open the Print - Handout dialog box and choose a handout option from the Print What drop-down list.

   B. Click the Print button.

   C. Choose File⇨Print to open the Print - Handout dialog box and then click OK.

   D. Press Ctrl+P to open the Print - Handout dialog box and select Notes Pages from the Print What drop-down list.

   E. Handouts prove that there is such a thing as a free lunch.

6. **Who said, "Few things are harder to put up with than the annoyance of a good example"?**

   A. H.L. Mencken.

   B. George Bernard Shaw.

   C. Mark Twain.

   D. S.J. Pearlman.

   E. Eric Hoffer.

Notes:

Unit 8 Exercise

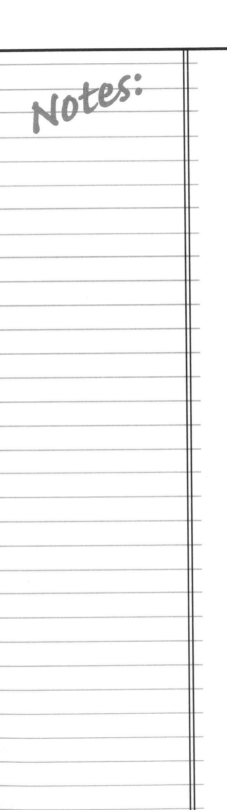

Notes:

on the CD

1. Open the Quiz 8 file in the Office 101 folder.
2. Switch to Slide Show view and press N or click on-screen to see the first three slides.
3. Go to slide 1 without pressing P.
4. Scribble on slide 1 with the pen.
5. End the slide show immediately.
6. Print a handout of the presentation.

Part III Review

Unit 7 Summary

▶ **Creating a presentation:** From the PowerPoint 97 dialog box, choose AutoContent Wizard to get help creating a preformatted presentation. You can also choose Template from that dialog box to choose a canned design. To insert slides one at a time, click the New Slide button on the Common Tasks toolbar, press Ctrl+M, click the New Slide button, or choose Insert⇨New Slide.

▶ **Viewing a presentation:** By clicking the view buttons in the lower-left corner of the screen or choosing options on the View menu, you can see a presentation in different ways. Switch to Outline view to see the text and get a better read of the content of a presentation. In Slide Sorter view, you can see how the slides follow one another. In Slide view, you see one slide at a time on-screen so that you can focus on each slide's layout and appearance. In Note Pages view, you can read and make notes on a slide.

▶ **Entering and formatting text:** Enter text in Outline view. To format text, switch to Slide view. The standard formatting techniques available in Word 97 — the buttons for boldfacing, italicizing, underlining, and aligning text — also are available in PowerPoint 97. To create a bulleted list, select the items in the list and click the Bullets button. PowerPoint 97 also offers buttons for increasing and decreasing font sizes and for increasing or decreasing the amount of space between lines.

▶ **Choosing a presentation design:** Click the Apply Design button to open the Apply Design dialog box, choose a design icon, and then click the Apply button.

▶ **Importing clip art:** On preformatted slides designed for clip-art images, double-click the icon to open the Microsoft Clip Art Gallery. Otherwise, click the Insert Clip Art button. In the Microsoft Clip Art Gallery dialog box, click a category name and then scroll through the images to find the one you want. After you find the right image, click it and then click Insert.

Unit 8 Summary

▶ **Previewing slides:** Click the Slide Show button or choose View⇨Show to see the slide at full-screen size. If you detect an error, right-click and choose End Show from the shortcut menu; then switch to another view and change the text or formatting. Click or press N (for Next) to move forward through the presentation; press P (for Previous) to move backward.

▶ **Giving presentations:** Click the Slide Show button to start a presentation. Click or press N (for Next) to go forward; press P (Previous) to go backward. You can go to any slide by right-clicking on-screen, choosing Go from the shortcut menu, clicking By Title, and choosing the slide's title from the drop-down list. To draw with the pen, right-click and choose Pen.

▶ **Giving automatic presentations:** In Slide Sorter view, right-click the first slide and choose Slide Transition. In the Advance area of the Slide Transition dialog box, click the On Mouse Click check box to remove the check mark, click the Automatically After check box, enter how long you want the slide to stay on-screen in the Seconds text box, and click Apply or Apply to All. Next, choose Slide Show⇨Set Up Show, click the Loop Continuously until Esc check box, and click OK. After you start the show, the presentation continues indefinitely or until you press Esc.

▶ **Printing handouts:** Choose File⇨Print and choose options in the Print-Handout dialog box. To tell PowerPoint 97 to print handouts, choose a handout option in the Print What drop-down list before clicking OK.

Part III Test

The Part III exam will test your survival skills. It will determine whether you are made of steel or soft putty. It will knock you down and dare you to stand up again. It will tip-toe behind your left shoulder and whisper, "You're not good enough." It will visit you in your sleep and flood your dreams with images of despair and hopelessness.

Actually, this test is pretty simple, especially if you completed Parts I and II of this book. By now, Office 97 must be getting very familiar to you. This test is simply meant to help you gauge what you learned in Part III and what you need to review. You will find the answers to this test in Appendix A (no peeking!). If you have trouble with a question, look at the preceding Review pages. Or thumb through Part III and look for the On the Test icons. Beside each On the Test icon is an answer to a question that follows.

True   False

T   F   1. Use the AutoContent Wizard if you want to change the formats and appearance of a presentation.

T   F   2. The View buttons are located in the lower-left corner of the screen.

T   F   3. Designing slides yourself is easier than using the PowerPoint 97 designs.

T   F   4. Press P to move backward in a presentation.

T   F   5. Right-click and choose Pen to draw on-screen in Slide Show view.

T   F   6. You can control how long each slide stays on-screen.

Multiple choice

Circle the correct answer or answers to the following questions. Each question may have more than one right answer.

7. **To insert a new slide in a presentation, you perform which of the following actions?**

    A. Click the New Slide button on the Common Tasks toolbar.

    B. Choose Insert⇨Slide Number.

    C. Press Ctrl+M.

    D. Click the New Slide button.

    E. Choose Insert⇨New Slide.

8. **To move a slide in a presentation, you perform which of the following actions?**

    A. Delete the slide and create it all over again.

    B. Click the Insert Slide button.

    C. Choose Edit⇨Move.

    D. Right-click, choose Cut, click elsewhere, and choose Paste.

    E. Switch to Slide Sorter View, click the slide, and drag it elsewhere.

9. **Which of the following views is best for focusing on the text in a presentation?**

    A. Outline view.

    B. Slide Sorter view.

    C. Slide view.

    D. Note Pages view.

    E. Slide Show view.

Part III Test

10. **To move forward through a slide presentation, you perform which of the following actions?**

    A. Right-click and choose <u>N</u>ext from the shortcut menu.

    B. Press N.

    C. Press P.

    D. Click on-screen.

    E. Double-click on-screen.

11. **To print a handout of a slide presentation, you perform which of the following actions?**

    A. Choose <u>F</u>ile⇨<u>P</u>rint.

    B. Choose <u>P</u>rint⇨<u>H</u>andout.

    C. Press Ctrl+P.

    D. Right-click a slide and choose <u>P</u>rint.

    E. Switch to Slide Sorter view.

12. **If you're in the audience at a presentation and the speaker can't get the slides to show correctly or the speaker puts the wrong set of slides on-screen, what is the best thing for you to do?**

    A. Cough into your closed fist.

    B. Say, "You're fired, buster!"

    C. Reach across the table for another doughnut.

    D. Draw caricatures of the other people in the room.

    E. Pull out your cell phone and use the opportunity to get some real work done.

Matching

13. **Match the following buttons with their names.**

    A. [icon]   1. New Slide

    B. [icon]   2. Decrease Paragraph Spacing

    C. [icon]   3. Bold

    D. [icon]   4. Increase Paragraph Spacing

    E. [icon]   5. Increase Font Size

14. **Match the following buttons with their names.**

    A. [icon]   1. Apply Design

    B. [icon]   2. Italic

    C. [icon]   3. New Slide

    D. [icon]   4. Insert Clip Art

    E. [icon]   5. Left Alignment

Part III Lab Assignment

If you've been doing the assignments at the end of the part tests, you already know that lab assignments give you practice in real-life situations. Instead of telling you exactly what to do to solve a problem, lab assignments give general instructions. The idea is for you to figure out or already know how to do a task — and then do it.

In the lab assignments at the end of Part I and Part II, you did some work for an outfit called Pierspont Property Management. You edited and formatted a rental agreement in Part I, and in Part II, you put the finishing touches on a worksheet. In this lab assignment, you polish a presentation that shows how successful Pierspont Property Management has become.

Part III Lab Assignment

To do the assignment, open the Test 3 file in the Office 101 folder and read on.

Step 1: Inserting and moving slides

Put a new slide in the presentation. Put the new slide between slides 2 and 3. And while you're at it, you may notice that the title slide is in the wrong place. That slide is now slide 2, but it should be slide 1. Move the title slide to the first position.

Step 2: Editing and formatting text

One of these sides has Latin script! Better erase that and put English script in its place. Would you like to change the format in this slide? The heading isn't the same size as the other headings in the presentation. Maybe you need a bulleted list on this slide. And I think the text lines on the slide are too far apart.

Step 3: Choosing a "look" for the presentation

Experiment with different designs for this presentation. Who will the audience be? Do you want a flashy design or a quiet, confident design? While you're at it, one of these slides needs clip art. Better put a clip-art image in that slide.

Step 4: A really big show

Give the presentation. Don't forget to use the pen to highlight the most important parts. After you're done, set up the presentation so that it can run in your absence. In other words, set up a timed, automatic presentation. Then set the presentation in motion, watch it twice, and turn it off.

Step 5: Printing handouts

Print two handouts of the presentation.

Outlook

Part IV

In this part...

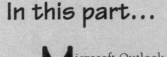icrosoft Outlook is actually two programs in one. On one hand, you can use Outlook to communicate with the outside world by sending, receiving, storing, and organizing e-mail.

On the other hand, Outlook is also a personal organizer. You may use it to schedule appointments and meetings, maintain a detailed list of the people you know and do business with, and track tasks and projects.

Unit 9 covers the communications side of Outlook, and Unit 10 covers the personal organizer side of the program. If your computer is not connected to the Internet or a network and you want to use Outlook solely to bring organization to the chaos of your life, complete Lesson 9-1, which offers a quick tour of Outlook, and then skip ahead to Unit 10. Otherwise, if your computer is connected to the Internet or a network, read straight through Part IV.

Look out, because you are about to embark on a journey through the wonderful world of Outlook.

Communicating with Outlook

Objectives for This Unit

✓ Learning how the parts of Outlook fit together

✓ Sending e-mail messages

✓ Receiving and reading e-mail

✓ Storing and organizing e-mail messages

✓ Replying to and forwarding e-mail messages

Prerequisites

▶ Starting an Office 97 program (Lesson 1-1)

▶ Opening and closing a file (Lesson 1-2)

▶ Saving a file (Lesson 2-1)

▶ Entering and editing text (Lesson 2-2)

Unit 9 explores the online communications side of Outlook. In this unit, you learn how to send, receive, read, reply to, organize, and sort e-mail messages with Outlook. Outlook, you will be glad to know, makes sending and receiving e-mail messages over a computer very easy.

Before you dive headlong into learning about e-mail, Lesson 9-1 starts off with an introduction to the different features of the program. On the surface anyway, the program is considerably different from the other four Office 97 programs. For one thing, you start from different screens, depending on what you want to do. And you find a lot of as-yet-unfamiliar buttons and command names. After you get the hang of Outlook, however, you discover that Outlook is the simplest and easiest to use of the Office 97 programs.

It almost goes without saying, but you must be connected to the Internet, a network, an e-mail server, or e-mail transmission service to send and receive e-mail messages with Outlook.

Notes:

After you install Outlook, the program endeavors to find out what your e-mail connection is. Outlook recognizes the following programs and makes using them for sending and receiving e-mail easy:

- ◗ Internet Mail
- ◗ Lotus cc:Mail
- ◗ Microsoft Exchange Server
- ◗ Microsoft Mail
- ◗ The Microsoft Network (MSN)

If you use one of these programs to connect to the Internet or a network, you've got it made. You are ready to send and receive e-mail messages with Outlook.

heads up

If you use a private Internet provider such as America Online or another service that competes with the Mighty Microsoft Monopoly, you must tell Outlook which provider you use and where to find its program on your computer. For guidance on how to do so, go to the Outlook Help program. Choose Help➪Contents and Index, click the Index tab in the Help Contents dialog box, type **information services**, click Display, choose Install an information service, and click Display again. That takes you to the "Install an information service" Help screen, where, at the bottom (scroll to get there), you find a shortcut to a topic called "Install an information service not provided by Outlook." Click the shortcut button to see the Help screen for installing your service, and follow its directions.

If you need help with the Internet and Internet e-mail, pick up a copy of *Dummies 101: The Internet For Windows 95,* by Margy Levine Young and Hy Bender, published by IDG Books Worldwide, Inc.

Lesson 9-1

Finding Your Way around Outlook

At first glance, the Outlook screen is kind of intimidating. What are all those buttons, icons, and menus for? To help you get acquainted with Outlook, this lesson takes you on a quick tour of the program and shows you how to get to the commands for writing and sending e-mail messages, maintaining a contact list, scheduling projects, and maintaining a task list. Put on your seatbelts, ladies and gentlemen.

To get the lay of the land in Outlook, follow these steps:

1 **Click the Inbox icon in the Outlook bar.**

Inbox icon

As Figure 9-1 shows, the *Outlook bar* is the box on the left side of the screen. By clicking icons in the Outlook bar, you can get to different parts of the Outlook program. Notice the down arrow at the bottom of the Outlook bar. Later in Unit 9, I ask you to click that arrow to access other buttons in the Outlook bar.

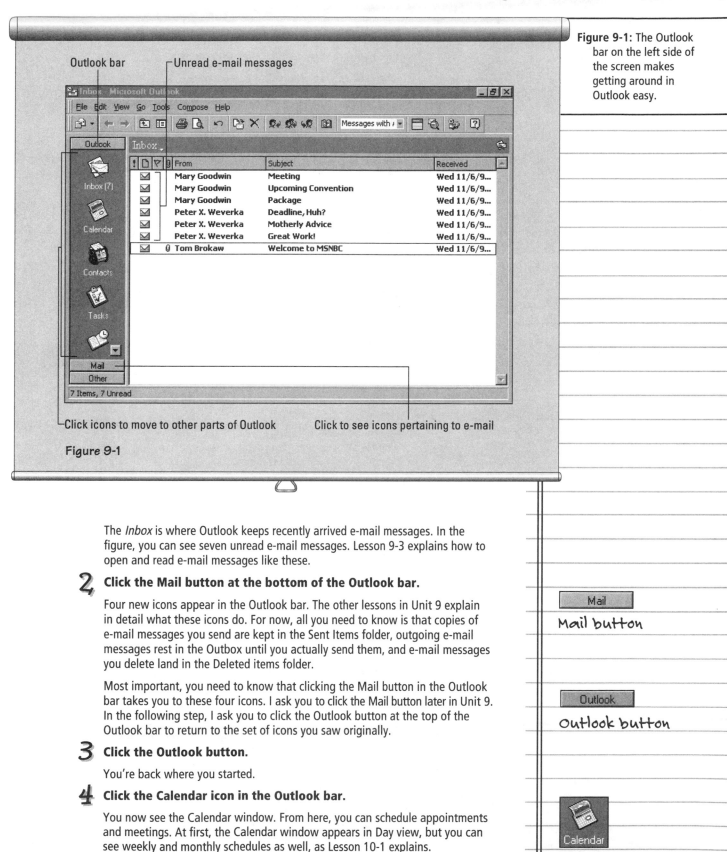

Outlook bar —|

—Unread e-mail messages

Figure 9-1: The Outlook bar on the left side of the screen makes getting around in Outlook easy.

—Click icons to move to other parts of Outlook

Click to see icons pertaining to e-mail

Figure 9-1

The *Inbox* is where Outlook keeps recently arrived e-mail messages. In the figure, you can see seven unread e-mail messages. Lesson 9-3 explains how to open and read e-mail messages like these.

2 Click the Mail button at the bottom of the Outlook bar.

Four new icons appear in the Outlook bar. The other lessons in Unit 9 explain in detail what these icons do. For now, all you need to know is that copies of e-mail messages you send are kept in the Sent Items folder, outgoing e-mail messages rest in the Outbox until you actually send them, and e-mail messages you delete land in the Deleted items folder.

Most important, you need to know that clicking the Mail button in the Outlook bar takes you to these four icons. I ask you to click the Mail button later in Unit 9. In the following step, I ask you to click the Outlook button at the top of the Outlook bar to return to the set of icons you saw originally.

3 Click the Outlook button.

You're back where you started.

4 Click the Calendar icon in the Outlook bar.

You now see the Calendar window. From here, you can schedule appointments and meetings. At first, the Calendar window appears in Day view, but you can see weekly and monthly schedules as well, as Lesson 10-1 explains.

Mail

Mail button

Outlook

Outlook button

Calendar

Calender icon

Contacts icon

Tasks icon

✓ Progress Check

If you can perform the following tasks, you've mastered this lesson:

❑ Click icons to go to different parts of Outlook.

❑ Click the Mail button on the Outlook bar to see different icons related to e-mail.

❑ Click the down arrow on the Outlook bar to see more icons.

5 **Click the Contacts icon in the Outlook bar.**

In the Contacts list, you can store the addresses and phone numbers of colleagues, clients, relatives, and friends. Lesson 10-3 explains how to enter contacts and find them in the list. When you send e-mail messages in Outlook, the program gets e-mail addresses from the Contacts list.

In Lesson 9-2, I ask you to send an e-mail message to me, so if you intend to complete that lesson, please perform the following four steps, which explain how to enter my name and e-mail address in the Contacts list. (Skip to Step 10 if you aren't going to use Outlook to send e-mail.)

6 **Press Ctrl+N to open the Contact dialog box.**

Lesson 10-2 explains everything you need to know about this intimidating dialog box. For now, just enter my name and e-mail address.

7 **Type the following in the Fu̲ll Name box:** Peter Weverka.

8 **Type Peter_Weverka@msn.com in the text box to the right of the E-mail drop-down list.**

To enter the underscore between my first and last name (_), hold down the Shift key and press the key to the right of the zero on your keyboard.

9 **Click the S̲ave and Close button.**

You're ready for Lesson 9-2. Meanwhile, on with the tour of Outlook.

10 **Click the Tasks icon in the Outlook bar.**

You see the Tasks list. Here you can enter the tasks you are supposed to complete for your work, tell when the tasks are overdue, and arrange a schedule so that you can meet deadlines. Lesson 10-3 explains the Tasks list.

11 **Click the Calendar icon again.**

Notice the Task list in the lower-right corner of the window. Tasks entered on the Task list also appear in the Calendar window so you can manage time better.

12 **Click the Inbox icon to return to the Inbox.**

I hope you enjoyed this little tour. No tipping. A pleasure to be of service.

Lesson 9-2

Writing, Editing, and Sending Messages

Lesson 9-2 explains how to write an e-mail message and send the message to one, two, or a hundred people. In the course of this lesson, you write a message to yours truly, the author of this book.

on the test

Outlook gets the e-mail addresses you need to send e-mail from the Outlook Contacts list. To send a message, you must have entered the recipient's name and e-mail address in the Contacts list, you must be replying to a message that someone has sent to you, or you must know the person's e-mail address and be able to type it in. Lesson 9-1 explained how to enter my name and e-mail

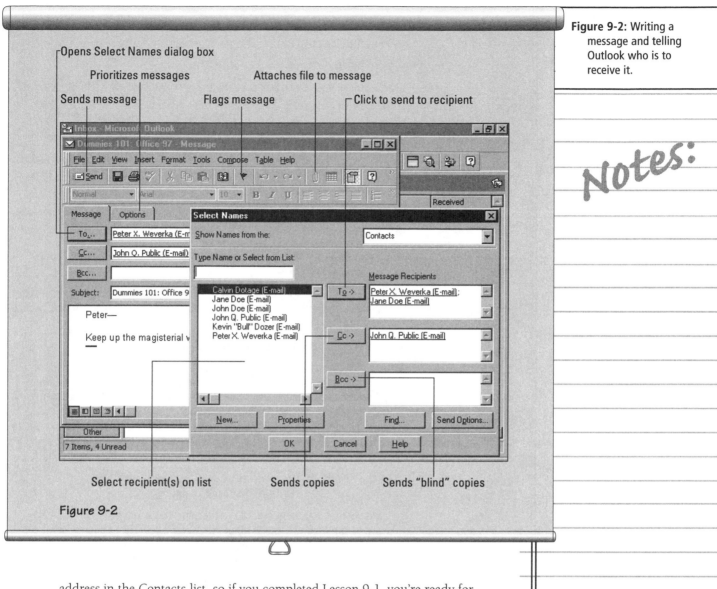

Figure 9-2

Figure 9-2: Writing a message and telling Outlook who is to receive it.

address in the Contacts list, so if you completed Lesson 9-1, you're ready for this lesson. If you skipped Lesson 9-1 and you want to work through this lesson, you need to do some back-tracking.

To compose and send an e-mail message to one or more people, make sure that you enter all the recipients' names on the Contacts list or that you know the recipients' e-mail addresses, and then follow these steps:

1 **Click the Inbox icon at the left side of the screen if you're not already in the Inbox.**

As you know from Lesson 9-1, the Inbox is one of several screens that appear in the Outlook bar.

2 **Click the New Mail Message button.**

You open the Message dialog box, which you can see behind the Select Names dialog box in Figure 9-2. You can also get to this dialog box by choosing Compose⇨New Mail Message or by pressing Ctrl+N.

Inbox icon

New Mail Message button

click Cc to send a
copy of a message

click Bcc to send
a copy without the
main recipient
knowing

In the following step, you tell Outlook to whom the message goes.

3 **Click the To button.**

The Select Names dialog box appears, as shown in Figure 9-2. On the left side of this dialog box, below the Type Name or Select from List box, are the names of all the people in the Contacts list for whom e-mail addresses are listed.

4 **Click my name on the list and then click the To button.**

My name appears in the Message Recipients list to the right of the To button. If you want to send your message to more than one person, you click the name of each recipient in the box on the left and then click the To button again.

Select a name and click the Cc button to send a copy of a message to someone other than the person to whom you addressed the message. The letters *CC* date to the typewriter era and stand for *carbon copy*. When you send a copy of an e-mail message this way, the recipients in the To box know to whom copies of the message were sent.

Click the Bcc button to send a *blind carbon copy* of a message to others besides the people listed in the To box. If you go this route, the recipients in the To box do *not* know that copies of the message were sent to others.

5 **Click OK to close the Select Names dialog box.**

The recipient's name, or the recipients' names if you are sending the message to more than one person, appear beside the To... button. If you send carbon copies or blind carbon copies of the message, the names of those recipients appear beside the Cc and Bcc buttons. If you change your mind at this point about who is to receive your message, you can click one of the three buttons to return to the Select Names dialog box, where you can delete names or select new names.

heads up

6 **Let the recipient know what your message is about by typing** Dummies 101: Office 97 **in the Subject box.**

Make sure that you write descriptive titles in the Subject box. After others receive your messages, the first thing they see is your name and the title you type in the Subject box. The fastest way for recipients to find out which messages are important and need to be answered first is by looking at the subject.

Speaking of importance, you can flag your messages to tell others how important they are.

7 **Click the Message Flag button.**

You see the Message Flag dialog box. From here, you can tell recipients how to handle messages and when or whether you expect a response.

Message Flag
button

8 **Click the arrow to open the Flag drop-down list, select For Your Information, and click OK.**

The drop-down list offers many choices for flagging the message. If you want recipients to reply by a certain date, you can open the By drop-down list and click a date on the calendar. Red flags appear beside flagged messages in the Inbox.

9 **Click the message box and write me a note about the book you're reading.**

Do you find this book useful? Should I have explored a certain topic more thoroughly? Lemme know.

on the test

While you are typing your message, you can take advantage of most of the Word 97 formatting commands on the toolbars and menus. You can, for example, boldface, italicize, and change the size of text. (Office 97 asks when you first open the program whether you to use the Word 97 formatting commands in Outlook. If you answered No, do the following after you finish this lesson so that you can use the Word 97 formatting commands to write e-mail messages: Choose Tools⇨Options, click the E-Mail tab in the Options dialog box, click the Use Microsoft Word as an E-Mail Editor check box, and click OK.)

extra credit

Miss Cyber-Manners discusses smileys

Dear Miss Cyber-Manners:

I just love getting e-mail from friends all around the world. But sometimes, the messages include parentheses and colons that look like chicken scratches. Is my computer broken, or are my friends using a secret code? I'm too embarrassed to ask them myself, Miss Cyber-Manners. Help!

> Embarrassed E-Mailer

Dear Embarrassed E-Mailer:

Those parentheses and colons you mentioned are called *smileys*. Smileys are meant to mimic the facial expressions that accompany real conversations. Turn this book sideways and you will see, instead of punctuation marks, a frown, a wink, a smile, and former President Ronald Reagan:

- 7:^]

- : -)

- ; -)

- (: -(

Miss Cyber-Manners does not recommend using smileys often. They are a bit like the laugh tracks one hears on television. On television, even jokes that aren't funny are greeted by loud, artificial laughter. Similarly, bad jokes in e-mail messages are usually accompanied by a smiley. Miss Cyber-Manners is of the opinion that if something is humorous, sad, or playful, the reader will know it without the e-mailer having to include a smiley. Indeed, if you decide to include a smiley, it is likely because you suspect that your message is not as funny, sad, or playful as you would like it to be, in which case Miss Cyber-Manners suggests dropping the smiley and rewriting the message.

---

10 **Click the Options tab, click the Importance down arrow to open the drop-down list, select High from the list, and click the Message tab.**

Messages to which you give "important" status display a red exclamation point next to their names in the Inbox.

on the test

11 **Click the Send button.**

Whether the message is sent right away depends on whether you're connected to a network or the Internet. Network messages are sent right away. Internet messages are sent the next time you choose Tools⇨Check for New Mail or press F5 to connect with your Internet provider.

Send

Send button

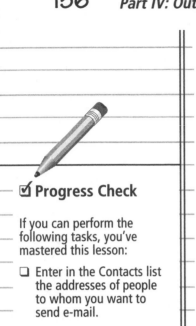

☑ Progress Check

If you can perform the following tasks, you've mastered this lesson:

❑ Enter in the Contacts list the addresses of people to whom you want to send e-mail.

❑ Compose an e-mail message.

❑ Assign a priority to or flag a message.

❑ Send an e-mail message.

12 **Click Mail at the bottom of the Outlook bar on the left side of the screen and then click the Outbox icon.**

on the test

Messages that haven't gone out yet appear in the Outbox. If you decide not to send such a message, open the Outbox, click the message, and click the Delete button. You can also edit a message from the Outbox by double-clicking that message to open the Message dialog box (refer to Figure 9-2).

13 **Click the Outlook button at the top of the Outlook bar and then click the Inbox icon.**

14 **Choose Tools⇨Check for New Mail or press F5 to send your message.**

Wave good-bye. After Outlook connects with the Internet provider, the message sails across cyberspace. Outlook also retrieves Messages others sent to you after you choose Tools⇨Check for New Mail.

extra credit

Miss Cyber-Manners discusses e-mail etiquette

Dear Miss Cyber-Manners:

Recently I began using my computer to send and receive e-mail messages. While I am delighted to communicate so swiftly with other people on the Internet, I have discovered that some people in cyberspace are not nice. In fact, some of them are downright rude. Why is that?

Hurt and Aggrieved

Dear Hurt and Aggrieved,

Indeed, Miss Cyber-Manners herself has received e-mail messages with language so vile she instinctively covered her ears, even though the messages were delivered on a computer screen, not in person or by telephone. And that is precisely the point, Hurt and Aggrieved: E-mail offers a degree of anonymity, and the uncouth among us think that e-mail's anonymity gives them a license to say whatever they please, no matter how rude or insulting. There is even a word for vile, insulting e-mail messages. They are called *flames*. Gently remind the e-mailers with whom you correspond that rules of civility and good conduct apply in cyberspace, too. If someone persists in flaming you, tell him or her that you don't wish to correspond any longer.

To make sure that you never commit such a grievous breach of e-mail etiquette, Miss Cyber-Manners recommends the following golden rules of e-mail etiquette:

▶ Never forward a message to others without getting permission from its author. If you write an e-mail message that someone can forward, tell the recipient that he or she has permission to forward the message.

▶ When you write a message, make sure that you also write a descriptive heading in the Subject line. Some people receive many e-mail messages each day. By writing a descriptive heading, you help people decide how important messages are and which ones to answer first.

▶ Don't use capital letters unnecessarily in e-mail messages. If you do, recipients will get the impression THAT YOU ARE SHOUTING AT THEM.

▶ Certain topics are not suitable for e-mail. Imagine, gentle reader, how horrified you'd be if you received the following e-mail message from your boss: "You're fired!" For messages such as that one, be brave and honorable and deliver the message in person.

Receiving and Reading Messages

Lesson 9-3

This lesson is a short one, because after you know the ins and outs of sending messages, receiving messages is pretty easy. To complete the following lesson, you must have received an e-mail message or two. A sure way to receive e-mail is to send yourself a couple of messages. Simply follow the directions in Lesson 9-2 and put your own e-mail address and name in the To box. (I tried it, and the messages I sent to myself arrived at almost the same time that I sent them.)

The following steps explain how to receive and read e-mail messages:

1 **Click the Inbox icon in the Outlook bar if you're not already in the Inbox.**

2 **Choose Tools⇨Check for New Mail or press F5.**

Another way to retrieve messages is to send outgoing messages. Whenever Outlook sends messages, it retrieves messages from others as well.

Next, you likely have to click a Connect button and go through the rigmarole of connecting to your network or Internet provider. And, depending on how your system is set up, you may see the Check For New Mail On dialog box, which asks you to click next to the names of the services from which you want to get mail and then to click OK.

Soon Outlook tells you that it is delivering your messages, searching for new messages, and receiving new messages. Then Outlook disconnects from the Internet or network and your screen looks something like the one in Figure 9-3.

on the test

Senders' names appear in the From column. In the Subject column are the all-important descriptions of what is in the messages. Unread messages show a sealed envelope icon and appear in boldface in the Inbox. Messages you have read are not boldfaced and show an open envelope icon. (Notice the exclamation points, flags, and paper clips in Figure 9-3. You learned what exclamation points and flags mean in Lesson 9-2. A paper clip means that a file is being sent along with the message.)

3 **Click the AutoPreview button.**

on the test

You see the first couple of lines in unopened messages in blue type. Click AutoPreview when you want to glimpse what is in unread messages.

4 **Click the AutoPreview button again.**

The blue lines disappear.

5 **Double-click a message — on its icon, sender name, or subject — to open and read the message.**

on the test

The Message window appears and shows you the text of the message. Read away. The next lesson explains how to store messages, and the lesson after that explains how to reply to or forward messages from the Message window.

6 **Click the Previous Item or Next Item button to close the message and open the previous or next one in the Inbox.**

on the test

You don't need to return to the Inbox, necessarily, to read other messages, as this step demonstrates, but you do need to go back there sooner or later.

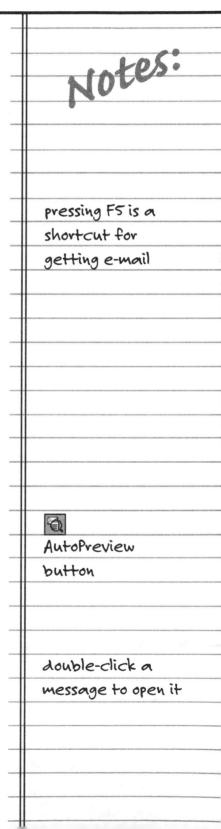

Notes:

pressing F5 is a shortcut for getting e-mail

AutoPreview button

double-click a message to open it

Figure 9-3: Messages in
the Inbox, some read
and some unread.

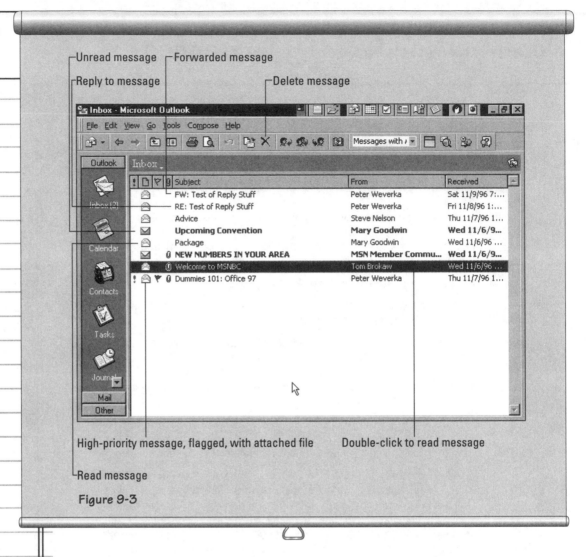

─Unread message   ─Forwarded message

─Reply to message   ─Delete message

High-priority message, flagged, with attached file   Double-click to read message

└Read message

Figure 9-3

click the Close
button (X) to close
the Message
window

Delete button

7 **Choose File⇨Close, press Alt+F4, or click the Close button (the *X*) in
the upper-right corner of the Message window.**

Each message is a file. As such, you close it as you would a file in Word 97, for
example. If you make changes to a message — if you delete part of it or type
words on it — Outlook asks if you want to save those changes before you close
the file that your message is saved in.

Back in the Inbox, the message or messages you just read now show an open
envelope icon. You can double-click another message to open it. Or you can
delete a message by selecting it and clicking the Delete button (or pressing
Ctrl+D). Messages stay in the Inbox until you delete them or store them in a
folder. Storing and organizing messages is the subject of the next lesson.

heads up

By the way, if you opened more than one e-mail message in this lesson, a "Message" button appears on the taskbar at the bottom of the screen. Outlook treats messages like computer programs. Each time you open a new message, another button appears on the taskbar. To close the extra Message window, click its button on the taskbar and then click the window's Close button.

Recess

Time for recess. You've learned a lot in the last three lessons, and you deserve a break. And as soon as the "freeze bell" sounds at the end of recess, I want you to stand stock-still. I want you to freeze in the position you were in as the freeze bell rang. No talking. No moving around. Or else I'll send you to the principal's office.

☑ **Progress Check**

If you can perform the following tasks, you've mastered this lesson:

❏ Retrieve e-mail messages.

❏ Preview what is in messages.

❏ Open and read an e-mail message.

❏ Close the Message window.

Storing and Sorting Messages   Lesson 9-4

The further you explore cyberspace, the more e-mail messages you get. And how to keep track of, organize, and sort all those messages can become a giant-sized problem. To help you keep your e-mail in order, Outlook offers the opportunity to store messages in different folders.

This lesson explains how to create folders for different kinds of messages. You may put correspondence from different people in different folders, for example, or store all messages that pertain to a project in one folder. Lesson 9-4 also tells you how to open a message stored in a folder.

To complete this lesson, at least one message must be in the Inbox. Send an e-mail message to yourself to put a message in the Inbox, if necessary.

Creating folders and storing messages in them

Follow these steps to create folders and store e-mail messages in the folders:

1 **In the Inbox, select the message that you want to store in a folder.**
Select the message by clicking it.

2 **Click the Move to Folder button and choose Move to Folder from the drop-down list.**

Move to Folder button

Figure 9-4: Moving a message into a folder.

Figure 9-5: Opening a folder from the folder list (left) and from the Go to Folder dialog box (right).

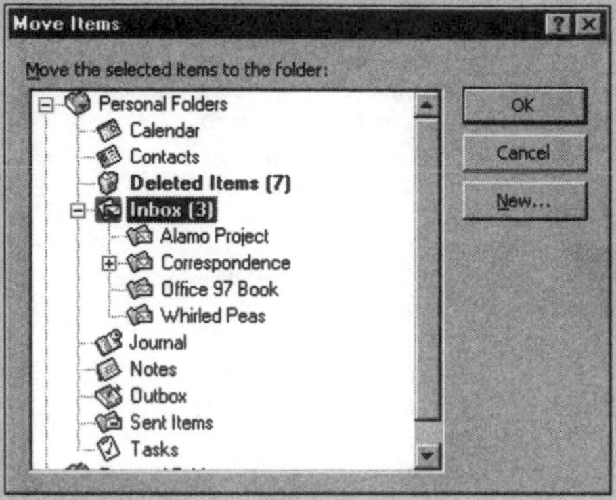

Figure 9-4

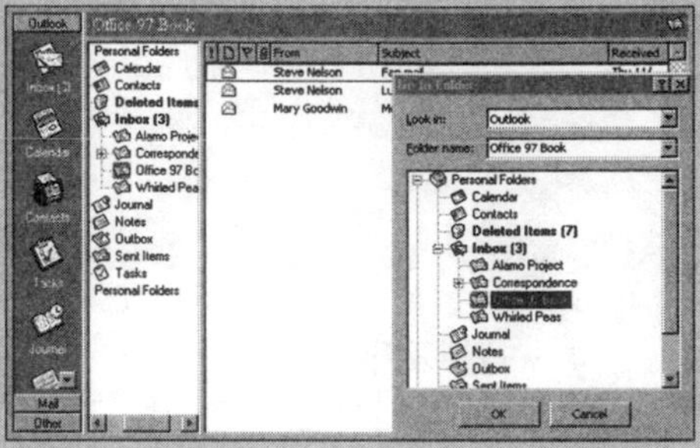

Figure 9-5

You can also choose Edit⇨Move to Folder or press Ctrl+Shift+V. The Move Items dialog box appears, as shown in Figure 9-4. This dialog box works much like the Windows Explorer. To get to the folder where you want to store a message, you click the plus signs to the left of folders. In the figure, I clicked the plus sign beside the Inbox folder to see the subfolders where I store e-mail correspondence for different projects.

heads up

By the way, you can store a message from the Message window as well. You learned about the Message window in Lesson 9-3. The Message window is the window in which e-mail messages appear after you open a message. The Message window also offers the Move to Folder button.

In the following step, you create a subfolder for your messages.

3 **Make sure the Inbox folder is selected and then click the New button in the Move Items dialog box.**

The Create New Folder dialog box appears.

4 **In the Name text box, type a descriptive name for the folder; in the Description box, write a few words about the messages you intend to store in the folder (if you want); then click OK.**

Back in the Move Items dialog box, your new folder appears below the Inbox folder. You may repeat Steps 3 and 4 to create other folders for the different kinds of e-mail messages you receive.

The following step explains how to actually store a message in a subfolder.

5 **Click the subfolder in which you want to store the message and then click OK in the Move Items dialog box.**

The message you store in the subfolder does not appear in the Inbox anymore — it's moved to the subfolder.

6 **Click the Move to Folder button.**

This time when you click the button, you see the name of the subfolder in which you stored the message on the drop-down list. If you want to store another message from the Inbox in the same subfolder, all you need to do now is click the subfolder's name on the Move to Folder menu. You don't need to open the Move Items dialog box again, although you still can store a message in a subfolder that way if you want.

on the test

As a matter of fact, you can store several messages at once in a subfolder by Ctrl+clicking them in the Inbox and then either choosing a subfolder name from the Move to Folder drop-down list or opening the Move Items dialog box. (*Ctrl+click* means to press and hold the Ctrl key as you click messages to select them.)

7 **Click the Mail button at the bottom of the Outlook bar and then click the Sent Items icon.**

What's this? Why, it's the Sent Items window, which keeps a copy of all the e-mail messages you send. To delete one of these messages, click it and press the Delete button. If you want to move one of these messages to a folder, you can follow Steps 2 and 5 in this lesson.

8 **Click the Inbox icon on the Outlook bar.**

You land back at the Inbox.

Reading messages in folders

After you store a message in a folder, how do you get to it, read it, and perhaps reply to it? Good questions. To read a message in a folder, follow these steps:

1 **Click the Inbox icon in the Outlook bar to open the Inbox window, if necessary.**

2 **Click the Folder List button.**

As shown on the left side of Figure 9-5, the Outlook folders appear immediately to the right of the Outlook bar. You can also see the folder list by choosing View⇨Folder List.

3 **Double-click folders until you find the subfolder you want and then click the name of the subfolder.**

You see a list of messages similar to the one shown back in Figure 9-3. To read or reply to one of these messages, double-click it. The next lesson explains how to reply to an e-mail message.

4 **Click the Folder List button to enlarge the Message window and remove the folder list.**

Another way to get to the messages in a folder also is shown in Figure 9-5. Click the Inbox icon to return to the Inbox and try the second method; then follow these steps:

1 **Choose Go⇨Go to Folder or press Ctrl+Y.**

The Go to Folder dialog box appears, as shown on the right side of Figure 9-5.

2 **Double-click folders until you reach the one you want to open.**

3 **Click the folder you want to open and then click OK.**

You see the list of messages in the folder.

Ctrl+click to select several messages

Folder List button

☑ **Progress Check**

If you can perform the following tasks, you've mastered this lesson:

❏ Create a folder for storing messages.

❏ Store a message in a folder.

❏ Open a folder from the Folder List and use the Go⇨Go to Folder command.

❏ Delete a message.

Deleting messages

Eventually, no matter how much you love getting e-mail, you need to delete messages, especially the unsolicited messages you get from Internet sales people.

After you delete a message by clicking the message and then clicking the Delete button, it isn't removed entirely from the computer's hard disk. Instead, the message goes in the Deleted Items folder, in case you regret deleting it and want to get it back again. That's good, of course, but it also means that files you don't regret deleting remain on-disk and take up valuable space on your computer. The following instructions explain how to recover a message you delete and how to permanently delete a message.

To retrieve a message you deleted, follow these steps:

1 **Scroll down the Outlook bar until you see the Deleted Items icon and then click that icon.**

The Deleted Items window appears.

2 **Right-click the message you want to resuscitate and choose Move to Folder.**

The Move Items dialog box appears (refer to Figure 9-4).

3 **Find and click the folder in which you want to put the deleted message and then click OK.**

To delete a message once and for all, follow these steps:

1 **Open the Deleted Items window by scrolling down the Outlook bar and clicking the Deleted Items icon.**

2 **Press and hold the Ctrl key and click each message you want to delete.**

3 **Click the Delete button or right-click and choose Delete.**

4 **Click Yes after Outlook asks whether you want to delete the messages permanently.**

Lesson 9-5

Replying to and Forwarding Messages

This lesson explains how to reply to or forward messages. When you reply to or forward a message, you can start either from the Inbox or from a subfolder in which you store messages.

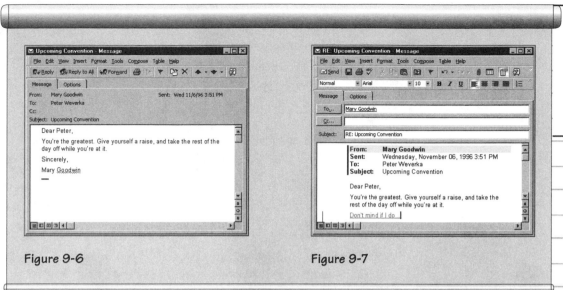

Figure 9-6: The original message, ready for you to reply to or forward.

Figure 9-7: If you want, you can make the original message part of the reply.

Figure 9-6   Figure 9-7

Lesson 9-2 explained that you need to know the recipient's e-mail address to send an e-mail message, but that isn't the case if you reply to a message. Whenever Outlook receives a message, the program "remembers" the address of the person who sent it. So when you reply to messages, you don't need to concern yourself with e-mail addresses. To forward a message, however, you do need to know the e-mail address of the person to whom you want to forward the message.

To complete this lesson, you must have at least one message in the Inbox or in a subfolder where you store messages.

Follow these steps to learn how to reply to and forward messages:

1 Locate the message you want to reply to or forward.

If the message is in the Inbox, click the Inbox icon in the Outlook bar. If you stored the message in a subfolder, open that subfolder. (Lesson 9-4 explains how.)

2 Double-click the message to open it.

The familiar Message window appears, as shown in Figure 9-6. (You learned about this window in Lesson 9-3.)

3 Click the Reply button.

The RE: Message window appears, as shown in Figure 9-7. This window works exactly like, and looks similar to, the window that you use to compose messages. The difference is that the sender's name already appears next to the To... button. In this window, you don't need to enter the recipient's name. Because you are replying to a message, the recipient's name is already there.

The message you're replying to appears in the text box along with a memo heading that lists the name of the person who sent the original message (From), the date and time the message was sent (Sent), the name of the person — you — to whom the message was sent (To), and the topic of the message (Subject). Outlook puts the original message and the memo heading in the text box in case you want to include this information as part of your reply.

Reply button

Message Header
button

Notes:

Send button

Reply to All button

Reply to All sends a
reply to everybody
who got copies of
the first message

Forward button

☑ **Progress Check**

If you can perform the
following tasks, you're
ready to move on to the
Unit 9 quiz:

❑ Send a reply to a message.

❑ Reply to the sender and
all who got copies of the
message.

❑ Forward a message.

---

4 **Click the Message Header button.**

After you click this button, the Cc line and Subject line disappear from the screen so that you have more room to type your reply.

5 **Click in the text box below the message you're replying to and type a reply.**

The words you type appear in red and are underlined. A vertical line appears in the left margin next to the words you type. After the person you're replying to receives the reply, this text appears in blue on the recipient's screen (provided that the recipient also uses Outlook).

Including the entire message in the reply isn't always necessary. You can delete all or part of the original message by selecting what you want to remove and pressing Del. (Lessons 2-3 and 2-5 in this book explain how to select and delete text.)

6 **Click the Message Header button again to see the Cc and Subject lines.**

Notice that the Subject line reads RE: and lists the subject of the original message. You can enter a subject of your own on this line if you want.

To send a copy of your reply to another person, click the Cc button to open the Select Names dialog box and start from there. (Lesson 9-2 explains how to handle that dialog box.)

7 **Click the Send button.**

The next time you choose Tools➪Check for New Mail or press F5, Outlook sends your reply. Meanwhile, you land back in the Message window, in case you want to forward the message or reply to all the people who received the original message.

8 **Click the Reply to All button.**

Click the Reply to All button if you want to reply to the sender of the original message as well as to all the people who received copies of that message. The names of everyone who received the original message, as well as the sender of the original message, now appear next to the To... button. Otherwise, this dialog box looks and works exactly like the RE: Message window shown in Figure 9-7. Refer to that lesson if you want your reply to be sent to all who received the original message as well as to its author.

9 **Click the Forward button in the Message window.**

The FW: Message window appears. In this window, no name or names appear beside the To... button, and you have to enter the names of the people to whom the message will be forwarded yourself.

10 **Click the To... button.**

The Select Names dialog box appears. Does this dialog box look familiar? You learned how to enter names in this dialog box in Lesson 9-2. Go there if you need help entering names for forwarding a message.

11 **Click Cancel (or OK if you're indeed forwarding a message) to close the Select Names dialog box.**

12 **Click the Close button (the X) to close the FW: Message window (or click the Send button to forward the message).**

You land back in the Inbox.

Unit 9 Quiz

For the following questions, circle the letter of the correct answer or answers. I designed this short quiz to help you remember what you learned in Unit 9. Each question may have more than one right answer.

1.   **Where is the Outlook bar located?**

A. At the top of the screen.

B. At the bottom of the screen.

C. At the left side of the screen.

D. At the top of a hill. It overlooks the entire city.

E. Click the Outlook button to see the Outlook bar.

2.   **To start writing an e-mail message, you perform which of the following actions?**

A. Press Ctrl+N.

B. Click the New Mail Message button.

C. Choose Compose⇨New Mail Message.

D. Click the Reply button.

E. All of the above.

3.   **If you want someone to reply to an e-mail message by a certain date, you perform which of the following actions?**

A. Call them on the phone and say so.

B. Send a fax.

C. Click the Message Flag button and fill in the For Your Information dialog box.

D. Threaten, bully, and cajole.

E. Ask them to do so in the e-mail message.

4.   **What happens if you click the Send button after you compose an e-mail message?**

A. Nothing happens.

B. You send the message.

C. The message goes to the Inbox.

D. The message goes to the Outbox.

E. You send the message if you're on a network.

5. **To retrieve e-mail messages sent to you, you perform which of the following actions?**

   A. Press F5.

   B. Click the Send button.

   C. Choose Tools⇨Check for New Mail.

   D. Click the AutoPreview button.

   E. Log on to your Internet provider.

6. **To reply to the person who sent you a message as well as to all others who received copies of the message, you perform which of the following actions?**

   A. Send each person a copy of your reply.

   B. Click the Reply to All button in the Inbox.

   C. Click the Reply to All button in the Message dialog box.

   D. Forward the reply to everybody.

   E. Use the telephone for a task such as this. It's too complicated in e-mail.

7. **The B-movie classic *The Incredibly Strange Creatures Who Stopped Living and Became Mixed-Up Zombies* (1963) was filmed by using which of the following advanced cinematic techniques?**

   A. Blood-o-rama.

   B. Terrorama.

   C. Blinding color.

   D. Ink-processed flesh-o-scope.

   E. Horrorama.

Unit 9 Exercise

1. Send an e-mail message to President Clinton (his address is president@whitehouse.gov) and express yourself.

2. Send a message to yourself and give the message a low priority.

3. Retrieve your e-mail messages.

4. Create a subfolder for storing files and put a message in the subfolder.

5. Reply to the message you sent to yourself.

6. Forward the message you sent to yourself. Forward it to yourself.

7. Delete the reply and the forwarded message.

Staying Organized with Outlook

Objectives for This Unit

✓ Entering appointments and meetings in the Outlook calendar

✓ Viewing, moving, and deleting appointments

✓ Keeping a Contacts list of people you know and with whom you do business

✓ Recording and tracking the tasks you need to accomplish

Prerequisites
▶ Starting an Office 97 program (Lesson 1-1)
▶ Entering and editing text (Lesson 2-2)
▶ Finding your way around Outlook (Lesson 9-1)

Unit 10, the shortest unit in the book, explores the personal organizer side of Outlook. You can use this side of the program to schedule meetings and appointments; keep a detailed list of the names, addresses, and phone numbers of your friends and colleagues; and maintain a task list of projects.

heads up

Unit 9 deals with the e-mail side of Outlook, for which you need a connection to the Internet or a network to use. You don't need a network or Internet connection to complete the lessons in Unit 10. All you must do is sit up straight, prick up your ears, and watch and listen attentively.

Lesson 10-1

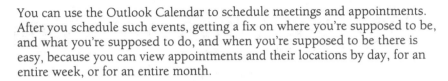

Scheduling Meetings and Appointments on the Calendar

You can use the Outlook Calendar to schedule meetings and appointments. After you schedule such events, getting a fix on where you're supposed to be, and what you're supposed to do, and when you're supposed to be there is easy, because you can view appointments and their locations by day, for an entire week, or for an entire month.

This lesson explains how to enter a meeting or appointment, schedule the event in a time slot, move the event, and delete the event from the Calendar. It also explains how to jot down addresses for and directions to meetings and appointments. You needn't open a practice file for this exercise. All you need to do is click the mouse and wiggle your fingers over the keyboard.

Follow these steps to learn how to manage meetings and appointments with Outlook:

1 **Click the Calendar icon on the Outlook bar.**

You see the Calendar in Day view, as shown in Figure 10-1. The hours of the day appear on the left side of the screen, beside the appointments and meetings that you scheduled for the day. By clicking the arrows on the scroll bar, you can move backward or forward through the day. In the upper-right corner of the screen are minicalendars for the current month and the following month. Days on which meetings or appointments are scheduled appear in boldface.

For this exercise, you go to April Fool's Day and schedule appointments and meetings for that day and for the week in which it falls.

2 **Click the left-pointing or right-pointing arrow to the left or right side of the month names as many times as it takes to reach the month of April, and then click the *1* in April to see April first in Day view.**

You can also get to a specific day by choosing Go⇨Go to Date (or by pressing Ctrl+G), entering a new date in the Date text box of the Go To Day dialog box, and clicking OK.

3 **Click in the box beside** 9:00, **type** Buy public access TV show, **and click outside the** 9:00 **box.**

Congratulations. You just recorded a half-hour meeting at 9:00. In fact, unless you tell Outlook to do otherwise, the program automatically makes all your appointments a half hour. But suppose that you want to record a meeting that lasts longer than half an hour.

4 **Click beside** 10:00 **and then click the New Appointment button.**

The Appointment dialog box appears, as shown in Figure 10-2. In this dialog box, you enter the subject of the appointment or meeting, its location (if necessary), and how long it will last, among other things.

click calendar
arrows to move
through months

New Appointment
button

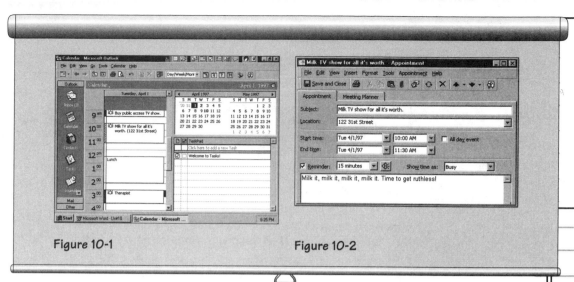

Figure 10-1: The Day view in the Calendar. You can also view appointments by week or by month.

Figure 10-2: From this dialog box, you can schedule a long-running appointment, make notes about the appointment, and describe its location.

Figure 10-1   Figure 10-2

5 **Use your imagination and enter a subject for the meeting in the Subject text box and a location in the Location drop-down list box; then click the down arrow beside the second End time drop-down list box and select 1.5 Hours from the list that appears.**

From the End time drop-down list, you can tell Outlook how long the meeting or appointment will last.

6 **Click the down arrow next to the Show time as box to open the drop-down list and then select Tentative from the list that appears.**

The Show time as list offers four selections. Depending on which selection you make from the drop-down list, Outlook marks the meeting or appointment in a different way in the Day view window of the Calendar. Busy appointments are marked in dark blue, Tentative appointments in pale blue, and Out of Office appointments in purple. Free appointments — time set aside for smelling the roses, for example — aren't marked in any color.

The Reminder check box is already checked. Unless you tell it otherwise, Outlook tells you 15 minutes beforehand that an appointment or meeting is scheduled. The program tells you by playing a two-note chime through the computer's speaker. Uncheck the Reminder box if you don't wish to hear a reminder notice; click the down arrow beside the minutes box and choose a different time period if you want to be forewarned earlier or later than the default 15-minute setting.

7 **Enter a few words in the text box to describe what the meeting or appointment is all about, if you want to, and then click the Save and Close button.**

Back in the Calendar window, the hour-and-a-half meeting is now blocked off. Notice the alarm bell icon. (If you unchecked the Reminder check box in Step 6, the alarm bell icon does not appear.)

Notes:

🖫 Save and Close

Save and Close button

Notes:

8 Click April 2 on the April calendar page in the upper-right corner of the screen and then repeat Steps 4 through 7 — but this time, click the All day event check box in the Appointment dialog box.

That's the fast way to mark off an entire day on the calendar. In fact, if you were going on vacation for a week, you could select all the days in the week (by dragging over them), and then block off all the days in the calendar from the Appointment dialog box.

Besides scheduling one-time appointments and meetings, you can schedule appointments that occur daily, weekly, monthly, or annually, as the following step demonstrates.

9 Click April 3 on the April calendar page, right-click the 10:00 time slot, and then choose New Recurring Appointment from the short-cut menu.

The Appointment Recurrence dialog box appears. How to fill out this dialog box is fairly self-explanatory. If you click OK to accept the default options (as you do in the following step), you schedule an infinite number of weekly recurring meetings of 30 minutes' duration, but you can adjust these options to taste, as the cookbooks say.

10 Click OK to close the Appointment Recurrence dialog box and then fill in the the Appointment dialog box (refer to Figure 10-2).

If you need help filling in the Appointment dialog box, review Steps 5 through 7 in this lesson.

So far you have been working in Day view, but the next several steps demonstrate different ways to view the meetings and appointments you've scheduled.

11 On the April calendar page in the upper-right corner, drag across all the days in the week in which April 1 falls.

The left side of the screen shows all the days, and you get a good sense of how time is blocked off this week.

12 Click the Week button or choose View⇨Week.

The days of the week and the appointments and meetings you've scheduled appear one after the other in boxes. By glancing at your schedule in Week view, you get a feel for whether this is a busy week. Suppose someone calls and has to reschedule a meeting. Can you simply move it? You sure can.

13 Click the meeting at 10:00 on April 1, drag the cursor over the time designation (10:00), and after the cursor changes into a four-headed arrow, click and drag the meeting to the April 4 box.

The meeting is now rescheduled for 10 a.m. on April 4. You can drag meetings and appointments to new places in Day view and Month view as well. What's more, if you must change the details of a meeting, all you need to do is double-click the event in Day view, Week view, or Month view.

14 Double-click the meeting on April 4 and then, in the Appointment dialog box that appears (refer to Figure 10-2), click the down arrow to open the Start time drop-down list (the second of the two, with time periods, not dates), choose 12:30, and click the Save and Close button.

The meeting is now rescheduled for 12:30 p.m.

Week button

☑ **Progress Check**

If you can perform the following tasks, you've mastered this lesson:

❑ Schedule meetings and recurring meetings.

❑ Move and delete a meeting.

❑ Change to Day view, Week view, and Month view.

on the test

15 **Click the Month button or choose <u>V</u>iew⇨<u>M</u>onth.**

You see a huge calendar page with this month's appointments and meetings. Suppose a meeting or appointment has been canceled and you need to delete it.

16 **Click any meeting in April and then click the Delete button.**

If you click a one-time meeting or appointment, Outlook deletes it, but if you click a recurring meeting, Outlook asks whether you want to delete a single meeting or all the recurring meetings that you scheduled. Choose an option and click OK.

Month button

Delete button

Go to Today button

Recess

Break time. Put your feet up. Sit a spell. Take five. Cop some Zs. Take a breather. Call a time out. Rest your dogs. Take a snooze.

Creating and Maintaining a Contacts List

Lesson 10-2

Personally, I think that the Contacts list is one of the most useful features in Office 97. Instead of thumbing through a tattered address book with dog-eared pages, erasure marks, and illegible letters to find an address or phone number, you can keep addresses and phone numbers in the Contacts list and find them instantly. You can even dial a telephone number from the Contacts list (see "Autodialing a contact" at the end of this lesson for the details). Entering the names and addresses in a Contacts list requires a little work, but after you do it, you won't regret the time it took.

The first part of this lesson explains how to enter contact names and addresses. In the second part of the lesson, you learn how to find a contact on the Contacts list. You also learn how to change what is on the Contacts list and to delete a contact.

Entering names, addresses, and other information

Follow these steps to learn how to enter contact names and addresses:

1 **Click the Contacts icon.**

The Contacts list appears, as shown in Figure 10-3. Later in this lesson, you learn how to find a name on this list. For now, I show you how to enter contact names, addresses, and whatnot.

Contacts

Figure 10-3: Click a letter button on the right side of the Contacts list to see the names and addresses of different contacts.

Figure 10-4: Enter names and information about contacts in this dialog box.

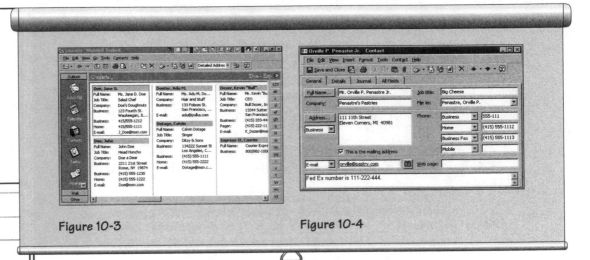

Figure 10-3   Figure 10-4

New Contact button

2. Click the New Contact button.

The Contact dialog box appears, as shown in Figure 10-4. You can also get here by pressing Ctrl+N or choosing Contacts⇨New⇨Contact. The Contact dialog box offers places for entering almost anything you care to enter about a client, coworker, friend, or relative. Except for a name and phone number, however, you needn't fill out all parts of the Contact dialog box if you don't want to. "Just the facts ma'am," as Sgt. Joe Friday used to say.

To complete the following steps, get out your well-thumbed address book or Rolodex and enter the name, address, and phone number of someone whose address and phone number you often need but always forget.

3. Click the Full Name button and, in the Check Full Name dialog box, enter as much information about the contact's name as you deem fit; then click OK.

This task is pretty simple, isn't it?

4. If the contact is a business associate or client, enter a company name and job title in the Company and Job title boxes.

In the following step, you enter an address. Before you do that, however, you must tell Outlook what kind of address you want to enter. You can enter a business address, a home address, or a generic "other" address.

5. Click the down arrow below the Address button and select the type of address you want to enter from the drop-down list.

You can record more than one address for a contact by going back to this drop-down list after you complete the following step.

you can enter more than one address for a contact

6. Click the Address button, fill in the Check Address dialog box that appears, and click OK.

The address now appears in the text box.

7. Go to the right side of the dialog box and enter a phone number or phone numbers for the contact.

If the contact's phone number is in the same area code as your phone number, you needn't enter the three-number area code prefix.

Try clicking the down arrow next to a phone number drop-down list box to see the many different ways of describing phone numbers. You can record a car phone number or pager number, among other types of phone numbers.

8 **If you intend to send e-mail messages to the contact, enter the contact's e-mail address in the text box next to the E-mail drop-down list.**

The E-mail drop-down list offers opportunities for entering more than one e-mail address. You can even enter a Web page address in the <u>W</u>eb page text box to the right of the E-mail text box.

9 **If necessary, move the pointer over the bottom border of the Contact dialog box and, after the pointer turns into a double-headed arrow, click and drag the border toward the bottom of the screen to make the dialog box larger.**

heads up

You may need to enlarge the dialog box to see the text box at the bottom of the Contact dialog box. In this text box, you can jot down notes about the contact. I strongly suggest jotting down a note. After your Contacts list gets very large, you may have trouble remembering who all the contacts on the list are. By jotting down a note about the contact, you will always be able to tell how this person came into your life, whether the person's name should remain on the Contacts list, and whether you can delete this person from the list.

10 **Write a note about the contact in the text box at the bottom of the Contact dialog box.**

11 **Click the <u>S</u>ave and Close button.**

You land back in the Contacts list.

Entering names and recording pertinent information about all the people you know and do business with takes a bit of time. As the next part of this lesson shows, however, looking up a contact name in the Contacts list is much easier than looking up a name in a tattered address book or a gummed-up Rolodex.

Finding names in and maintaining a Contacts list

This part of the lesson explains how to find people on the Contacts list and how to delete a name or change the information you recorded. Follow these steps:

1 **Click the Contacts icon in the Outlook bar if you are not already in the Contacts list.**

You see the people at the top of the list. Outlook offers two ways to get to other parts of the list.

on the test

2 **Click the right-pointing arrow on the scroll bar at the bottom of the screen several times.**

By clicking this scroll bar, you can see different parts of the list.

3 **Click the wx button on the right side of the Contacts list window.**

You see the names of people at the end of the list, including my name if you entered it back in Lesson 9-1. The fastest way to get to other parts of the Contacts list is to click a letter button on the right side of the Contact window.

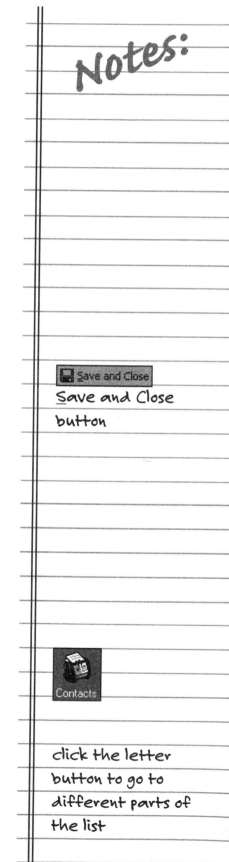

Notes:

Save and Close button

Contacts

click the letter button to go to different parts of the list

on the test

double-click a
name to change
information on the
list

Delete button

☑ **Progress Check**

If you can perform the
following tasks, you've
mastered this lesson:

❏ Enter a new contact on
the Contacts list.

❏ Find a contact on the
list.

❏ Delete a contact.

❏ View the Contacts list in
different ways.

4 **Double-click my name or another name on the list.**

The Contact dialog box appears (see Figure 10-4). You can always double-click a name to open the Contact dialog box and read all the information about a contact.

If someone changes phone numbers or addresses, double-click that person's name on the list and then change the information in the Contact dialog box.

5 **Click the Close button (the *X* in the upper-right corner) to close the Contact dialog box without making any changes to the information you recorded.**

In the following step, you learn how to delete a contact.

6 **Click my name on the Contacts list and then click the Delete button.**

All you need to do to remove a contact from the list is to select the contact and click the Delete button, press Ctrl+D, or choose Edit⇨Delete.

The following three steps explain how to view the list in different ways.

7 **Move the cursor to the Current View box, click the down arrow to open the drop-down list, and select Phone List.**

The Current View box is the third button from the left on the toolbar. If you're in a hurry to find a phone number, you can switch to Phone List view.

8 **Open the Current View drop-down list again but, this time, select Address Cards.**

In Address Cards view, you see only addresses and phone numbers, so more contacts fit on-screen.

9 **Open the Current View drop-down list and select Detailed Address Cards.**

You can now see everything you could possibly know about the people on the Contacts list — except their deepest, darkest secrets.

---

extra credit

Autodialing a contact

You can tell Outlook to dial a telephone number. I'm not kidding. As long as you have your computer and telephone line connected to a modem, you can "autodial" telephone numbers on the Contacts list. Here's how:

1. **Open the Contacts list and click the name of the person you want to call.**

2. **Click the AutoDialer button in the toolbar (the one with the telephone on it) or, if the contact has more than one telephone number, click the down arrow next to the**

AutoDialer button and select the number you want to dial from the drop-down list.

The New Call dialog box appears. Make sure that the number you want to call appears in the Number text box.

3. **Click the Start Call button in the New Call dialog box.**

4. **Lift the telephone receiver to your ear and click the Talk button.**

5. **After you finish the conversation, hang up the phone and click the End Call button.**

Maintaining and Prioritizing a Task List

Lesson 10-3

To help plan how much time you have and how to spend that time to complete the tasks you're assigned, Outlook offers you the Tasks list. The Tasks list shows all the tasks that need doing and when those tasks are due. From the Tasks list, you can see how close you've come to completing a project, which tasks are overdue, and which tasks you've completed. After you record a task, it appears on the Calendar window so that you can tell which tasks to focus on during a given day or week.

To learn how to record tasks and make them appear in the Tasks and Calendar windows, do the following:

on the test

1 Click the Tasks icon in the Outlook bar.

The Tasks window appears, as shown in Figure 10-5. You see a few tasks in this window. Completed tasks are crossed out and checked off in the check mark column. Overdue tasks appear in — what else? — bright red. The Due Date column tells you when the tasks are supposed to be completed.

2 To record a new task, click the New Task button in the upper-left corner of the window.

The Task dialog box appears, as shown in Figure 10-6. This is where you describe the task to Outlook.

3 In the Subject text box, enter the following: Moving Mountains.

The subject you type appears in the Task window. Be sure to type descriptive names in this text box. Next, you tell Outlook when the task is due and when you started or intend to start the task.

4 Click the Due radio button, click the down arrow to open the drop-down list, and select tomorrow's date by clicking it in the calendar. For the Start date, click to open the drop-down list and choose yesterday's date by clicking that date in the calendar.

To get to different dates in the drop-down lists, click the arrows to the left or right of the month names. Notice that the calendars offer the Today and None buttons, which you can click to enter today's date or no date at all.

In the Status, Priority, and % Complete text boxes, you tell Outlook how the task is progressing, how important the task is, and how close you are to finishing the task.

5 Click the Status drop-down list and select In Progress; click the Priority drop-down list and select High; click the up arrow beside the % Complete box twice to enter 50%.

As you learn later in this lesson, you can see Status, Priority, and % Complete settings on the Tasks list.

As you know from Lesson 10-1, Outlook chimes at you before you are scheduled to appear at a meeting or appointment. The program does the same before a task is due if you leave the check mark in the Reminder check box. You can remove the check mark if you don't want to be chimed at, however, or change the time and date of the reminder by making new choices from the drop-down lists next to the Reminder check box.

New Task button

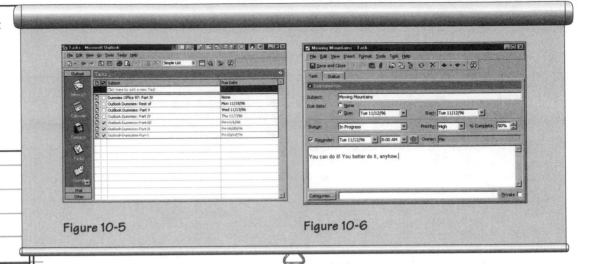

Figure 10-5: The Tasks list shows you all the work that lies ahead — and your completed work, too.

Figure 10-6: Entering a new task for the Tasks list.

Figure 10-5   Figure 10-6

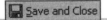

☑ Progress Check

If you can perform the following tasks, you're ready to take the Unit 10 quiz:

❑ Record a new task.

❑ View tasks in the Tasks window in different ways.

❑ Delete a task from the Tasks window.

🖫 Save and Close

Save and Close button

double-click the task to update your progress

AutoPreview button

6 Jot a few words about the task in the text box at the bottom of the screen.

As you see later, in Step 10, you can make the words you enter in the text box appear in the Tasks list.

7 Click the Status tab of the Task dialog box.

This tab offers places for tracking how many hours you work on a project and how many hours you expect to work. You can also track such things as mileage and contact names from this tab.

8 Click the Save and Close button.

Your new task appears on the Tasks list. By entering several tasks, you can get a fix on what needs doing and what has been done. As you complete tasks, open the Task dialog box and update your progress. The following step explains how.

9 Double-click the task you just recorded and then click the Close button in the upper-right corner of the Task dialog box to close the dialog box.

After the Task dialog box appears, you can record changes in the status of the task and then click the Save and Close button to stay up to date.

In the next several steps, you learn ways to examine and, with luck, manage all the tasks you need to accomplish.

10 Click the AutoPreview button, glance at the Tasks window, and click the button again.

You see the words you entered in the Task dialog box's text box back in Step 6. Clicking the AutoPreview button is a good way to find out what all the tasks on the list really consist of.

11 Click the down arrow next to the Current View drop-down list box.

As you can see on the drop-down list, Outlook gives you several ways to find out which tasks are pressing. You can, for example, select Overdue Tasks to see only the tasks that are overdue. Or click Tasks Timeline to see a timeline with all the tasks you've been assigned laid side by side.

12 Click Detailed List in the drop-down list.

You see the status of tasks and how complete they are.

13 **Click the Calendar icon in the Outlook bar.**

The task you entered appears on the Task Pad (tasks do not appear in Month view, however). Now you can compare the appointments and meetings you are supposed to attend with the tasks you are supposed to complete, get stressed out, and scream.

To remove a task when you no longer want to see it in the Tasks window, select it (by clicking) and then click the Delete button (which looks like an X on the toolbar), or press Ctrl+D.

Unit 10 Quiz

For the following questions, circle the letter of the correct answer or answers. I designed this short quiz to help you remember what you learned in Unit 10. Each question may have more than one right answer.

1. **To move from month to month in a calendar, you...**

   A. Type in a date.

   B. Click the Today button.

   C. Click the arrow to the right or left side of the month name.

   D. Use the scroll bar.

   E. Click a day.

2. **A recurring meeting is which of the following?**

   A. One that recurs.

   B. A meeting you go to often.

   C. A meeting that everyone has to go to but doesn't want to go to.

   D. A meeting where doughnuts are served.

   E. A meeting that takes place on the same day, at the same time, each week or month.

3. **What happens after you click this button in the Calendar window?**

   A. You see the schedule for the month.

   B. You get seven wishes.

   C. You see the first seven messages in the Inbox.

   D. You see the schedule for the week.

   E. You see today's schedule in Day view.

4. **To enter a new contact on the Contacts list, you...**

   A. Click the New Contact button.

   B. Click the Contacts icon.

   C. Press Ctrl+N.

   D. Choose Contacts⇨New Contact.

5. **To see all the information about a contact in the Contacts window, you must perform which of the following actions?**

    A. Double-click the contact's name.

    B. Click arrows on the scroll bar at the bottom of the screen.

    C. Choose Phone List from the Current View drop-down list.

    D. Click a letter button.

    E. Call the contact and ask for the information.

6. **Click this button to perform which of the following actions?**

    A. Delete a contact.

    B. Delete a scheduled appointment or meeting.

    C. Delete a task in the Tasks list.

    D. Delete an e-mail message in the Inbox.

    E. All of the above.

7. **If a task appears in red in the Tasks window, it means which of the following?**

    A. The project is running in the red.

    B. You completed the task.

    C. The task is overdue.

    D. Time to call your supervisor and grovel.

    E. The task is a high-priority task.

Unit 10 Exercise

1. Schedule a meeting for next Monday at 11 a.m.

2. Move the meeting to the following Tuesday at 3 p.m.

3. View your weekly meetings, and then your monthly meetings (if you've scheduled any).

4. Enter President Bill Clinton on the Contacts list. Enter his e-mail address, which is `president@whitehouse.gov`.

5. Move to the end of the Contacts list and then to the start of the list.

6. Set yourself the task of cleaning the garage (or some applicable part of your domicile) by next November.

7. No way can you complete the garage-cleaning task in time. Better delete it from the Tasks list.

Part IV Review

Unit 9 Summary

▶ **Getting around in Outlook:** To access different parts of Outlook, click icons in the Outlook bar along the left side of the screen. Click the Mail button to access folders and windows that pertain to sending, storing, and deleting e-mail. Click the Outlook button on the Outlook bar to see the icons for accessing different parts of the program.

▶ **Sending e-mail:** From the Inbox, click the New Mail Message button to compose an e-mail message. In the Message dialog box, click the To... button to open the Select Names dialog box. Select names in the box on the left side of the screen and then click the To button to name the people who are to receive the message. You can also click the Cc button or Bcc button to send copies of the message to others. Click OK and, in the Message dialog box, click the Send button.

▶ **Receiving e-mail:** From the Inbox, choose Tools⇨Check for New Mail or press F5 and then click the necessary buttons to connect with your Internet provider. The messages appear in the Inbox. Double-click a message to read it.

▶ **Storing and sorting messages:** To create a subfolder for storing messages, choose Move to Folder from the drop-down list next to the Move to Folder button. In the Move Items dialog box, make sure that the Inbox folder is selected and then click the New button. In the Create New Folder dialog box, enter a name for the subfolder and click OK. To move messages to a subfolder, click the Move to Folder button, find the subfolder in the Move Items dialog box, select the folder, and click OK. To read a message stored in a folder, click the Folder List button, double-click folders until you see the subfolder you want, click the name of that folder, and then double-click the message you want to read.

▶ **Replying to and forwarding messages:** Open the message you want to reply to or forward in the Message window and click the Reply button (or the Reply to All button if you want to send your reply to all who received the original message). Type your reply in the RE: Message dialog box and click Send. To forward a letter, click the Forward button. In the FW: Message dialog box, click the To... button and then, in the Select Names dialog box, name the people you want to receive the forwarded message. Click OK and then click the Send button.

Unit 10 Summary

▶ **Scheduling meetings and appointments:** Click the Calendar icon in the Outlook bar to open the Calendar window. In the calendar in the upper-right corner, click the day on which you want to schedule an appointment and then click the hour of the appointment on the left side of the screen. Either type the subject of the appointment in the hour box on the left side of the screen or, if the appointment lasts longer than a half hour, click the New Appointment button and fill in the requested information in the Appointment dialog box. To change appointment times and dates, drag the appointment to another time or date. Select an appointment and click the Delete button to delete it.

▶ **Using the Contacts list:** Click the Contacts icon to see the Contacts list. To find a contact, either scroll through the list or click a letter button and then double-click the contact's name if the information you want doesn't already appear in the listing on-screen. To enter a contact's name, address, and so on, click the New Contact button and fill in the requested information in the Contact dialog box.

▶ **Maintaining a Tasks list:** Click the Tasks icon on the Outlook bar, click the New Task button, and fill in the requested information in the Task dialog box to record a new task. Tasks that are overdue appear in red in the Tasks list. You can see tasks in the Calendar window as well.

Part IV Test

The Part IV test will intimidate you. It makes you wonder if this cyber, e-mail, electronic superhighway stuff is really for you. Maybe you're not forward-looking enough. Maybe you're not ready for the future. Maybe time is passing you by and you have nothing to show for it. Maybe you're not ready for the "paperless" office when schedules, addresses, and mail are all electronic and the uninitiated get tossed aside like so much highway litter. This test finds out if you are ready for the future.

Actually, this test does nothing of the kind. This test is meant to help you review what you learned in Part IV. If you have trouble finding an answer, look for the On the Test icons throughout Part IV. You can find the answer to each question on this test next to one of those icons. You can also look at the summary reviews at the start of this test to find answers and, if worse comes to worst, look in Appendix A, which provides the answers to this test.

True   False

T   F   **1.** Computers are our friends.

T   F   **2.** To send an e-mail message, the person to whom you're sending the message and that person's e-mail address must be on the Contacts list.

T   F   **3.** You can boldface, italicize, and change the font of e-mail messages.

T   F   **4.** A paper clip next to an e-mail message in the Inbox means that the message is important.

T   F   **5.** Double-click a message to open and read it.

T   F   **6.** You can store e-mail messages in separate folders to organize and sort them.

T   F   **7.** If you delete a message from the Inbox, the message isn't really deleted from your computer's hard disk.

T   F   **8.** Click a name on the Contacts list to enlarge the listing and read all its information.

T   F   **9.** The computer has fingers and can dial a telephone number for you.

T   F   **10.** In the Tasks list, overdue tasks appear in red.

Multiple choice

Circle the correct answer or answers to the following questions. Each question may have more than one right answer.

11. A red exclamation point next to an e-mail message means the following:

A. The message is surprising.

B. A file is attached to the message.

C. The message is important.

D. You must reply by a certain date.

E. The message brings bad news.

12. To access the Outbox and review outgoing messages, you must perform which of the following actions?

A. Click the Outbox button.

B. Go to the Inbox.

C. Scroll to the bottom of the Outlook bar and click the Outbox icon.

D. Click the Sent Mail icon.

E. Click the Mail button at the bottom of the Outlook bar and then click the Outbox icon.

Part IV Test

13. **In the Inbox, you can tell which messages haven't been read because:**

    A. They appear in boldface.

    B. An exclamation point appears beside the envelope.

    C. They're still in the Inbox.

    D. A sealed envelope icon appears next to the subject name.

    E. They're not open.

14. **What happens in the Inbox after you click the AutoPreview button?**

    A. You can see the messages you're about to send.

    B. You see a description of each task in the Tasks list.

    C. You see the first couple lines in each message.

    D. You see the first couple lines in unread messages.

    E. You get to see a movie trailer.

 15. **Click this button in a Message window to perform which of the following actions?**

    A. Explore the Internet.

    B. Reply to a message.

    C. Go to the previous item in the Inbox.

    D. "Auto-preview" a message.

    E. Go to the next item in the Inbox.

16. **To delete a message, select it in the Inbox and perform which of the following actions?**

    A. Click the Delete button.

    B. Press Ctrl+D.

    C. Choose Edit⇨Delete.

    D. Right-click and choose Delete from the shortcut menu.

    E. All of the above.

17. **To select several different messages at once in the Inbox, perhaps to delete each one, perform which of the following actions?**

    A. Drag over the messages.

    B. Choose Edit⇨Select All.

    C. Press and hold the Ctrl key and click each message.

    D. Shift+click each message.

    E. Press Ctrl+A.

18. **To find someone's name on the Contacts list, perform which of the following actions?**

    A. Type a name.

    B. Click the scroll bar.

    C. Click a letter button on the right side of the screen.

    D. Choose Edit⇨Retrieve.

    E. Ask for it.

Part IV Test

Matching

19. Match the "smileys" in the left-hand column with the thing they are supposed to represent in the right-hand column.

     A.   `<:-I`   1. A pout.

     B.   `:c`   2. A cool guy in sunglasses.

     C.   `3:-o`   3. A dunce.

     D.   `B-)`   4. A cow.

     E.   `d:-)`   5. A baseball player.

20. Match the following buttons with the correct button names:

     A.   1. AutoPreview

     B.   2. Message Flag

     C.   3. Insert File

     D.   4. Delete

     E.   5. Mail Message

21. Match the following buttons with the correct button names:

     A.   1. Delete

     B.   2. Month

     C.   3. New Appointment

     D.   4. Go to Today

     E.   5. Week

22. Match the following movie genre in the left-hand column with the correct circa 1955–1965 B-movie title in the right-hand column:

     A. Science Fiction   1. *Barbed Wire Dolls*

     B. Beach Party   2. *Plan Nine from Outer Space*

     C. Women in Prison   3. *Juvenile Jungle*

     D. Juvenile Delinquency   4. *It's a Bikini World*

     E. Horror   5. *The Corpse Grinders*

Part IV Lab Assignment

So far in the lab assignments, you've been playing the role of the manager and sole employee of Pierspont Property Management in Pierspont, Pennsylvania. For this lab assignment, you pretend that you recently acquired the capability to send e-mail messages to the property owners for whom you work. You are to send them e-mail messages, enter a few of their names in the Contacts list, schedule a meeting or two with them, and set yourself a monumental task on the Tasks list.

Step 1: Composing e-mail messages

Write an e-mail message informing the owners whose property you manage that an important meeting is being held on the last day of the month. Send a copy of the message to yourself to see how fast it gets there. (Actually, because you don't have the addresses of a bunch of property owners, send a message and a copy of the message to yourself.)

Step 2: Receiving and reading e-mail

After the message arrives, store it in a subfolder. Make sure that you create a subfolder first to keep the message in. In the meantime, delete the copy of the message that you sent yourself.

Step 3: Replying to messages

Reply to the message that you sent yourself (ridiculous, I know, but the object here is to make you comfortable with the Outlook e-mail features). After the reply arrives, delete it.

Step 4: Scheduling a meeting

The Big Meeting takes place at the end of the month. Make it an important meeting that you just can't miss and then reschedule the meeting because you must miss it after all. Move the meeting to the first week of next month.

Step 5: Entering contacts on the Contacts list

This lab assignment calls for you to enter the names, addresses, and so on of property owners. Get out your address book or Rolodex, pretend that 15 of your friends and coworkers are property owners, and enter their names and addresses.

Part IV Lab Assignment

Step 6: Maintaining a Tasks list

Set yourself the task of finishing this book within the next week. As you record the task in the Tasks list, make the task a high-priority one. Throughout the week, open the Task dialog box and upgrade your progress in getting through the book. After you finish studying this book, mark the task as complete and eat a pistachio ice cream cone.

Access 97

Part
V

In this part...

Part V takes on Microsoft Access 97, the database program in Office 97. Don't let the technical-sounding word *database* scare you, because databases can be very useful indeed. Among other things, you can use databases for record keeping, to store client information, to keep inventories, and to create and maintain an address list. And after you enter information in a database, you can manipulate it different ways. For example, you can arrange the data by name or by address. Or you can find out how many items of a certain kind sold last month, who lives in a certain state, or whose income falls within a certain income range.

If I had been in the room when the word *database* was coined, I would have objected. I would have said, "No, it's not a database, it's a *superlist*. It's a list you can arrange any way you want and draw almost any kind of information from."

In Part V, I'll show you how to set up a database. I'll show you how to arrange and rearrange its data and how to grill a database to squeeze out every last drop of information.

Learning Your Databasics

Objectives for This Unit

✓ Creating a database

✓ Entering data on a datasheet

✓ Creating and entering data in a form

✓ Moving and deleting fields

✓ Moving and deleting records

Prerequisites

▶ Starting an Office 97 program (Lesson 1-1)

▶ Opening and closing a file (Lesson 1-2)

▶ Using scroll bars to get around (Lesson 1-4)

▶ Creating and saving a file (Lesson 2-1)

▶ Entering and editing text (Lesson 2-2)

on the CD

▶ Input Mask

▶ Enter Data

▶ Move and Delete

▶ Quiz 11

A *database* is a collection of data that pertains to a particular topic. You may not know it, but you have been creating and using databases for a long time. An address book, for example, is a database. It stores data — telephone numbers and addresses — that pertains to the people you know and with whom you do business. If you've ever arranged a CD collection in a certain way — in alphabetical order or by musical genre — you created a database of CDs, one that makes finding a particular CD easy.

The telephone directory is a classic example of a database that everyone knows and uses. In a telephone directory, data is arranged, or *sorted,* in alphabetical order by last name or business name, and the data is presented in two catego-ries, or *fields*: Name and Telephone Number. To find someone's phone number, you look in the Name category, and when you've found the name of the person whose telephone number you need, you look in the Telephone Number category.

The difference between a conventional database, such as a telephone directory or address book, and a computerized database is that computerized databases make storing, finding, and manipulating data much, much easier and faster. Suppose, for example, that you find a mysterious telephone number, 555-5432, in your purse or wallet and you want to know to whom the number belongs. Unless you live in a very small town, finding the name would take

days, because data in telephone directories is arranged by name, not by telephone number. You would need to read down the Telephone Number category in the directory and hope for the best. With a database program such as Access 97, however, you can ask, or *query,* the database to find the number 555-5432 and have the name to which the number belongs in about three seconds. Or you can sort (that ugly word again!) the database so that names and numbers are listed in phone number order, not name order, and find the owner of the mysterious telephone number that way.

Before you can start manipulating data, however, you must enter the data in a database table, which is the subject of Unit 11. (Unit 12 explains how to pester a database for the information you need.) Both Units 11 and 12 define dreary database terminology, three terms of which you have already encountered: *sort, field,* and *query.* Of all the computer terminology, database terminology is the ugliest and hardest to understand, but don't worry about that. I demystify database terms in these units. For you — and for you only — I unscrew the inscrutable.

Lesson 11-1   Creating a Database Table

heads up

This long lesson, followed by a short recess, explains how to create a new database. When you create a database, you actually create a table for storing the data. A database can include one or more tables. In fact, if you intend to store a lot of data in a database, you should consider dividing the data among two, three, or ten tables, as necessary. By storing data in different tables, you make entering and finding information much easier. And if you want to combine the data from different tables, Access 97 enables you to do so with ease (Lesson 12-2 explains how).

As you create a database, your first task is to figure out what kind of information you want to store and how many tables you need for storing your data. In this lesson, you create a database table for storing names and addresses. Later on, you see how to combine data from different database tables.

After you start Access 97, you see the Microsoft Access dialog box, which bids you to create a new, empty database; create a database from a Database Wizard; or open an existing database. After you become familiar with databases, you might try creating a predefined, preformatted database by using the Database Wizard. In this lesson, you create a database from scratch.

To create a new database, follow these steps:

1 **Open Access 97, click the Blank Database radio button in the Microsoft Access dialog box that appears, and click OK.**

The File New Database dialog box appears. It asks you to name and save your database. Access 97 behaves differently than do the other Office 97 programs in saving files and giving them names. Normally, you open and work on a file before you save and name the file, but Access 97 requires you to save and name databases from the get-go.

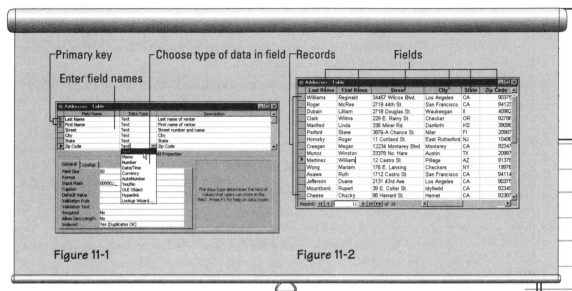

Figure 11-1: Creating the fields for the database table in Design view.

Figure 11-2: In Datasheet view, you can see the fields and records in the database table.

Figure 11-1   Figure 11-2

(***Note:*** If the Microsoft Access dialog box isn't on-screen after you start the program, you can create a new database without exiting and restarting Access 97. Click the New button, press Ctrl+N, or choose File⇨New Database. The General tab of the New dialog box appears. Click the Blank Database icon and then click OK. The File New Database dialog box appears.)

2 **In the File New Database dialog box, type** First Try **in the File name text box, find the Office 101 folder, and click Create to save the file in that folder.**

The Database window appears with its six tabs: Tables, Queries, Forms, Reports, Macros, and Modules. You learn what four of these tabs are throughout Part V. This Database window is not a dialog box, but an actual window that you return to whenever you want to create another arm of the database.

3 **Click the Tables tab and then click New.**

You see the New Table dialog box, which asks how you want to enter data in the first table in your new database.

on the test

4 **Click Design view and then click OK.**

You see the table in Design view, as shown in Figure 11-1. This dialog box asks you to name the fields in the table and tell which kind of data is stored in each field. Fields are similar to columns in a table. They divide the information about each person or thing into distinct sections.

In the following step, you create the field names shown in Figure 11-2. The database table you create in this lesson has six fields: Last Name, First Name, Street, City, State, and Zip Code.

5 **Type the names of the fields you see in Figure 11-1** (Last Name, First Name, Street Name, City, State, and Zip Code) **in the text boxes in the Field Name column.**

To move from field to field, either click or press the Tab key. Notice that Access 97 enters Text in the Data Type column automatically. It does that because you entered text — letters, not numbers — in the Field Name column.

fields =
information
categories

Notes:

primary key = a unique field or fields in table

click or Ctrl+click boxes next to fields to select the fields

6 **Click the Data Type column and then click the down arrow to open the Data Type drop-down list.**

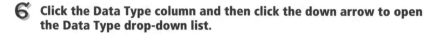

on the test

You can see Data Type menu in Figure 11-1. In this sample table, all the data falls in the Text category, but if you wanted to categorize the data in a different way, you would choose a data type from the drop-down menu.

It seems odd, doesn't it, to categorize the Zip Code field as a text field instead of a number field? However, Zip codes are text, not numbers. You cannot, or at least you wouldn't want to, perform mathematical equations on Zip codes. Zip codes identify data, they don't quantify it, so they belong in the Text category, as do social security numbers, telephone numbers, and item numbers. Only assign the Number category to fields in which quantities are entered. Assign the Currency category to fields where monetary values are stored.

7 **Scroll to the top of the Design view window and click the first field, Last Name.**

on the test

In the next step, you will tell Access 97 which field in the table is the *primary key.* If a database includes more than one table and you intend to generate reports — that is, get information from — both tables, you have to name a primary key in each table. The primary key is the field (or combination of fields) that is unique to both tables and is found in both tables. For the primary key field, you must choose a field in which information is never duplicated.

In the table you are creating, you couldn't use the Street, City, State, or Zip Code field as the primary key field because, presumably, some of the people whose addresses you will enter live on the same street or in the same city, state, or zip code. For the sample table, you will use the Last Name and First Name fields as the primary key. Of course, an address database table could have two John Smiths, two Maria Martinezes, or two other people with common first and last names. However, for this exercise, you will pretend that two identical names can never appear in the database table in the First Name and Last Name fields, and you will make those fields the primary key. In a large table with many names, you would have to create another field, such as a social security number field, whose data is sure to be unique to each person in the table.

The reason primary keys have to be unique is because, when Access 97 gathers information for a report from different database tables, it compares the primary fields in each table and looks for matches. For example, Access 97 looks in the primary key field of one table for Lemuel Gulliver, and it looks in the primary key field in the other table for Lemuel Gulliver. When the match has been struck, it combines the information in both tables that belongs to Gulliver. But if there are two Gullivers in the second table, it won't know which Gulliver to match with the Gulliver in the first table, so the report couldn't be generated.

8 **Click the small square to the left of the Last Name field and, after Access 97 highlights the field, press and hold the Ctrl key and click the square to the left of the First Name field.**

You selected both fields. You are ready to make these two fields the primary key for the database table.

9 **Click the Primary Key button on the Standard toolbar or choose Edit⇨Primary Key.**

Little keys appear in the squares to identify the Last Name and First Name fields as the primary key.

In the next step, you will put a limit on the number of characters that can be entered in the State field.

on the test

10 **Click the State field name, click the Field Size text box at the bottom of the screen, and then delete the 50 that is there and enter 2 in its place.**

You can keep the number of letters or numbers in a field to a minimum by entering a number in this text box. In this case, by entering **2** in the Field Size text box, you can make sure that no one accidentally enters a three-letter state abbreviation.

11 **Click the Save button, press Ctrl+S, or choose File⇨Save.**

When you choose the Save command, you aren't actually saving the database file. You did that back in Step 2. In this step and the following one, you are saving the Addresses table as part of the First Try database.

12 **In the Save As dialog box, type** Addresses **and click OK.**

13 **Click the down arrow next to the View button and choose Datasheet View.**

You can also change to Datasheet view by choosing View⇨Datasheet View. Your screen looks like Figure 11-2. In the next lesson, you enter *records* in the datasheet. As Figure 11-2 shows, a record is similar to a row in a table. Each record holds all the data that pertains to one person or thing. Each record, you may notice, divides up into fields, where you can record specific types of information about the person or thing.

14 **Choose File⇨Close twice, once to save and close the table in the Design View window and once to save and close the First Try database; click Yes after Access 97 asks whether you want to save your changes.**

Recess

A recess after the first lesson in the unit! Well, you deserve a recess. Lesson 11-1 certainly filled your plate with new things to learn. Take a few minutes to recall what *field, input mask,* and the other weird words that I introduced in this lesson mean. Give Lesson 11-1 a chance to soak into your gray matter before you go on to the next lesson, which is considerably easier than this one.

Save button

☑ **Progress Check**

If you can perform the following tasks, you've mastered this lesson:

❑ Create a new database.

❑ Enter and assign data types to field names.

❑ Assign the primary key to a database table.

Entering the Data in a Datasheet   Lesson 11-2

This lesson describes how to enter data in a datasheet. You saw a datasheet in the last lesson, as you created and saved the Addresses database table.

heads up

Before you start entering data, you need to know that the order in which you enter records doesn't matter at all. It doesn't matter because Access 97 gives you ample opportunities to rearrange records after you enter them. So don't worry about order as you enter records — concentrate on entering the data accurately instead.

Figure 11-3: Entering data in Datasheet view.

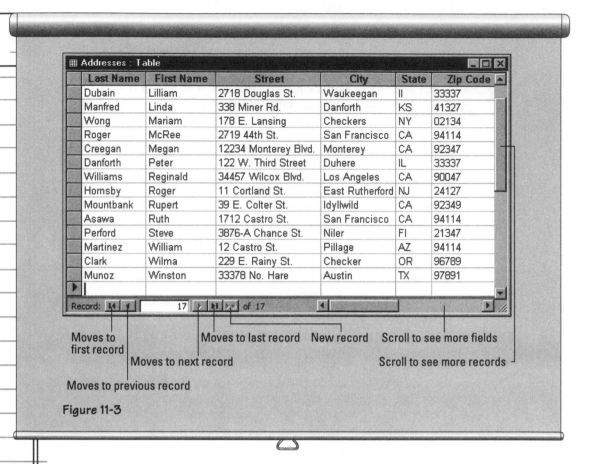

Last Name	First Name	Street	City	State	Zip Code
Dubain	Lilliam	2718 Douglas St.	Waukeegan	Il	33337
Manfred	Linda	338 Miner Rd.	Danforth	KS	41327
Wong	Mariam	178 E. Lansing	Checkers	NY	02134
Roger	McRee	2719 44th St.	San Francisco	CA	94114
Creegan	Megan	12234 Monterey Blvd.	Monterey	CA	92347
Danforth	Peter	122 W. Third Street	Duhere	IL	33337
Williams	Reginald	34457 Wilcox Blvd.	Los Angeles	CA	90047
Hornsby	Roger	11 Cortland St.	East Rutherford	NJ	24127
Mountbank	Rupert	39 E. Colter St.	Idyllwild	CA	92349
Asawa	Ruth	1712 Castro St.	San Francisco	CA	94114
Perford	Steve	3876-A Chance St.	Niler	Fl	21347
Martinez	William	12 Castro St.	Pillage	AZ	94114
Clark	Wilma	229 E. Rainy St.	Checker	OR	96789
Munoz	Winston	33378 No. Hare	Austin	TX	97891

Record: 17 of 17

Moves to first record
Moves to next record
Moves to previous record
Moves to last record   New record   Scroll to see more fields
Scroll to see more records

Figure 11-3

Access 97 offers two ways to enter data: on the datasheet and on a form. Forms are the subject of the next lesson. For now, follow these steps to try your hand at entering data in a datasheet:

on the CD

1 Open the Enter Data file in the Office 101 folder.

To open a database file, choose File⇨Open Database, press Ctrl+O, or click the Open button. Then, in the Open dialog box, find the database file in the Office 101 folder and double-click it.

If you just started Access 97, you can open a database that you have worked on before from the Microsoft Access dialog box. Names of the databases you've worked on appear at the bottom of the dialog box. Click a name (or click More Files first if the database you want to open isn't on the list) and then click OK.

After the file opens, you see the Table tab of the Database window. This database has two tables, Addresses and Phone Numbers. The Addresses table is selected and ready for you to open.

2 Either double-click the Addresses table or click the Open button.

As shown in Figure 11-3, you now see the Addresses table in Datasheet view. But some of the information in this table is hard to see. Better make the columns wider.

3 **Move the pointer to the top of the table window, over the dividing line between the Street and City field names; after the cursor changes into a double-headed arrow, click and drag the dividing line to the right until the Street field is wide enough to read all the house numbers and street names in the column.**

You can adjust the width of fields by clicking and dragging in the row of field names at the top of the database table.

4 **Click the New Record button.**

The cursor lands in the last row, or record, of the database table so that you can enter a new record. You can also choose Insert⇨New Record or click the New Record button in the table window's status bar to enter a new record.

Notice that the status bar at the bottom of the table window reads `Record 18 of 18`. This database table holds 18 records, and the cursor is currently in the eighteenth record.

What's more, the status bar gives you a description of the field the cursor is in. You learned how to enter field descriptions in the Design view window in the last lesson. If you're in doubt concerning what to enter in a field, glance at its description in the status bar.

5 **Use your imagination and fill in all the first five fields in this record, from the Last Name field to the State field, and after you reach the State field, try to enter three letters.**

To move from one field to the next, press the Tab or → key or else click a new field. You can delete text inside a field by pressing Del or the Backspace key.

When you try to enter the third number in the State field, Access 97 beeps at you. It does so because no more than two characters can be entered in the State field. Step 10 in the previous lesson explains how to establish how many characters can be entered in a field. Now you can see why putting a limit on the number of characters makes data entries more accurate.

6 **Make sure that you enter only two letters in the State field; then enter four numbers in the Zip Code field and try to press the → key to move to the next record.**

You hear another beep, and a dialog box tells you that the value you entered is inappropriate for this field.

7 **Click OK in the dialog box, enter the fifth number in the Zip Code field, and then press the → or Tab key to move to the next record.**

When the cursor is in the last field of a record and you want to continue entering records, press → or Tab. Of course, you can also click a New Record button, either the one on the toolbar or the one on the Datasheet window's status bar, or choose Insert⇨New Record.

In the following three steps, you learn how to get around in Datasheet view by clicking the buttons in the status bar or the table.

8 **Click the leftmost arrow on the status bar, the one next to the word** `Record`.

The cursor moves to the first row in the database table. You can also get there by pressing Ctrl+Home.

on the test

---

click and drag between field names to change a field's width

▶*
New Record button

press the Tab or → key or click to move from field to field

☑ Progress Check

If you can perform the following tasks, you've mastered this lesson:

❏ Open a database.

❏ Move around in Datasheet view.

❏ Enter data in a data sheet

9 **Click the fourth arrow from the left on the status bar, the one that shows a right-pointing triangle with a line next to it.**

Clicking this button takes you to the last record in the database table. You can also press Ctrl+End to go to the last record.

10 **Click the left-pointing triangle, the one to the left of the box that tells you in which record the cursor is located.**

After you click this button, the cursor moves up one record. Click the right pointing arrow, the one on the other side of the box with the record number in it, to move to the next record.

11 **Click the up arrow at the top of the vertical scroll bar.**

Besides clicking buttons and pressing shortcut keys, you can always zip from place to place or from side to side by using the scroll bars. Clicking the up arrow moves the cursor up a record.

12 **Click the New Record button and enter another record (using your imagination to fill in the fields).**

This time, I trust, you don't make the same mistakes as you enter data in the State and Zip Code fields.

Don't close the Addresses datasheet yet. You need it for Lesson 11-3, which explains how to enter data by way of a form.

Lesson 11-3

Creating and Using Forms to Enter Data

In the last lesson, you learned how to enter data in a database table in Datasheet view. But Datasheet view, depending on your tastes and inclinations, isn't necessarily the easiest way to enter data. You can also enter data on a form. An Access 97 form is similar to a paper form you might fill out to apply for a job or a driver's license. Labels tell you exactly what kind of information you are supposed to enter, and space is provided beside the labels for entering information.

The last lesson left you hanging in the Address database table. Starting from there, follow these steps to learn how to create and use a form to enter data in a database table:

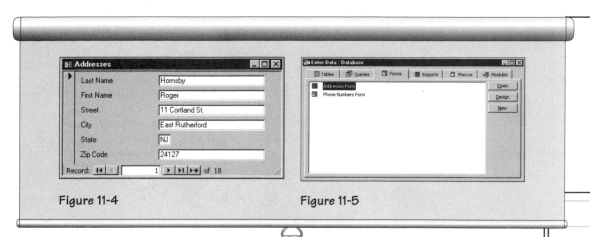

Figure 11-4: Besides entering data in Datasheet view, you can enter data on forms.

Figure 11-5: To open a form, double-click the form name on the Forms tab of the Database window.

Figure 11-4   Figure 11-5

1 **Click the down arrow next to the New Object button and select AutoForm from the drop-down list.**

You see a form similar to the one on the left side of Figure 11-4. Do you recognize the field names in this form? They're the same names that appeared on the datasheet.

In the following two steps, you save and name the form so that you can use this form to enter data.

2 **Click the Save button.**

The Save As dialog box appears and asks you to name the form.

3 **Type** Address Form **and click OK.**

Now that you saved the form, you can use it to enter data in the Addresses database table.

4 **Click the Close button (the *X*) in the upper-right corner of the form to close the form.**

You land back at the datasheet.

5 **Click the Database window button.**

Clicking this button, not unexpectedly, takes you to the Database window. So far, you've only explored the Table tab in this window. The form you just created is now on the Forms tab, as shown in Figure 11-5.

6 **Click the Forms tab and then double-click the Address Form icon to open the form you created.**

You now see a form for entering data. Information in the first record of the database table appears in the form. Notice that the top of the form reads Addresses. That tells you that data you enter in this form appears on the Addresses database table.

7 **Click the New Record button to enter a new record.**

A new, empty form, ready to be filled out, appears. The buttons along the bottom of the form look and work the same way as the buttons along the bottom of a table in Datasheet view (refer to Figure 11-3 to learn how these buttons work). Having clicked the New Record button, you see a blank form in which to enter a new record.

New Object button

Save button

Database Window button

8 Use your imagination to enter data in the form.

Press the Tab key or click to move from field to field. You can also press Shift+Tab to move the cursor backward through the fields. Remember or jot down the last name of the fictional person you enter on the form, because I ask you in Step 9 to find that person's name in the database table.

One of the advantages of forms over a datasheet is that forms clearly show which data belongs in each field. All you have to do is look to the left of a text box to see the field names. And forms also show how much data is to be entered in each field. In the State field, for example, you can plainly see that only two characters are expected. There isn't room for more than two characters.

9 Choose <u>Window</u>⇨<u>2</u> Address: Table to view the Address database table and then look in the table for the record you just added.

Go to the <u>W</u>indow menu if you want to bounce back and forth between the database tables and forms with which you are working. You can also click the Minimize and Maximize buttons to shrink and enlarge the different tables and forms you are working on.

10 Choose <u>File</u>⇨<u>C</u>lose three times to close the database table, the form you created, and finally, the Enter Data database file.

I trust this lesson has proven how efficient forms are for entering data. Whether you enter data in datasheets or forms is up to you. Some like it hot and some like it cold, as the nursery rhyme so wisely states.

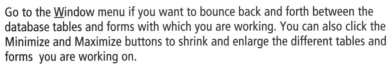

Lesson 11-4

Moving and Deleting Records and Fields

☑ Progress Check

If you can perform the following tasks, you've mastered this lesson:

❏ Create a new form for entering data in a database table.

❏ Open a form from the Forms tab of the Database window.

❏ Enter data on a form.

on the test

Notes:

After you have recorded information in the fields and records of the database, you might discover that you don't need as many fields or records as you thought, in which case you can delete fields and records. This short and very easy lesson explains how to delete unnecessary fields and records. It also describes how to move records and fields in a database.

on the test

About deleting, you need to know before you delete anything that fields and records are irrecoverable after they have been deleted. Throughout this book, I have pointed out that you can click the Undo button or choose <u>E</u>dit⇨<u>U</u>ndo to reverse a command or deletion, but Access 97 doesn't offer Undo commands for getting fields and records back after they have been deleted. So before you delete fields or records, take a deep breath and ask yourself if you really want to delete them. Entering information in a database can be a tedious and time-consuming chore. It becomes doubly tedious and time-consuming when you have to enter data you deleted accidentally.

on the CD

To learn how to delete and move records and fields, open the Move and Delete file in the Office 101 folder and follow these steps:

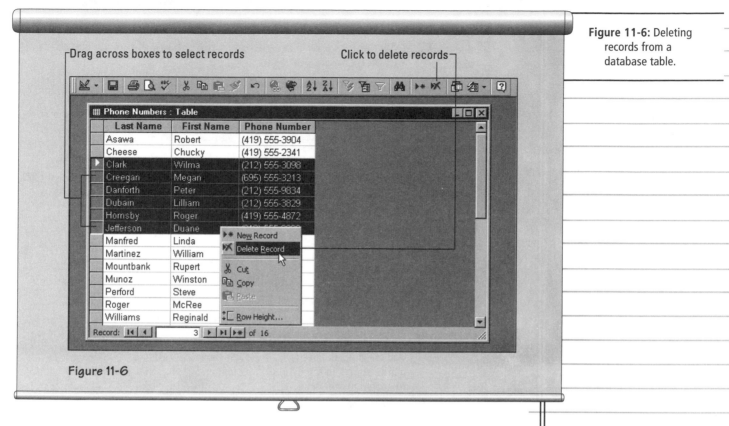

Figure 11-6: Deleting records from a database table.

Drag across boxes to select records   Click to delete records

Figure 11-6

---

on the test

1 **On the Tables tab of the Database window, double-click Phone Numbers to open the Phone Numbers database table.**

Before you can delete or move records, you must select them. To select a single record, click the small box to its left. You can select several records at once by dragging the mouse across the boxes to the left of the records you want to select.

2 **Click and drag the mouse across the boxes to the left of several records in the database table.**

If you perform this action correctly, the records are highlighted, as shown in Figure 11-6.

3 **Click the Delete Record button.**

You can also choose Edit➪Delete Record, right-click and choose Delete Record from the shortcut menu, or press the Del key. A warning box appears and tells you what I already told you at the start of this lesson — that you can't undo a Delete operation.

4 **Click Yes to delete the records forever.**

heads up

In the following two steps, you move records in a database by cutting and pasting them. You can't, however, move records at will in a database table. You can move the records only to the last, empty record at the bottom.

click boxes to the left of records to select them

Delete Record button

View button

drag field name
boxes to change
the location of
fields

☑ **Progress Check**

If you can perform the
following tasks, you're
ready to move on to the
Unit 11 quiz:

❑ Delete records in a
database table.

❑ Rearrange the fields in a
database table.

❑ Delete a field and its
contents.

5 **Select any two or three records from the middle of the database and then choose Edit⇨Cut.**

You can also cut records by clicking the Cut button, pressing Ctrl+X, or right-clicking and choosing Cut from the shortcut menu. Access 97 tells you that you can't undo the Delete operation, but don't worry about that. You *can* paste these records at the bottom of the database table. What you can't do is paste the records at the start or anywhere in the middle of the table.

6 **Click Yes in the message box, move to the empty record at the bottom of the database table, choose Edit⇨Paste Append, and click Yes after Access 97 asks whether you really want to paste these records.**

Not being able to move records wherever you want to move them seems like a failure on the part of Access 97. However, it is much easier to move records by sorting them, as Lesson 12-2 will prove beyond the shadow of a doubt.

The rest of this lesson focuses on deleting and moving fields. To do that, you are better off in Design view than in Datasheet view.

7 **Click the down arrow beside the View button and select Design view from the drop-down list, or else choose View⇨Design View.**

You see the database table in Design view. In this database table, last names appear in the first field, or column. Suppose that you want first names to appear in the first field.

8 **Click the box to the left of First Name in the Field Name column.**

The field is selected and is highlighted.

9 **Click in the box again, but this time hold down the mouse button and drag the box upward, to where the Last Name field box is, and release the mouse button.**

First Name becomes the first field in the Field Name column and, therefore, the first column in the database table. By dragging the boxes to the left of the field names in Design view, you can change the location of fields in a database table.

10 **Click the box to the left of Last Name field to select that field and then press the Del key.**

You see the message box again. It warns you that you are about to delete the field from the database table, as well as all the data you entered in the field. This time, you will heed this very important warning.

11 **Click the No button to keep the Last Name field intact.**

12 **Choose File⇨Close and click Yes when Access 97 asks whether you want to keep your changes to the Phone Numbers database table.**

13 **Choose File⇨Close again to close the Move and Delete database file.**

Earlier in Unit 11, you learned how to enter and edit data in a database. Unit 12 explains how to make use of the data you so carefully entered.

Unit 11 Quiz

For the following questions, circle the letter of the correct answer or answers. I designed this short quiz to help you remember what you learned in Unit 11. Each question may have more than one right answer.

1. **Which of the following is *not* a database?**

    A. A cookbook.

    B. A telephone directory.

    C. A list of registered voters.

    D. An address book.

    E. A zoo.

2. **In which view do you name and set up fields for a database table?**

    A. Datasheet view.

    B. Database Window view.

    C. Field view.

    D. Design view.

    E. Good view.

3. **To move from field to field in a datasheet or form, you perform which of the following actions?**

    A. Press Shift+Tab.

    B. Press Tab.

    C. Press the → key.

    D. Click a new field.

    E. All of the above.

 4. **Click this button to perform which of the following actions?**

    A. Delete a record.

    B. Go to the Database window.

    C. Change views.

    D. Enter a new record.

    E. Sort a database.

5. **To create a form for entering data in a database table, you perform which of the following actions?**

    A. Click the down arrow beside the New Object button and select AutoForm from the drop-down list.

    B. Click the Form button.

C. Choose Tools⇨Form.

D. Save the database table as a form.

E. Right-click and choose Form.

6. **To open and work on a form you created, you perform which of the following actions?**

A. Open the database file as a form.

B. Choose Insert⇨Form.

C. Click the down arrow beside the View button and choose Form View.

D. From the Database window, click the Forms tab and then double-click the form.

E. Choose Window⇨Form.

7. **To change the position of a field in a database table, you perform which of the following actions?**

A. Drag the field in Design view.

B. In Design view, click the selection box beside the field name; then click the box again and drag the field.

C. Cut and paste the field to a new location.

D. Choose Field⇨Move.

E. In Datasheet view, drag the field to a new location.

Unit 11 Exercise

on the CD

1. Open the Quiz 11 file in the Office 101 folder.

2. Switch to Design view and create a new field called Phone Numbers for the database table.

3. Enter a few phone numbers in the database field and adjust column widths in the table while you're at that task.

4. Create a form for entering data in the database table and enter new records from the form.

5. Switch to Design view and move the Phone Number field between the Last Name and First Name field.

6. Delete the Phone Number field and all its contents.

Getting the Data Out

Objectives for This Unit

✓ Finding, or filtering, information in a database table

✓ Querying a database table to get specific information

✓ Sorting records to rearrange them in a table

✓ Creating and printing a report

Prerequisites

◆ Move to the Database window (Lesson 11-3)

◆ Open a form (Lesson 11-3)

◆ Printing a file (Lesson 3-6)

on the CD

◆ Filter

◆ Query

◆ Query Combo

◆ Report

◆ Quiz 12

In Unit 11, you learned how to cram data into a database. In this unit, you learn how to get the data out so you can examine it closely. In Unit 12, you learn how to filter, sort, and query databases. Or, to put it in plain English, you learn how to find data in a database, rearrange the records in different ways, and find records that meet different criteria. This unit also explains how to generate and print reports that describe the data in a database.

Filtering a Database to Find Information

Lesson 12-1

In the peculiar jargon of databases, finding data that match a set of criteria is called *filtering*. Perhaps the person who invented the term owned a swimming pool and often found unusual objects — hairpins, I suppose — in the pool's filter. I can think of no other reason why the word *filter* describes finding information in a database.

In this lesson, you will learn two ways to filter data. You can either start from Datasheet view and search for records that match what is in one field of a record, or you can switch to Form view and narrow your search by requiring the records you are filtering to match the data in more than one field.

Figure 12-1: Using a form, you can narrow the search by looking in several fields at once.

Notes:

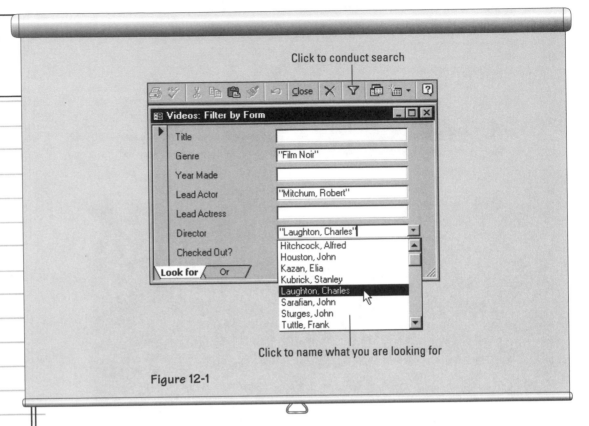

Click to conduct search

Figure 12-1

Click to name what you are looking for

To learn how to find specific records in a database, open the Filter file in the Office 101 folder and follow these steps:

1 In Database view, double-click the Videos table to open the Videos datasheet.

For this lesson, you will pretend that you manage a video rental store. People often call to find out if such-and-such a movie is in stock, and whether you have movies that star or were directed by so-and-so. Rather than search your memory or the store shelves for the answers to customers' questions, you have put together a database of the videos in the store so you can search the database for answers. In the database, records are divided into seven fields: Title, Genre, Year Made, Lead Actor, Lead Actress, Director, and Checked Out?, which tells whether the video has been rented.

The first caller wants to know if you stock comedies. In the following two steps, you will find out by doing a simple *filter by selection*.

2 Click the Genre field of the fourth record, City of Women.

By clicking in the Genre field, you have told Access 97 that you want to "filter by genre."

3 Click the Filter by Selection button.

You now see a list of all the comedies in the database. In addition to clicking the Filter by Selection button, you can also find records in a database by choosing Records➪Filter➪Filter by Selection.

Filter by Selection button

4 **Click the Remove Filter button.**

Now you see the entire database again and you're ready for the next caller. If you're not the button-clicking kind, you can also remove a filter by choosing Records⇨Remove Filter/Sort.

The next caller also wants to know whether you stock comedies. To find out, you could repeat Steps 2 and 3, but that isn't necessary, as the following step demonstrates.

5 **Click the Apply Filter button or choose Record⇨Apply Filter/Sort.**

The Remove Filter button has changed names — now the button is called Apply Filter. Access 97 remembers the last filtering operation you did. Rather than tell the program all over again what you searched for last time around, you can simply click the Apply Filter button.

6 **Click the Remove Filter button — it's changed names again — to view the entire database table.**

The next caller is looking for a movie but she can't remember the title. It starred Robert Mitchum as this whacko guy who just got out of prison. And it was directed by Charles Laughton. In fact, it was the only movie he ever directed. Roger Ebert said it was one of the ten best film noirs ever made.

To find out whether this movie is in stock, you will have to switch to a form and do the filter job there. By filtering from a form, you can search by more than one criterion.

7 **Click the Database Window button to open the Database window; then click the Forms tab and double-click the Videos Form icon.**

You see a form with the first record in the database in it. You know three things about the video this customer is looking for: it starred Robert Mitchum, it falls in the film noire genre, and it was directed by Charles Laughton.

8 **Click the Filter by Form button.**

Now you're ready to ask the database what it knows about the video your customer wants.

9 **Delete the title in the Title field and then click the Genre field.**

If you forget to delete the title field, Access 97 will think it is one of the criteria you are using in the search. A down arrow appears next to the Genre field. On the Genre drop-down list are the names of all the genres in the database. The other fields also offer drop-down lists for choosing parts of records in the database.

10 **Click the down arrow and select Film Noir from the list; then click the Lead Actor field and select Robert Mitchum from that drop-down list; finally, click the Director field and select Charles Laughton.**

Figure 12-1 demonstrates how to choose a name or genre from a drop-down list. You often have to scroll down the lists to find what you are looking for. All three criteria have been entered on the form, so now you can conduct the search.

11 **Click the Apply Filter button.**

Access 97 searches the database table and fills in the missing pieces. The film is titled *Night of the Hunter* and is not checked out.

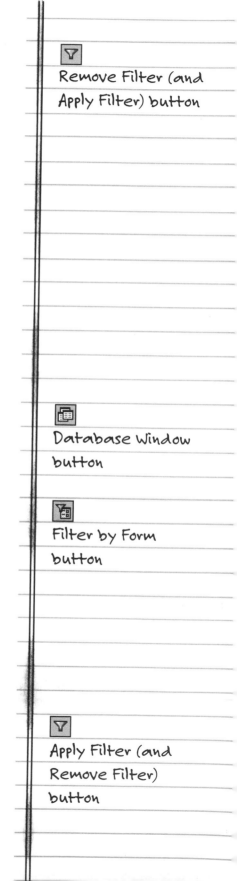

Remove Filter (and Apply Filter) button

Database Window button

Filter by Form button

Apply Filter (and Remove Filter) button

☑ Progress Check

If you can perform the following tasks, you've mastered this lesson:

❏ Filter a database table by selecting part of a record.

❏ Search in Form view by selecting from the drop-down lists.

12 Click the Close button in the form to remove the form from the screen.

If two records had matched the search criteria, the bottom of the dialog box would read, "Record 1 of 2 (Filtered)." Then you would click the right-pointing arrow to see the second record. By the way, the films in the Filter database are superb. You can't go wrong if you rent any of these films.

Lesson 12-2

Querying to Find Data and Combine Database Tables

In the previous lesson, you learned how to mine a database table for records that match criteria. Suppose, however, that you need to find data that doesn't match, but falls in a certain range. For example, to get the records of all people between the age of 40 and 49, you can't filter a database. It would take too long to search for all the 40-year-olds, then all the 41-year-olds, and so on. Instead of filtering, you would query the database.

A *query* is a question you ask of the database: "Can you show me the records of all people between the age of 40 and 49 who live in Nevada and whose incomes are above $45,000?" Junk-mailers query their databases all the time to answer questions like these. Then they print mailing labels from the query and send advertisements to the people who are most likely to buy their products.

This lesson explains how to query a database. It also explains how you can run a query to combine the data that is in two or more database tables.

Querying to get the data out

on the CD

To learn how to query a database, open the Query file in the Office 101 folder and follow these steps:

1 Click the Queries tab in the Database window.

As shown in Figure 12-2, the names of three queries I have already constructed appear on the Queries tab. When you construct and save a query, Access 97 "remembers" it in case you want to run it again.

For this lesson, you pretend that you run a mail-order house. Over the years, you have built a large database with the names, addresses, phone numbers,

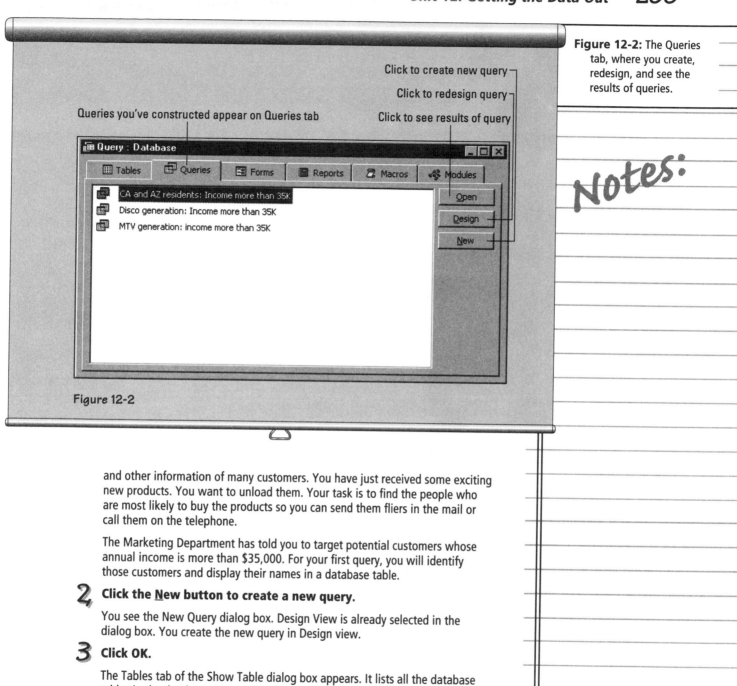

Figure 12-2: The Queries
tab, where you create,
redesign, and see the
results of queries.

Click to create new query

Click to redesign query

Click to see results of query

Queries you've constructed appear on Queries tab

Figure 12-2

Notes:

and other information of many customers. You have just received some exciting new products. You want to unload them. Your task is to find the people who are most likely to buy the products so you can send them fliers in the mail or call them on the telephone.

The Marketing Department has told you to target potential customers whose annual income is more than $35,000. For your first query, you will identify those customers and display their names in a database table.

2 **Click the New button to create a new query.**

You see the New Query dialog box. Design View is already selected in the dialog box. You create the new query in Design view.

3 **Click OK.**

The Tables tab of the Show Table dialog box appears. It lists all the database tables in the database. From this tab, you can query more than one table to gather information, as the second part of this lesson demonstrates, but for this exercise you only need the Addresses table.

4 **The Addresses table is already selected, so click the Add button to add the Addresses table to the list of tables in your query and then click Close.**

As shown in Figure 12-3, the Select Query window appears. This window is where you tell Access 97 which fields to query in the database table and how to query those fields.

Figure 12-3: Choosing
fields and entering
criteria for the query.

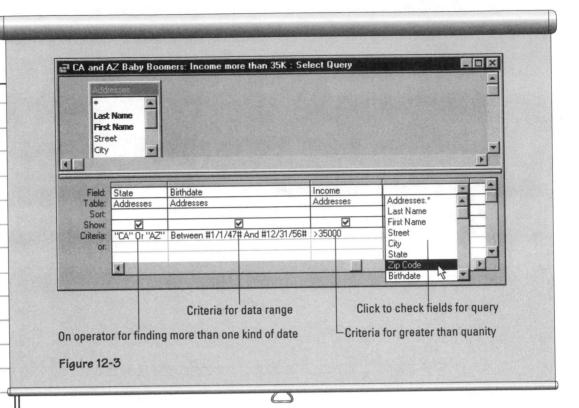

Criteria for data range

Click to check fields for query

On operator for finding more than one kind of date

Criteria for greater than quanity

Figure 12-3

5 **Click the Field text box in the first column and, after the down arrow appears, click the arrow and select Last Name from the drop-down list of field names in the database table.**

You just told Access 97 to include last names in the records that the query will turn up. Notice the check mark in the Show check box — it means that the Last Name field will indeed appear in the database table that results from this query. The Table row tells you that the Addresses database table is going to be queried.

6 **Go down the Field columns, click the down arrows, and choose the following fields for the query: First Name, Street, City, Zip Code, and Income.**

You have to use scroll bars to move across the Field columns, and you have to use the scroll bar in the drop-down menu to find Income at the bottom of the list. If you want, you can adjust column widths by dragging the dividing lines between columns.

In the next step, you make an entry in the Criteria box below the Income field to instruct the query to seek out people whose income is above $35,000.

7 **Click the Income field Criteria box and type the following: >35000.**

The greater than symbol (>) tells Access 97 to find incomes above $35,000. If you were seeking people who make less than that amount, you would use the less than symbol (<).

Don't enter dollar signs or commas in monetary figures as you construct a query.

You're ready to conduct the query, but first you need to save and name the query so that you can use it again in the future.

heads up

8 **Click the Save button and, in the Save As dialog box, type** Income over 35K; **then click OK.**

At last, the query is ready to go. Good thing you saved it so that you don't need to go to all this trouble months from now, after you enter more names in the Addresses database table.

on the test

9 **Click the Run button or choose Query⇨Run.**

You see a database table with the names and addresses of everyone whose income is more than $35,000.

10 **To see the Database window again, click the Close button (the *X*) in the Income more than 35K Query window.**

The MTV generation query on the Queries tab was designed to find people in the Addresses database table who were born between 1/1/67 and 12/31/76, and whose income is above $35,000. I constructed this query because the Marketing Department told me it has a warehouse full of old Brady Bunch videos to move. To see how you can query for a range of data, in this case all birthdays between 1/1/67 and 12/31/76, do the following step.

11 **Select the MTV generation query on the Queries tab, click the Design button, and in the Select Query window, scroll to the Birthdate field.**

Click the Design button if you want to see how a query was fashioned and perhaps redesign it.

on the test

The Criteria box in the Birthday field says, Between #1/1/67# And #12/ 31/76#. Access 97 added the number signs (#) to the box. When I entered this criterion, I did it like so: **Between 1/1/67 And 12/31/76**. To tell Access 97 to query for a range of data, enter the word **Between**, write the lowest number or date in the range, enter the word **And**, and then enter the highest number in the range. Make sure *Between* and *And* are capitalized.

12 **Click the Select Query window's Close button to return to the Database window, click the CA and AZ baby boomers query, and then click the Design button.**

For this query, I asked the database table for people born between 1/1/47 and 12/31/56 who live in Arizona or California and make at least $35,000 a year. The company has a number of hot tubs to unload and wants to unload the items in California and Arizona to the health-conscious but somewhat vain members of the Baby Boom generation.

13 **Scroll to the State field to see how to enter criteria for finding two kinds of data in a field.**

To query for people in two states, I used the Or operator. Access 97 added the quotation marks. To enter these criteria, I typed **CA Or AZ**. To find two types of data in a query field, enter the first type, enter **Or**, and enter the second type.

14 **Click the Close button in the Select Query window to return to the Database window and then choose File⇨Close to close the Query database file.**

When you are on the Queries tab of Database window, you can click a query and then click the Open button to see the results that the query generates.

Save button

Run button

click the Design button to redesign the query

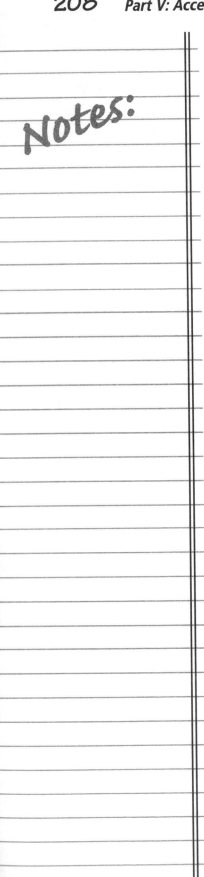

Notes:

Queries for combining data from different tables

The start of Part V mentioned the importance of keeping data of different kinds in separate database tables. By doing so, you can enter and manipulate data easily. But what if you want to combine data from different database tables? One way to do so is to construct a query that draws data from different places.

on the CD

To learn how to combine data from different tables by using a query, open the Query Combo file in the Office 101 folder and follow these steps:

1 **In the Database window, click the Queries tab and then click the New button.**

The New Query dialog box appears.

2 **Design view is already selected, so click the OK button.**

To design a query, do so in Design view. In Step 4 of the preceding exercise, you selected only one table, Addresses, for the query, but this time you select two.

3 **In the Show Table dialog box, click Add to query the Addresses table, click Phone Numbers, click Add again, and then click Close.**

Two tables appear in the Select Query window, as shown in Figure 12-4. Notice, in each table, that the Last Name and First Name fields appear in boldface type. These fields are the primary key for each table. (Step 7 in Lesson 11-1 described at tedious length what the primary key is and does.) The primary keys of both tables or of all the tables you query at the same time must be the same for the query operation to work.

In the following six steps, you construct a query that brings together the names in both tables as well as the cities in the Addresses table and the telephone numbers in the Phone Numbers table.

4 **Click the Last Name field in the Addresses field list in the box at the top of the Select Query window. Click and hold down the mouse button, and then drag the words Last Name across the dialog box and drop them on the words Last Name in the Phone Numbers field list box.**

A tricky operation, I know. If you do it right, however, Access 97 draws a line between the two fields, as shown in Figure 12-4. What you've done is tell Access 97 to join these two fields so that, as data from the two tables combine, the program knows in which field to look for matches.

5 **Repeat Step 5 but, this time, drag the First Name field name from one list box to the other.**

Two lines appear, as shown in Figure 12-4. Now it's time to focus on the Field and Table boxes in the bottom half of the Select Query window.

6 **In the first field, click the Table box, click the down arrow, and select Addresses from the drop-down list.**

You just told Access 97 to show only fields from the Addresses table after you click the Field down arrow in the following step.

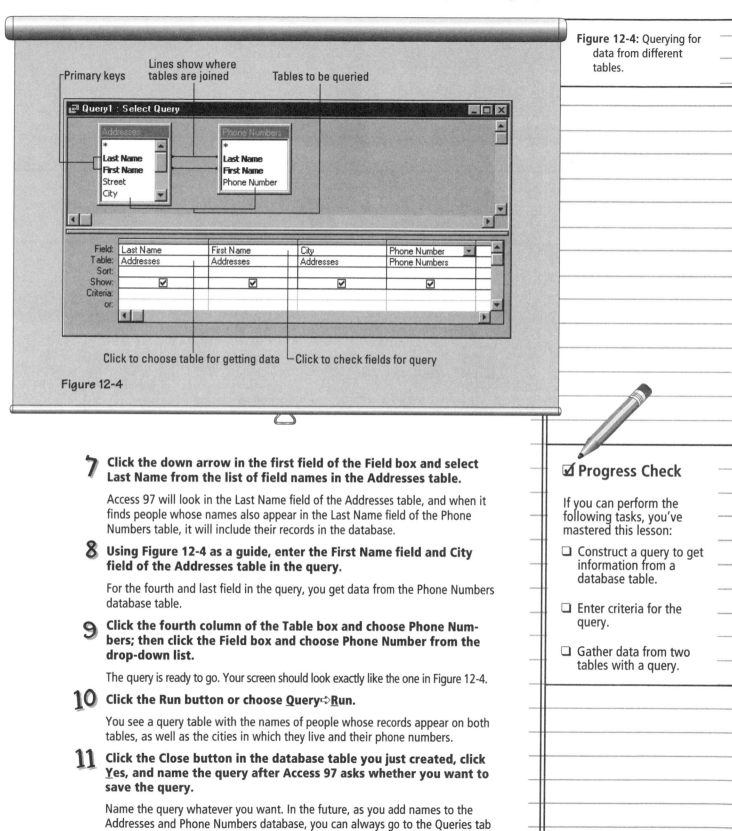

Figure 12-4: Querying for data from different tables.

Primary keys

Lines show where tables are joined

Tables to be queried

Click to choose table for getting data └Click to check fields for query

Figure 12-4

7 **Click the down arrow in the first field of the Field box and select Last Name from the list of field names in the Addresses table.**

Access 97 will look in the Last Name field of the Addresses table, and when it finds people whose names also appear in the Last Name field of the Phone Numbers table, it will include their records in the database.

8 **Using Figure 12-4 as a guide, enter the First Name field and City field of the Addresses table in the query.**

For the fourth and last field in the query, you get data from the Phone Numbers database table.

9 **Click the fourth column of the Table box and choose Phone Numbers; then click the Field box and choose Phone Number from the drop-down list.**

The query is ready to go. Your screen should look exactly like the one in Figure 12-4.

10 **Click the Run button or choose Query⇨Run.**

You see a query table with the names of people whose records appear on both tables, as well as the cities in which they live and their phone numbers.

11 **Click the Close button in the database table you just created, click Yes, and name the query after Access 97 asks whether you want to save the query.**

Name the query whatever you want. In the future, as you add names to the Addresses and Phone Numbers database, you can always go to the Queries tab and draw on this query for a concise list of customers, their phone numbers, and the cities where they live.

☑ Progress Check

If you can perform the following tasks, you've mastered this lesson:

❑ Construct a query to get information from a database table.

❑ Enter criteria for the query.

❑ Gather data from two tables with a query.

Recess

Take a recess. In fact, take the rest of the day off, curl up with a good book, and relax. Learning about databases is a grueling business. Microsoft has tried to make the task easier for you with the many tools in the Access 97 program, but still . . . this stuff is hard work!

Lesson 12-3

Sorting a Database

Notes:

When you sort a database table, you arrange the records in a new way. Database tables are sorted by field. For example, to make the records appear in alphabetical order by last name, sort the Last Name field. Or, to put the records in order from the oldest person in the database table to the youngest, sort the Birthdate field.

on the test

Access 97 offers two ways to sort the data in fields, in *ascending order* or in *descending order:*

- In ascending order, the program sorts text fields from A to Z (Anderson, Hernandez, Zalopa); number and currency fields from smallest to largest (1, 10, 10,000); and date and time fields from the oldest in time to the most recent (1901, 1958, 1997).

- In descending order, the program sorts text fields from Z to A (Zimbabwe, Martinique, Addis Ababa); number and currency fields from largest to smallest (10,000, 10, 1); and date and time fields from the most recent in time to the oldest in time (1997, 1958, 1901).

This lesson explains how to sort data in a database table, and, I'm pleased to say, it is a very easy lesson.

To find out about sorting, open the Sort file in the Office 101 folder and follow these steps:

1 In the Database window, click the Queries tab and then double-click the Sort Me query.

Can you tell how this database table is sorted? (*Hint:* On the Last Name field in ascending order.)

2 Click Last Name at the top of the field to select the Last Name field.

The field appears in black, as shown in Figure 12-5. The field is selected and ready for you to sort.

3 Click the Sort Descending button.

The records are arranged in the Last Name field from Z to A instead of A to Z.

Sort Descending
button

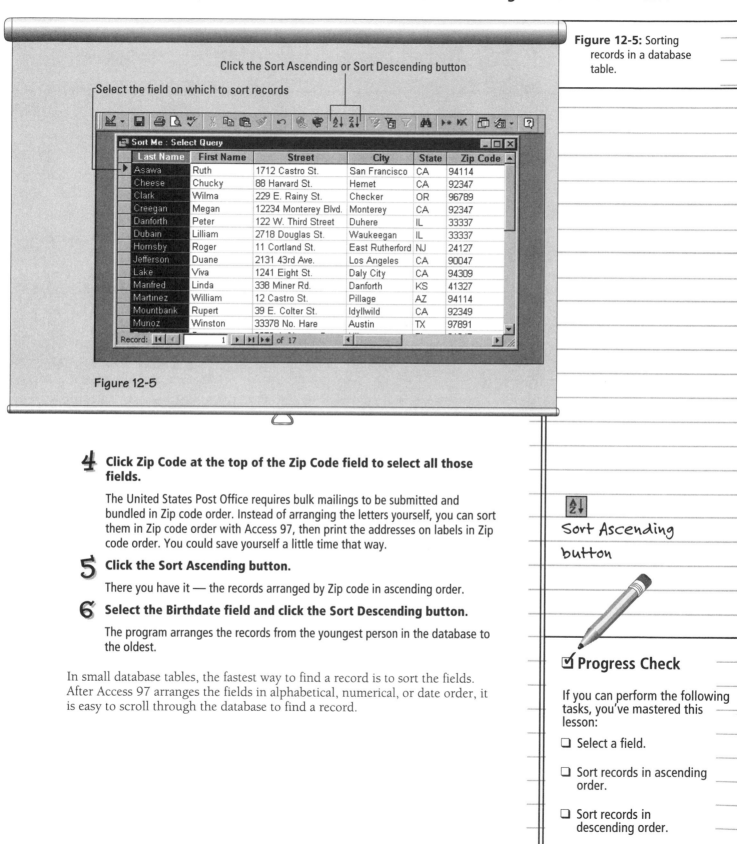

Click the Sort Ascending or Sort Descending button

Select the field on which to sort records

Sort Me : Select Query

Last Name	First Name	Street	City	State	Zip Code
Asawa	Ruth	1712 Castro St.	San Francisco	CA	94114
Cheese	Chucky	88 Harvard St.	Hemet	CA	92347
Clark	Wilma	229 E. Rainy St.	Checker	OR	96789
Creegan	Megan	12234 Monterey Blvd.	Monterey	CA	92347
Danforth	Peter	122 W. Third Street	Duhere	IL	33337
Dubain	Lilliam	2718 Douglas St.	Waukeegan	IL	33337
Hornsby	Roger	11 Cortland St.	East Rutherford	NJ	24127
Jefferson	Duane	2131 43rd Ave.	Los Angeles	CA	90047
Lake	Viva	1241 Eight St.	Daly City	CA	94309
Manfred	Linda	338 Miner Rd.	Danforth	KS	41327
Martinez	William	12 Castro St.	Pillage	AZ	94114
Mountbank	Rupert	39 E. Colter St.	Idyllwild	CA	92349
Munoz	Winston	33378 No. Hare	Austin	TX	97891

Record: 1 of 17

Figure 12-5

Figure 12-5: Sorting records in a database table.

4 Click Zip Code at the top of the Zip Code field to select all those fields.

The United States Post Office requires bulk mailings to be submitted and bundled in Zip code order. Instead of arranging the letters yourself, you can sort them in Zip code order with Access 97, then print the addresses on labels in Zip code order. You could save yourself a little time that way.

5 Click the Sort Ascending button.

There you have it — the records arranged by Zip code in ascending order.

6 Select the Birthdate field and click the Sort Descending button.

The program arranges the records from the youngest person in the database to the oldest.

In small database tables, the fastest way to find a record is to sort the fields. After Access 97 arranges the fields in alphabetical, numerical, or date order, it is easy to scroll through the database to find a record.

Sort Ascending button

☑ **Progress Check**

If you can perform the following tasks, you've mastered this lesson:

❑ Select a field.

❑ Sort records in ascending order.

❑ Sort records in descending order.

Lesson 12-4   # Generating and Printing Reports

on the CD

In Access 97, a *report* is information that you've formatted and made presentable for others. If someone in Timbuktu asks, "Can you send me a copy of that data?" all you need to do is to print a report and send it. This lesson explains how to generate and print reports.

To learn how to generate and print a report, open the Report file in the Office 101 folder and follow these steps:

1 **Click the Reports tab in the Database window and then click the New button.**

The New Report dialog box appears. For reports, you may as well choose the Report Wizard in the New Report dialog box. By letting the Wizard do the work, you save yourself the trouble of formatting the report on your own.

2 **Click Report Wizard and then click OK.**

After a bit of bumping and grinding on the computer's part, you see the first Report Wizard dialog box. It asks which fields to include in the report. To include a field, select it and then click the > button. Or, if you want to include all the fields in the report, click the >> button, as you will do in the next step.

3 **Click the >> button.**

All the fields in the Available Fields box move to the Selected Fields box.

4 **Click the Next button.**

The next dialog box asks about grouping levels. A *grouping level* is like a report subheading. The grouping level you choose, if you indeed choose one, stands out and in larger type in the report. For this report, you make last names the grouping level.

5 **Last Name, the first field for grouping, is already selected, so click the > button.**

Last Name appears in tall blue letters in the preview box on the right side of the dialog box.

6 **Click Next.**

You can sort records in the next dialog box. To sort the records by a particular field, select the field from the first drop-down list. For this exercise, you skip this step.

7 **Click Next.**

The next dialog box you see is the important one. This is where you decide what the report will look like. By clicking the Layout radio buttons, you can see in the preview box what the Layout choices mean.

8 **Click a Layout radio (your choice).**

If you're printing a large database report, you may also click the Landscape radio button in the Orientation area. In landscape mode, the page prints out wider than it is long, so you can fit more records across a page.

Notes:

grouping level =
report subheading

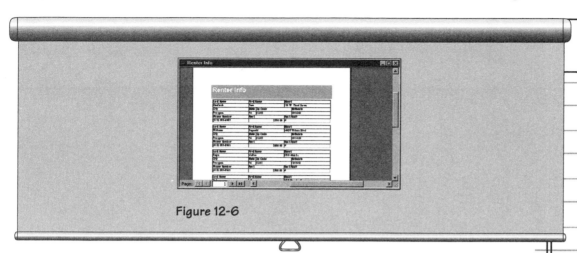

Figure 12-6: A report on the Print Preview screen.

Figure 12-6

9 **Click Next again.**

Now you must decide on a style for the title of the report. Click a few choices and check the preview box to see how these choices appear.

10 **Choose Soft Gray and click the Next button.**

The next dialog box asks for a title for the report. This dialog box is the last in the Reports Wizard. After you enter a title and click Finish, you get to see a preview of how the report should look after you print it.

11 **Enter** Reenter List **in the Title text box and click Finish.**

heads up

The report appears on a Print Preview screen, as shown in Figure 12-6. Take a good look at it now, because the only way to view reports is on the Print Preview screen. As you will see after the next step, reports are fairly incomprehensible after you leave Print Preview.

12 **Click the Close button to leave the Preview window and then squint at the strange-looking report that appears on-screen.**

Perhaps you can make more sense of the thing after you print it.

13 **Click the Print button.**

14 **After the report prints, click the Close button to remove it from your screen.**

You can call up this report again after you add more records to the table. The report is right there, waiting just for you, on the Reports tab of the Database window.

☑ **Progress Check**

If you can perform the following tasks, you're ready to move on to the Unit 12 quiz:

❏ Create a report with the Report Wizard.

❏ Print the report.

Print button

Unit 12 Quiz

For the following questions, circle the letter of the correct answer or answers. I designed this short quiz to help you remember what you learned in Unit 12. Each question may have more than one right answer.

 1. **Clicking this button performs which of the following actions?**

A. Opens the Database window.

B. Constructs a query so that you can find data.

C. Finds, or filters, all records in the database that match the data in the field in which the cursor is located.

D. Makes lightening strike twice.

E. Opens the Find dialog box.

2. **The query criterion "<38.50" finds which of the following?**

A. Records with number or currency figures between 38 and 50.

B. Records with number or currency figures of exactly 38.50.

C. Records with number or currency figures less than 38.50.

D. House numbers between 38 and 50.

E. It doesn't find anything.

3. **The query criterion "Between #1/1/49# and #12/31/51" finds which of the following?**

A. All records in the years 1949, 1950, and 1951.

B. All records from January 1 and December 31 in the years 1949, 1950, and 1951.

C. All records between those two days, but not including those two days.

D. All the records in the database.

E. It wouldn't find anything, because you must capitalize the word *And* for the query to work.

4. **Which of the following is sorted in descending order?**

A. $10.99, $25.49, $45.29, $91.33.

B. Arkansas, Hawaii, Kansas, Rhode Island.

C. 11/10/96, 12/2/96, 1/2/97, 2/14/97.

D. Zed, Timmy, Jake, Darnell.

E. 12144, 31245, 53206, 94114.

5. **In Access 97, a report is which of the following?**

    A. A detailed explanation of what is in the fields.

    B. A comprehensive description of the database.

    C. A printout of the information in a database table.

    D. A concise, summary account of the database's findings.

    E. A bulletin with the latest news and weather.

6. **Who said, "The problem with a self-made man is that he inherits all the faults of his creator"?**

    A. Woody Allen.

    B. George Bernard Shaw.

    C. Mark Twain.

    D. Groucho Marx.

    E. Louis Erdrich.

Unit 12 Exercise

on the CD

1. Open the Quiz 12 file in the Office101 folder.

2. Open the Subscribers database table and filter the table to find all the people who live in California.

3. Go back to the Database window, click the Forms tab, open the Subscribers form, and use the form to find all people in the 94114 zip code who live in San Francisco.

4. Conduct a query to find all people who live in Oregon and Washington state.

5. Sort the database table in alphabetical order by last name.

6. Create a report from the database table. Include only the Last Name, First Name, City, and State fields in the report.

Part V Review

Unit 11 Summary

▶ **Creating a database:** To create a database, click the Blank Database option button in the Microsoft Access dialog box and click OK. You can also click the New button, and, in the General tab of the New dialog box, double-click the Blank Database icon. Switch to Design view and enter the field names. In Design view, you also choose which type of data is to be kept in each field and tell Access 97 which field or fields in the database table form the primary key.

▶ **Entering data in Datasheet view:** Click the New Record button, choose Insert⇨New Record, or click the New Record button in the table window's status bar to create a new record. Press the Tab or → key or click a new field to move from field to field. Press Del or the Backspace key when you need to erase the characters or numbers you have entered.

▶ **Entering data on a form:** To create a form, click the down arrow beside the New Object button and choose AutoForm, and then click the Save button to save the form and give it a name. To open a form, click the Datasheet Window button to get to the Datasheet window; if necessary, click the Forms tab, and double-click the name of the form you want to enter data on. Enter the data on the form and press Tab or click to get from field to field.

▶ **Moving and deleting records and fields:** To delete records, select them by dragging across the small squares to their left in Datasheet view, and then click the Delete Record key. To delete a field and all its contents, switch to Design view, click the field you want to delete, press Del, and click Yes when Access 97 asks if you really want to delete the field. To move a field, click its selection box. Then click the selection box again and drag the field upward or downward to a new position.

Unit 12 Summary

▶ **Finding, or filtering, data:** To look for data in a database table in Datasheet view, click a field in a record that matches the data you are looking for, and then click the Apply Filter button. To look for matches in several different fields, switch to Form view, click the down arrow in the fields in which you are seeking matches, choose criteria from the drop-down menus, and then click the Apply Filter button.

▶ **Constructing a query:** Click the Queries tab in the Database window, and then click the New button. Choose Design View in the New Query dialog box and click OK. On the Table tab of the Show Table dialog box, click each table you want to query and click Add. Click Close when you're done selecting tables. In the Select Query window, click the down arrow in the Field boxes and choose fields to tell Access 97 which fields you want to query. If you are querying more than one database table, choose tables from the Table boxes as well, and join fields from the different tables. Click the Run button to run the query.

▶ **Sorting a database:** In Datasheet view, click a field name to select the field and then click the Sort Ascending or Sort Descending button. Ascending sorts arrange data from A to Z, from the smallest to the largest number, or from the oldest in time to the most recent. Descending sorts arrange data from Z to A, from the largest to the smallest number, or from the most recent in time to the oldest.

▶ **Generating and printing reports:** Go to the Reports tab in the Database window and click the New button. In the New Report dialog box, choose Report Wizard and click OK. In the first Report Wizard dialog box, tell Access 97 which fields to include in the report by clicking the > button or the >> button. Click Next and fill out the other Report Wizard dialog boxes as they appear, and then click Finish in the last dialog box.

Part V Test

This test will bowl you over. It will interrupt your sleep tonight. It will give you a guilty conscience because you didn't study for it hard enough. It will make you dream that you are roaming naked through the halls of your old high school, past your old friends and acquaintances, none of whom notice that you have no clothes on. This test will make you sweat and it will affect your breathing. It will make you scratch your head in dismay.

Actually, this simple test will do nothing of the kind. All it will do is help you remember what you learned in Part V. If you can't answer a question, turn backward through the pages of this book and look for the On the Test icons. Next to each icon is the answer to a question on this test. Appendix A lists all the answers, incidentally.

True   False

T   F   1. Use the Design View window to name the fields in a database table.

T   F   2. A database filter keeps all the bugs out of your data.

T   F   3. You can put a limit on the number of characters that can be entered in a field.

T   F   4. As you enter data, you can read a description of the field where the data is being entered on the status bar.

T   F   5. Click the Undo button after you have deleted records or fields to get them back again.

T   F   6. Filtering a database table means to search for data inside it.

T   F   7. [icon] Click this button to find, or filter, data in a database table.

T   F   8. The criteria *Between 450 And 1000* in a query finds records with numbers between 450 and 1,000 in the field.

T   F   9. [icon] Click this button to sort data in descending order.

T   F   10. A report summarizes the information in a database table.

Multiple choice

Circle the correct answer or answers to the following questions. Each question may have more than one right answer.

11. **When it comes to describing what kind of data goes in a field for storing Social Security numbers, which data type do you use?**

    A.   Number.

    B.   Memo.

    C.   Text.

    D.   AutoNumber.

    E.   Yes/No.

12. **Field is to database table as:**

    A.   Clothesline is to backyard.

    B.   Column heading is to text table.

    C.   Tail is to dog.

    D.   Corncob pipe is to chimney.

    E.   History is to butcher shop.

Part V Test

13. **A primary key is which of the following?**

    A. The field Access 97 uses to compare and join data from different database tables.

    B. The most important field in the database table.

    C. The field that provides knowledge and understanding.

    D. The field or fields in the database that are sure to contain different data from record to record.

    E. The field with the highest number values.

14. **To start entering a new record in Datasheet view, do the following:**

    A. Click the New Record button.

    B. Choose Insert⇨New Record.

    C. Click the New Record button in the table window's status bar.

    D. Scroll to the last field of the last record in the database table and press Tab.

    E. All of the above.

15. **When you've opened a form and a database table, you can get back and forth between the two by doing the following:**

    A. Clicking the Minimize and Maximize buttons to open and close the forms and tables you want to see or remove from the screen.

    B. Clicking the Database Window button.

    C. Making choices from the Window menu.

    D. Choose File⇨Close.

    E. Clicking the Save button.

16. **To select records in a database table, do the following:**

    A. Click in a record and choose Edit⇨Select.

    B. Click a field name along the top of the database table.

    C. Drag the mouse across the selection boxes to the left of the records.

    D. Drag down on column in the table.

    E. Right-click and choose Select.

17. **Which of the following is sorted in descending order:**

    A. 02134, 41295, 73216, 94114

    B. 11 Nov 96, 16 Dec 96, 11 Jan 97, 14 Feb 97

    C. $1000, $2500, $4500, $9000

    D. Zanzibar, Waukeegan, Motley, Dauran

    E. 2000 B.C., 11 A.D, 1012 A.D., 2001 A.D.

Part V Test

Matching

18. Match the buttons in the left-hand column with the correct names in the right-hand column.

   A.   1. New Record

   B.   2. New Object

   C.   3. Database Window

   D.   4. View

   E.   5. Save

19. Match the buttons in the left-hand column with the correct names in the right-hand column.

   A.   1. Print

   B.   2. New Object

   C.   3. Sort Ascending

   D.   4. Sort Descending

   E.   5. Run

20. Match the profession in the left-hand column with the jargon its practitioners use in the right-hand column.

   A. Sailor   1. *Jamb, girt, bucksaw, bevel, flush.*

   B. Jockey   2. *Joystick, altimeter, cockpit, tail.*

   C. Database propeller-head   3. *Query, data, filter, sort.*

   D. Pilot   4. *fo'c'sle, Spaniker boom, bosun, aft.*

   E. Carpenter   5. *Switch, snaffle, steeplechase, trotter.*

Part V Lab Assignment

If you completed the lab assignments at the end of Parts I, II, III, and IV, you know that those lab assignments had you pretend to be the manager and sole owner of a company called Pierspont Property Management in Pierspont, Pennsylvania. You have been keeping a detailed database with information about renters. In this lab assignment, you will enter data in the database and gather information from it in different ways.

To do the test, open the Renters file in the Office 101 folder and get to it.

Step 1: Entering the data

Open the Renter Info database table and add a couple of records. It's not easy to enter data in Datasheet view, is it? Create a form for entering data in the Renter Info table and enter two or three more records by way of the form.

Step 2: Moving and deleting data

Delete the last two records you entered — turns out you didn't need to enter them. And come to think of it, the Phone Number field belongs after the Zip Code field, where the Birthdate field is now. Move the Phone Number field so that it appears after the Zip Code field.

Step 3: Filtering, or finding information in, a database

It turns out that the Joost City Council is raising property taxes. That might affect your business. Find all the people in the database table who live in Joost, not Pierspont. Then, using the form you created in Step 1, find everybody in Joost who hasn't paid their rent this month.

Step 4: Querying a database

A notice just arrived from the Pierspont City Council. It says that the city, in its munificence, will pay part of the rent of all renters in Pierspont who were born before Janaury 1, 1926. Query the database to find Pierspont residents born before that date.

Step 5: Sorting a database

You decide to send a bulk mailing to all renters. That means you have to arrange the records in Zip Code order. Do that. Then sort the database by last name in ascending order.

Test Answers

No matter how well you rate, you will always rate well with me.

Part I Answers

Question	Answer	If You Missed It, Try This
1.	Dead false.	A computer is just a machine.
2.	False.	Review Lesson 1-1.
3.	False.	Choose File⇨Close. Review Lesson 1-2.
4.	True.	Review Lesson 1-4.
5.	True.	Review Lesson 2-1.
6.	False.	But you can press the Backspace key. Review Lesson 2-2.
7.	True.	Review Lesson 2-3.
8.	True.	Review Lesson 2-4.
9.	False.	False, at least, as of the writing of this book.
10.	True.	Review Lesson 3-5.
11.	B.	Review Lesson 2-1.
12.	D.	Review Lesson 1-2.
13.	A and E.	Review Lesson 1-5.
14.	C.	Of course!
15.	D.	Review Lesson 2-3.
16.	A.	Review Lesson 2-4.
17.	B and C.	Review Lesson 1-3.
18.	C.	Review Lesson 1-5.
19.	A3, B1, C4, D5, E2.	Review Lessons 1-2, 2-2, and 2-4.
20.	A4, B3, C1, D2, E5.	Review Lessons 2-1 and 2-4.
21.	A4, B3, C5, D1, E2.	Rock on, Beavis!
22.	A3, B1, C5, D4, E2.	Review Lessons 2-1 and 2-4.

Part II Answers

Question	Answer	If You Missed It, Try This
1.	True.	Review Lesson 4-1.
2.	True.	Review Lesson 4-2.
3.	False.	Review Lesson 5-3.
4.	False.	Review Lesson 5-3.
5.	True.	Review Lesson 5-5.
6.	True.	Review Lesson 5-2.
7.	True.	Review Lesson 5-4.
8.	True.	You can combine formulas this way by using parentheses. Review Lesson 5-1.
9.	False.	That is the Greek letter sigma on the AutoSum button, but no, it won't get you a glass of beer.
10.	True.	Review Lesson 6-2.
11.	E.	Review Lesson 4-2 and 4-4.
12.	B.	Review Lesson 4-4.
13.	C.	Review Lesson 4-5.
14.	A.	Yes, I hate questions like this too. Review Lesson 4-2.
15.	A, B, and C.	A trick question, because you can get two decimal places with all three. Review Lesson 5-1.
16.	E.	Review Lesson 6-1.
17.	B and E.	Review Lesson 6-2.
18.	D.	Review Lesson 6-4.
19.	A1, B3, C1, D5, E4.	Review Lesson 4-2.
20.	A2, B5, C4, D1, E3.	Review Lesson 4-2.
21.	A2, B3, C4, D1, E5.	Review Lesson 4-2.

Part III Answers

Question	Answer	If You Missed It, Try This
1.	False.	Review Lesson 7-1.
2.	True.	Review Lesson 7-2.

3.	Very false.	Lesson 7-4 explains how easy it is to use a PowerPoint 97 design.
4.	True.	Review Lesson 8-1.
5.	True.	Review Lesson 8-2.
6.	True.	Review Lesson 8-3.
7.	A, C, D, and E.	Review Lesson 7-1.
8.	A.	Review Lesson 7-2.
9.	A.	Review Lesson 7-2.
10.	A, B, and D.	Review Lesson 8-1.
11.	A and C.	Review Lesson 8-4.
12.	D.	Bad presentations gave many artists their big break.
13.	A4, B5, C3, D1, E2.	Review Lessons 7-1 and 7-3.
14.	A4, B1, C3, D2, E5.	Review Lessons 7-3, 7-4, and 7-3.

Part IV Answers

Question	Answer	If You Missed It, Try This
1.	False.	A computer is a dumb machine — one that you are learning to boss around in the worst possible way. Would you do that to a friend?
2.	True.	True, unless you are replying to a message. Review Lesson 9-2.
3.	True.	Review Lesson 9-2.
4.	False.	Review Lesson 9-2.
5.	True.	Review Lesson 9-3.
6.	True.	That is the subject of Lesson 9-4.
7.	True.	See the end of Lesson 9-4.
8.	False.	Actually, you double-click. Review Lesson 10-2.
9.	True, sort of.	The end of Lesson 10-2 explains "autodialing."
10.	True.	Review Lesson 10-3.
11.	C.	Review Lesson 9-2.
12.	E.	Review Lesson 9-2.
13.	A and C.	Review Lesson 9-3.
14.	D.	Review Lesson 9-3.
15.	C.	Review Lesson 9-3.
16.	E.	Review Lesson 9-3.

17.	C.	Review Lesson 9-4.
18.	B and C.	Review Lesson 10-2.
19.	A3, B1, C4, D2, E5.	See the end of Lesson 9-2 to learn about smileys.
20.	A4, B5, C1, D3, E5.	These buttons are explained throughout Unit 9.
21.	A3, B1, C5, D2, E4.	Review Lesson 10-1.
22.	A2, B4, C1, D3, E5.	Two hundred channels, and you still can't find this stuff on TV.

Part V Answers

Question	Answer	If You Missed It, Try This
1.	True.	Review Lesson 11-1.
2.	False.	Review Lesson 12-1.
3.	True.	Review Lesson 11-1.
4.	True.	Review Lesson 11-2.
5.	False.	Sad, but true. Review Lesson 11-4.
6.	True.	Review Lesson 12-1.
7.	True, but also false.	The button both starts a search in the database and removes the results of the search from the screen. Review Lesson 12-2.
8.	True.	Review Lesson 12-2.
9.	False.	Review Lesson 12-3.
10.	False.	Review Lesson 12-4.
11.	C.	Review Lesson 11-1.
12.	B.	I hate this kind of question, too. Review Lesson 11-1.
13.	A, D, and maybe B.	Review Lesson 11-1.
14.	E.	Review Lesson 11-2.
15.	A and C.	Review Lesson 11-3.
16.	C.	Review Lesson 11-4.
17.	D.	Review Lesson 12-3.
18.	A3, B4, C1, D2, E5.	Review Lessons 11-2 and 11-3.
19.	A5, B4, C1, D3, E5.	Review Lessons 12-2 and 12-3.
20.	A4, B5, C3, D2, E1.	Database jargon is hideous, isn't it?

About the CD

The CD that comes with *Dummies 101: Microsoft Office 97 For Windows* offers practice files and two extra units — Units 13 and Unit 14. You won't find Units 13 and 14 on the pages of this book, but after you have printed these units, you will get a handful of extra pages that are laid out and look exactly like the pages in this book. Or you can just read these extra units on-screen if you prefer to save a few sheets of paper.

Before you can make use of the CD files, you need to install them on your computer. Don't worry: Installing the files takes only a minute or two.

heads up

After you install the practice files, please don't open them. Wait until you read the lessons in the book. In the book, where I tell you to open a practice file, I tell you its name and put an on the CD icon on the margin of the page.

Each practice file has been carefully prepared so you can learn an Office 97 task. If you open a practice file and fool with it before you're ready, you may mess up the file. You may alter the file somehow, and if you do that, the instructions in the lesson that the practice file was meant for may become meaningless. Your best bet is to follow the installation instructions given in this appendix, go straight to Unit 1, and wait until I tell you to open a practice file.

System Requirements

Before you install the CD, make sure that your system meets the following system requirements. If your computer doesn't meet the minimum requirements, you may have trouble using the practice files and computer program on the CD.

- Computer with CD-ROM drive
- Microsoft Office 97 installed on your computer
- Microsoft Windows 95 installed on your computer
- At least 8MB of RAM installed on your computer
- At least 4MB of free hard-disk space available if you want to install just the exercise files; at least 8MB if you want to install all the programs

What's on the CD

Following is a list of everything that can be installed from the CD, along with the lesson in which the practice file or computer program is first used. In each lesson, you will find the name of the practice file you are to open.

Lesson 1-2	Open
Lesson 1-3	View
Lesson 1-4	Hurry Up
Lesson 2-3	Club Select
Lesson 2-4	Moving Sale
Lesson 2-5	Delete Me
Lesson 2-6	Fonts and Things
End of Unit 2	Quiz 2
Lesson 3-2	Indenting
Lesson 3-3	Line Spacing
Lesson 3-4	Alignment
Lesson 3-5	Miss Spalling
Lesson 3-6	Print Me
End of Unit 3	Quiz 3
Part I Lab Assignment	Test 1
Lesson 4-2	Tour
Lesson 4-3	Cell
Lesson 4-4	Copy Move
Lesson 4-5	View Data
Lesson 4-6	Print Me
End of Unit 4	Quiz 4
Lesson 5-1	Formatting

Lesson 5-2	Columns and Rows
Lesson 5-4	Align
Lesson 5-5	Borders and Colors
End of Unit 5	Quiz 5
Lesson 6-1	Formula
Lesson 6-2	Function
Lesson 6-3	Range
Lesson 6-4	Chart
End of Unit 6	Quiz 6
Part II Lab Assignment	Test II
Lesson 7-2	View
Lesson 7-3	Format
Lesson 7-4	Design
Lesson 7-5	Clip Art
Lesson 8-1	Rehearse
Lesson 8-2	Big Show
Lesson 8-3	Automatic
Lesson 8-4	Handout
End of Unit 8	Quiz 8
Part III Lab Assignment	Test 3
Lesson 11-2	Enter Data
Lesson 11-4	Move and Delete
End of Unit 11	Quiz 11
Lesson 12-1	Filter
Lesson 12-2	Query
Lesson 12-2	Query Combo

Notes:

Notes:

Lesson 12-3	Sort
Lesson 12-4	Report
End of Unit 12	Quiz 12
Part V Lab Assignment	Renters

Bonus Unit Practice Files

Lesson 13-1	Clipboard
Lesson 13-1	Receive
Lesson 13-1	Excel to Word
Lesson 13-2	Destination
Lesson 13-2	Source
Lesson 13-3	Access to Word
Lesson 13-4	PowerPoint Outline
Lesson 13-4	Bind1
Lesson 14-2	Excel Page
Lesson 14-3	PowerPoint Page
Lesson 14-4	Access Page
Lesson 14-5	Hyper 1, Hyper 2, Hyper 3, Hyper 4

Computer Program

| Adobe Acrobat Reader | You don't have to do much with this program. It's the program that helps you read the bonus units available on the CD. I just listed it here so that you know what Adobe Acrobat Reader is when you go to open one of the bonus units. |

Bonus Units

Unit 13: Bringing It All Together

Unit 14: Office 97 and the World Wide Web

Putting the CD Files on Your Hard Drive

The practice files you find on the CD are sample Word 97 documents, Excel 97 spreadsheets, PowerPoint 97 presentations, and Access 97 databases that accompany the lessons in the book. You need to put these files on your hard drive before you can use them. After you read this book, you can easily remove the files with a simple uninstall process.

The CD also features two additional units, Units 13 and 14, and the computer program Adobe Acrobat Reader, which you use to open, view, and print Units 13 and 14.

The first thing you need to do is install a couple of icons to the Start menu or Program Manager to make the CD easier to use. Then you install the exercise files.

heads up

If you have problems with the installation process, you can call the IDG Books Worldwide, Inc., Customer Support number: 800-762-2974 (outside the U.S.: 317-596-5261).

Installing the icons

With Windows 95 up and running, follow these steps:

1 **Insert the Dummies 101 CD (label side up) into your computer's CD drive and wait about 30 seconds to see whether Windows 95 starts the CD for you.**

Be careful to touch only the edges of the CD. The CD drive is the one that pops out with a circular drawer.

If your computer has the Windows 95 AutoPlay feature, the installation program should begin automatically. If the program does not start after 30 seconds, go to Step 2. If it does, go to Step 4.

2 **If the installation program doesn't start automatically, click the Start button and click Run.**

3 **In the dialog box that appears, type** d:\setup.exe **(if your CD drive is not drive D, substitute the appropriate letter for D) and click OK.**

A message informs you that the program is about to install the icons.

4 **Click OK in the message window.**

After a moment, a program group called Dummies 101 appears on the Start menu, with a set of icons. Then another message appears, asking whether you want to use the CD now.

5 **Click Yes to continue with the installation now or click No if you want to continue later.**

If you click No, you can continue with the installation simply by clicking the Dummies 101 - Office 97 For Windows CD icon in the Dummies 101 program group (on the Start menu).

Notes:

Installing the exercise files

If you closed the CD after you installed the icons, restart it by clicking the Start button, clicking Dummies 101, and clicking Dummies 101 - Office 97 For Windows CD. Then click the Install Exercise Files button and follow the instructions that appear on the screen to install the exercise (sometimes known as *practice*) files on your computer.

To make the installation and the exercises in this book as simple as possible, let the installer place the exercise files in the recommended location. If you really want to put the files somewhere else, you can change the location by following the on-screen instructions (make sure that you remember where you put them if you customize the location).

Unless you change the location, the exercise files are installed to C:\Office 101.

You don't have to do anything with the files yet — I tell you when you need to open the first file (in Unit 1).

Note: The files are meant to accompany the book's lessons. If you open a file prematurely, you may accidentally make changes to the file, which may prevent you from following along with the steps in the lessons. So please don't try to open or view a file until you've reached the point in the lessons where I explain how to open the file.

If at some point you accidentally modify an exercise file and want to reinstall the original version, just run the CD again and click on Install Exercise Files once more. If you want to save your modified version of the file, either move the file to another folder before reinstalling the original or tell the exercise file installer to place the new replacement file in a different folder.

Accessing the exercise files

You'll find detailed instructions on how to access the *Dummies 101: Microsoft Office 97 For Windows* files in Unit 1, where you first need to open a file. You can also refer to the Cheat Sheet (the yellow, perforated quick-reference card at the front of the book) for these instructions.

Removing the exercise files and icons

After you have read the book and no longer need the exercise files and icons, you can uninstall them.

To uninstall the exercise files, follow these steps:

1 **In Windows 95, click the Start button on the taskbar.**

2 **Click Programs.**

3 Click Dummies 101.

4 Click Uninstall Dummies 101 Office 97 CD.

To remove the icons, click the Automatic option in the Uninstall window. If you feel comfortable removing a few of the files instead of all of them, click the Custom button. Then follow the directions on-screen.

heads up

Caution: As soon as you click the Automatic button, the exercise files are as good as gone, and the only way to get them back is to go through the original installation process again. If you want to keep any of the files that were installed, move them to a different folder *before* you begin the uninstall process. You should be absolutely certain that you want to delete all the files before you choose the Automatic option.

Using the Acrobat Reader to Read and Print Units 13 and 14

The Acrobat Reader, from Adobe Systems, is a computer program for printing Portable Document Format (PDF) files, including Units 13 and 14 that come on the CD with this book. When you print Units 13 and 14 on the CD with the Acrobat Reader, you get book pages that are laid out and look exactly like the pages in the book.

This part of the appendix explains how to install the Acrobat Reader and use it to view and print Units 13 and 14.

Installing and running the Acrobat Reader

To install the Acrobat Reader, follow these steps:

1 Follow Steps 1-5 in the section "Installing the icons" in this appendix.

2 Click Choose Software.

3 On the next screen, click Adobe Acrobat Reader.

4 On the next screen, click Install Adobe Acrobat Reader.

A welcome screen appears.

5 Click Continue.

A screen appears asking if you really want to install Acrobat Reader.

6 Click <u>Y</u>es.

Two message boxes appear while the program loads onto your machine. After a while, a welcome screen appears. Now you are ready to set up the Acrobat Reader.

7 Click **Next**.

8 Follow the directions on-screen.

9 Glance at the readme file and then choose **File⇨Exit**.

10 Click **OK** in the message box that tells you that the installation is complete.

11 Click **Exit** and then click **Yes**.

You can run the Acrobat Reader at any time by clicking the Start button and choosing Programs⇨Adobe Acrobat⇨Acrobat Reader 3.0.

Reading and printing Units 13 and 14 with the Acrobat Reader

After you install the Acrobat Reader, you can use the program to read and print Units 13 and 14 on the CD.

To read Units 13 and 14, follow these steps:

1 Run the Acrobat Reader by clicking the Start button and choosing **Programs⇨Adobe Acrobat⇨Acrobat Reader 3.0**.

2 Choose **File⇨Open**.

The Open dialog box appears.

3 Click the down arrow next to the Look **in** box.

4 In the list that appears, choose **101office97 (D:)**.

5 Double-click the **Lessons** folder.

6 Double-click the name of the lesson you want to read.

To move around in the document, just move the scroll bar on the right side of the program's window.

After the files appear on-screen, you can print them, if you wish. Choose File⇨Print, make sure All is selected in the dialog box, and click OK.

To close the Acrobat Reader, choose File⇨Exit.

Index

The Fun & Easy Way™ to learn about computers and more!

7/29/96

Windows® 3.11 For Dummies,® 3rd Edition
by Andy Rathbone

ISBN: 1-56884-370-4
$16.95 USA/
$22.95 Canada

Mutual Funds For Dummies™
by Eric Tyson

ISBN: 1-56884-226-0
$16.99 USA/
$22.99 Canada

DOS For Dummies,® 2nd Edition
by Dan Gookin

ISBN: 1-878058-75-4
$16.95 USA/
$22.95 Canada

The Internet For Dummies,® 2nd Edition
by John Levine & Carol Baroudi

ISBN: 1-56884-222-8
$19.99 USA/
$26.99 Canada

Personal Finance For Dummies™
by Eric Tyson

ISBN: 1-56884-150-7
$16.95 USA/
$22.95 Canada

PCs For Dummies,® 3rd Edition
by Dan Gookin & Andy Rathbone

ISBN: 1-56884-904-4
$16.99 USA/
$22.99 Canada

Macs® For Dummies,® 3rd Edition
by David Pogue

ISBN: 1-56884-239-2
$19.99 USA/
$26.99 Canada

The SAT® I For Dummies™
by Suzee Vlk

ISBN: 1-56884-213-9
$14.99 USA/
$20.99 Canada

Here's a complete listing of IDG Books' ...For Dummies® titles

Title	Author	ISBN	Price
DATABASE			
Access 2 For Dummies®	by Scott Palmer	ISBN: 1-56884-090-X	$19.95 USA/$26.95 Canada
Access Programming For Dummies®	by Rob Krumm	ISBN: 1-56884-091-8	$19.95 USA/$26.95 Canada
Approach 3 For Windows® For Dummies®	by Doug Lowe	ISBN: 1-56884-233-3	$19.99 USA/$26.99 Canada
dBASE For DOS For Dummies®	by Scott Palmer & Michael Stabler	ISBN: 1-56884-188-4	$19.95 USA/$26.95 Canada
dBASE For Windows® For Dummies®	by Scott Palmer	ISBN: 1-56884-179-5	$19.95 USA/$26.95 Canada
dBASE 5 For Windows® Programming For Dummies®	by Ted Coombs & Jason Coombs	ISBN: 1-56884-215-5	$19.99 USA/$26.99 Canada
FoxPro 2.6 For Windows® For Dummies®	by John Kaufeld	ISBN: 1-56884-187-6	$19.95 USA/$26.95 Canada
Paradox 5 For Windows® For Dummies®	by John Kaufeld	ISBN: 1-56884-185-X	$19.95 USA/$26.95 Canada
DESKTOP PUBLISHING/ILLUSTRATION/GRAPHICS			
CorelDRAW! 5 For Dummies®	by Deke McClelland	ISBN: 1-56884-157-4	$19.95 USA/$26.95 Canada
CorelDRAW! For Dummies®	by Deke McClelland	ISBN: 1-56884-042-X	$19.95 USA/$26.95 Canada
Desktop Publishing & Design For Dummies®	by Roger C. Parker	ISBN: 1-56884-234-1	$19.99 USA/$26.99 Canada
Harvard Graphics 2 For Windows® For Dummies®	by Roger C. Parker	ISBN: 1-56884-092-6	$19.95 USA/$26.95 Canada
PageMaker 5 For Macs® For Dummies®	by Galen Gruman & Deke McClelland	ISBN: 1-56884-178-7	$19.95 USA/$26.95 Canada
PageMaker 5 For Windows® For Dummies®	by Deke McClelland & Galen Gruman	ISBN: 1-56884-160-4	$19.95 USA/$26.95 Canada
Photoshop 3 For Macs® For Dummies®	by Deke McClelland	ISBN: 1-56884-208-2	$19.99 USA/$26.99 Canada
QuarkXPress 3.3 For Dummies®	by Galen Gruman & Barbara Assadi	ISBN: 1-56884-217-1	$19.99 USA/$26.99 Canada
FINANCE/PERSONAL FINANCE/TEST TAKING REFERENCE			
Everyday Math For Dummies™	by Charles Seiter	ISBN: 1-56884-248-1	$14.99 USA/$22.99 Canada
Personal Finance For Dummies™ For Canadians	by Eric Tyson & Tony Martin	ISBN: 1-56884-378-X	$18.99 USA/$24.99 Canada
QuickBooks 3 For Dummies®	by Stephen L. Nelson	ISBN: 1-56884-227-9	$19.99 USA/$26.99 Canada
Quicken 8 For DOS For Dummies,® 2nd Edition	by Stephen L. Nelson	ISBN: 1-56884-210-4	$19.95 USA/$26.95 Canada
Quicken 5 For Macs® For Dummies®	by Stephen L. Nelson	ISBN: 1-56884-211-2	$19.95 USA/$26.95 Canada
Quicken 4 For Windows® For Dummies,® 2nd Edition	by Stephen L. Nelson	ISBN: 1-56884-209-0	$19.95 USA/$26.95 Canada
Taxes For Dummies,™ 1995 Edition	by Eric Tyson & David J. Silverman	ISBN: 1-56884-220-1	$14.99 USA/$20.99 Canada
The GMAT® For Dummies™	by Suzee Vlk, Series Editor	ISBN: 1-56884-376-3	$14.99 USA/$20.99 Canada
The GRE® For Dummies™	by Suzee Vlk, Series Editor	ISBN: 1-56884-375-5	$14.99 USA/$20.99 Canada
Time Management For Dummies™	by Jeffrey J. Mayer	ISBN: 1-56884-360-7	$16.99 USA/$22.99 Canada
TurboTax For Windows® For Dummies®	by Gail A. Helsel, CPA	ISBN: 1-56884-228-7	$19.99 USA/$26.99 Canada
GROUPWARE/INTEGRATED			
ClarisWorks For Macs® For Dummies®	by Frank Higgins	ISBN: 1-56884-363-1	$19.99 USA/$26.99 Canada
Lotus Notes For Dummies®	by Pat Freeland & Stephen Londergan	ISBN: 1-56884-212-0	$19.95 USA/$26.95 Canada
Microsoft® Office 4 For Windows® For Dummies®	by Roger C. Parker	ISBN: 1-56884-183-3	$19.95 USA/$26.95 Canada
Microsoft® Works 3 For Windows® For Dummies®	by David C. Kay	ISBN: 1-56884-214-7	$19.99 USA/$26.99 Canada
SmartSuite 3 For Dummies®	by Jan Weingarten & John Weingarten	ISBN: 1-56884-367-4	$19.99 USA/$26.99 Canada
INTERNET/COMMUNICATIONS/NETWORKING			
America Online® For Dummies,® 2nd Edition	by John Kaufeld	ISBN: 1-56884-933-8	$19.99 USA/$26.99 Canada
CompuServe For Dummies,® 2nd Edition	by Wallace Wang	ISBN: 1-56884-937-0	$19.99 USA/$26.99 Canada
Modems For Dummies,® 2nd Edition	by Tina Rathbone	ISBN: 1-56884-223-6	$19.99 USA/$26.99 Canada
MORE Internet For Dummies®	by John R. Levine & Margaret Levine Young	ISBN: 1-56884-164-7	$19.95 USA/$26.95 Canada
MORE Modems & On-line Services For Dummies®	by Tina Rathbone	ISBN: 1-56884-365-8	$19.99 USA/$26.99 Canada
Mosaic For Dummies,® Windows Edition	by David Angell & Brent Heslop	ISBN: 1-56884-242-2	$19.99 USA/$26.99 Canada
NetWare For Dummies,® 2nd Edition	by Ed Tittel, Deni Connor & Earl Follis	ISBN: 1-56884-369-0	$19.99 USA/$26.99 Canada
Networking For Dummies®	by Doug Lowe	ISBN: 1-56884-079-9	$19.95 USA/$26.95 Canada
PROCOMM PLUS 2 For Windows® For Dummies®	by Wallace Wang	ISBN: 1-56884-219-8	$19.99 USA/$26.99 Canada
TCP/IP For Dummies®	by Marshall Wilensky & Candace Leiden	ISBN: 1-56884-241-4	$19.99 USA/$26.99 Canada

DUMMIES PRESS™

7/29/96

The Internet For Macs® For Dummies® 2nd Edition	by Charles Seiter	ISBN: 1-56884-371-2	$19.99 USA/$26.99 Canada
The Internet For Macs® For Dummies® Starter Kit	by Charles Seiter	ISBN: 1-56884-244-9	$29.99 USA/$39.99 Canada
The Internet For Macs® For Dummies® Starter Kit Bestseller Edition	by Charles Seiter	ISBN: 1-56884-245-7	$39.99 USA/$54.99 Canada
The Internet For Windows® For Dummies® Starter Kit	by John R. Levine & Margaret Levine Young	ISBN: 1-56884-237-6	$34.99 USA/$44.99 Canada
The Internet For Windows® For Dummies® Starter Kit, Bestseller Edition	by John R. Levine & Margaret Levine Young	ISBN: 1-56884-246-5	$39.99 USA/$54.99 Canada

MACINTOSH

Mac® Programming For Dummies®	by Dan Parks Sydow	ISBN: 1-56884-173-6	$19.95 USA/$26.95 Canada
Macintosh® System 7.5 For Dummies®	by Bob LeVitus	ISBN: 1-56884-197-3	$19.95 USA/$26.95 Canada
MORE Macs® For Dummies®	by David Pogue	ISBN: 1-56884-087-X	$19.95 USA/$26.95 Canada
PageMaker 5 For Macs® For Dummies®	by Galen Gruman & Deke McClelland	ISBN: 1-56884-178-7	$19.95 USA/$26.95 Canada
QuarkXPress 3.3 For Dummies®	by Galen Gruman & Barbara Assadi	ISBN: 1-56884-217-1	$19.95 USA/$26.99 Canada
Upgrading and Fixing Macs® For Dummies®	by Kearney Rietmann & Frank Higgins	ISBN: 1-56884-189-2	$19.95 USA/$26.95 Canada

MULTIMEDIA

Multimedia & CD-ROMs For Dummies® 2nd Edition	by Andy Rathbone	ISBN: 1-56884-907-9	$19.99 USA/$26.99 Canada
Multimedia & CD-ROMs For Dummies® Interactive Multimedia Value Pack, 2nd Edition	by Andy Rathbone	ISBN: 1-56884-909-5	$29.99 USA/$39.99 Canada

OPERATING SYSTEMS:

DOS

MORE DOS For Dummies®	by Dan Gookin	ISBN: 1-56884-046-2	$19.95 USA/$26.95 Canada
OS/2® Warp For Dummies® 2nd Edition	by Andy Rathbone	ISBN: 1-56884-205-8	$19.99 USA/$26.99 Canada

UNIX

MORE UNIX® For Dummies®	by John R. Levine & Margaret Levine Young	ISBN: 1-56884-361-5	$19.99 USA/$26.99 Canada
UNIX® For Dummies®	by John R. Levine & Margaret Levine Young	ISBN: 1-878058-58-4	$19.95 USA/$26.95 Canada

WINDOWS

MORE Windows® For Dummies® 2nd Edition	by Andy Rathbone	ISBN: 1-56884-048-9	$19.95 USA/$26.95 Canada
Windows® 95 For Dummies®	by Andy Rathbone	ISBN: 1-56884-240-6	$19.99 USA/$26.99 Canada

PCS/HARDWARE

Illustrated Computer Dictionary For Dummies® 2nd Edition	by Dan Gookin & Wallace Wang	ISBN: 1-56884-218-X	$12.95 USA/$16.95 Canada
Upgrading and Fixing PCs For Dummies® 2nd Edition	by Andy Rathbone	ISBN: 1-56884-903-6	$19.99 USA/$26.99 Canada

PRESENTATION/AUTOCAD

AutoCAD For Dummies®	by Bud Smith	ISBN: 1-56884-191-4	$19.95 USA/$26.95 Canada
PowerPoint 4 For Windows® For Dummies®	by Doug Lowe	ISBN: 1-56884-161-2	$16.99 USA/$22.99 Canada

PROGRAMMING

Borland C++ For Dummies®	by Michael Hyman	ISBN: 1-56884-162-0	$19.95 USA/$26.95 Canada
C For Dummies® Volume 1	by Dan Gookin	ISBN: 1-878058-78-9	$19.95 USA/$26.95 Canada
C++ For Dummies®	by Stephen R. Davis	ISBN: 1-56884-163-9	$19.95 USA/$26.95 Canada
Delphi Programming For Dummies®	by Neil Rubenking	ISBN: 1-56884-200-7	$19.99 USA/$26.99 Canada
Mac® Programming For Dummies®	by Dan Parks Sydow	ISBN: 1-56884-173-6	$19.95 USA/$26.95 Canada
PowerBuilder 4 Programming For Dummies®	by Ted Coombs & Jason Coombs	ISBN: 1-56884-325-9	$19.99 USA/$26.99 Canada
QBasic Programming For Dummies®	by Douglas Hergert	ISBN: 1-56884-093-4	$19.95 USA/$26.95 Canada
Visual Basic 3 For Dummies®	by Wallace Wang	ISBN: 1-56884-076-4	$19.95 USA/$26.95 Canada
Visual Basic "X" For Dummies®	by Wallace Wang	ISBN: 1-56884-230-9	$19.99 USA/$26.99 Canada
Visual C++ 2 For Dummies®	by Michael Hyman & Bob Arnson	ISBN: 1-56884-328-3	$19.99 USA/$26.99 Canada
Windows® 95 Programming For Dummies®	by S. Randy Davis	ISBN: 1-56884-327-5	$19.99 USA/$26.99 Canada

SPREADSHEET

1-2-3 For Dummies®	by Greg Harvey	ISBN: 1-878058-60-6	$16.95 USA/$22.95 Canada
1-2-3 For Windows® 5 For Dummies® 2nd Edition	by John Walkenbach	ISBN: 1-56884-216-3	$16.95 USA/$22.95 Canada
Excel 5 For Macs® For Dummies®	by Greg Harvey	ISBN: 1-56884-186-8	$19.95 USA/$26.95 Canada
Excel For Dummies® 2nd Edition	by Greg Harvey	ISBN: 1-56884-050-0	$16.95 USA/$22.95 Canada
MORE 1-2-3 For DOS For Dummies®	by John Weingarten	ISBN: 1-56884-224-4	$19.99 USA/$26.99 Canada
MORE Excel 5 For Windows® For Dummies®	by Greg Harvey	ISBN: 1-56884-207-4	$19.95 USA/$26.95 Canada
Quattro Pro 6 For Windows® For Dummies®	by John Walkenbach	ISBN: 1-56884-174-4	$19.95 USA/$26.95 Canada
Quattro Pro For DOS For Dummies®	by John Walkenbach	ISBN: 1-56884-023-3	$16.95 USA/$22.95 Canada

UTILITIES

Norton Utilities 8 For Dummies®	by Beth Slick	ISBN: 1-56884-166-3	$19.95 USA/$26.95 Canada

VCRS/CAMCORDERS

VCRs & Camcorders For Dummies™	by Gordon McComb & Andy Rathbone	ISBN: 1-56884-229-5	$14.99 USA/$20.99 Canada

WORD PROCESSING

Ami Pro For Dummies®	by Jim Meade	ISBN: 1-56884-049-7	$19.95 USA/$26.95 Canada
MORE Word For Windows® 6 For Dummies®	by Doug Lowe	ISBN: 1-56884-165-5	$19.95 USA/$26.95 Canada
MORE WordPerfect® 6 For Windows® For Dummies®	by Margaret Levine Young & David C. Kay	ISBN: 1-56884-206-6	$19.95 USA/$26.95 Canada
MORE WordPerfect® 6 For DOS For Dummies®	by Wallace Wang, edited by Dan Gookin	ISBN: 1-56884-047-0	$19.95 USA/$26.95 Canada
Word 6 For Macs® For Dummies®	by Dan Gookin	ISBN: 1-56884-190-6	$19.95 USA/$26.95 Canada
Word For Windows® 6 For Dummies®	by Dan Gookin	ISBN: 1-56884-075-6	$16.95 USA/$22.95 Canada
Word For Windows® For Dummies®	by Dan Gookin & Ray Werner	ISBN: 1-878058-86-X	$16.95 USA/$22.95 Canada
WordPerfect® 6 For DOS For Dummies®	by Dan Gookin	ISBN: 1-878058-77-0	$16.95 USA/$22.95 Canada
WordPerfect® 6.1 For Windows® For Dummies® 2nd Edition	by Margaret Levine Young & David Kay	ISBN: 1-56884-243-0	$16.95 USA/$22.95 Canada
WordPerfect® For Dummies®	by Dan Gookin	ISBN: 1-878058-52-5	$16.95 USA/$22.95 Canada

Fun, Fast, & Cheap!™

NEW!

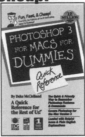

NEW!

SUPER STAR

SUPER STAR

The Internet For Macs® For Dummies® Quick Reference
by Charles Seiter

ISBN:1-56884-967-2
$9.99 USA/$12.99 Canada

Windows® 95 For Dummies® Quick Reference
by Greg Harvey

ISBN: 1-56884-964-8
$9.99 USA/$12.99 Canada

Photoshop 3 For Macs® For Dummies® Quick Reference
by Deke McClelland

ISBN: 1-56884-968-0
$9.99 USA/$12.99 Canada

WordPerfect® For DOS For Dummies® Quick Reference
by Greg Harvey

ISBN: 1-56884-009-8
$8.95 USA/$12.95 Canada

Title	Author	ISBN	Price
DATABASE			
Access 2 For Dummies® Quick Reference	by Stuart J. Stuple	ISBN: 1-56884-167-1	$8.95 USA/$11.95 Canada
dBASE 5 For DOS For Dummies® Quick Reference	by Barrie Sosinsky	ISBN: 1-56884-954-0	$9.99 USA/$12.99 Canada
dBASE 5 For Windows® For Dummies® Quick Reference	by Stuart J. Stuple	ISBN: 1-56884-953-2	$9.99 USA/$12.99 Canada
Paradox 5 For Windows® For Dummies® Quick Reference	by Scott Palmer	ISBN: 1-56884-960-5	$9.99 USA/$12.99 Canada
DESKTOP PUBLISHING/ILLUSTRATION/GRAPHICS			
CorelDRAW! 5 For Dummies® Quick Reference	by Raymond E. Werner	ISBN: 1-56884-952-4	$9.99 USA/$12.99 Canada
Harvard Graphics For Windows® For Dummies® Quick Reference	by Raymond E. Werner	ISBN: 1-56884-962-1	$9.99 USA/$12.99 Canada
Photoshop 3 For Macs® For Dummies® Quick Reference	by Deke McClelland	ISBN: 1-56884-968-0	$9.99 USA/$12.99 Canada
FINANCE/PERSONAL FINANCE			
Quicken 4 For Windows® For Dummies® Quick Reference	by Stephen L. Nelson	ISBN: 1-56884-950-8	$9.95 USA/$12.95 Canada
GROUPWARE/INTEGRATED			
Microsoft® Office 4 For Windows® For Dummies® Quick Reference	by Doug Lowe	ISBN: 1-56884-958-3	$9.99 USA/$12.99 Canada
Microsoft® Works 3 For Windows® For Dummies® Quick Reference	by Michael Partington	ISBN: 1-56884-959-1	$9.99 USA/$12.99 Canada
INTERNET/COMMUNICATIONS/NETWORKING			
The Internet For Dummies® Quick Reference	by John R. Levine & Margaret Levine Young	ISBN: 1-56884-168-X	$8.95 USA/$11.95 Canada
MACINTOSH			
Macintosh® System 7.5 For Dummies® Quick Reference	by Stuart J. Stuple	ISBN: 1-56884-956-7	$9.99 USA/$12.99 Canada
OPERATING SYSTEMS:			
DOS			
DOS For Dummies® Quick Reference	by Greg Harvey	ISBN: 1-56884-007-1	$8.95 USA/$11.95 Canada
UNIX			
UNIX® For Dummies® Quick Reference	by John R. Levine & Margaret Levine Young	ISBN: 1-56884-094-2	$8.95 USA/$11.95 Canada
WINDOWS			
Windows® 3.1 For Dummies® Quick Reference, 2nd Edition	by Greg Harvey	ISBN: 1-56884-951-6	$8.95 USA/$11.95 Canada
PCs/HARDWARE			
Memory Management For Dummies® Quick Reference	by Doug Lowe	ISBN: 1-56884-362-3	$9.99 USA/$12.99 Canada
PRESENTATION/AUTOCAD			
AutoCAD For Dummies® Quick Reference	by Ellen Finkelstein	ISBN: 1-56884-198-1	$9.95 USA/$12.95 Canada
SPREADSHEET			
1-2-3 For Dummies® Quick Reference	by John Walkenbach	ISBN: 1-56884-027-6	$8.95 USA/$11.95 Canada
1-2-3 For Windows® 5 For Dummies® Quick Reference	by John Walkenbach	ISBN: 1-56884-957-5	$9.95 USA/$12.95 Canada
Excel For Windows® For Dummies® Quick Reference, 2nd Edition	by John Walkenbach	ISBN: 1-56884-096-9	$8.95 USA/$11.95 Canada
Quattro Pro 6 For Windows® For Dummies® Quick Reference	by Stuart J. Stuple	ISBN: 1-56884-172-8	$9.95 USA/$12.95 Canada
WORD PROCESSING			
Word For Windows® 6 For Dummies® Quick Reference	by George Lynch	ISBN: 1-56884-095-0	$8.95 USA/$11.95 Canada
Word For Windows® For Dummies® Quick Reference	by George Lynch	ISBN: 1-56884-029-2	$8.95 USA/$11.95 Canada
WordPerfect® 6.1 For Windows® For Dummies® Quick Reference, 2nd Edition	by Greg Harvey	ISBN: 1-56884-966-4	$9.99 USA/$12.99/Canada

Order Center: **(800) 762-2974** *(8 a.m.–6 p.m., EST, weekdays)*

7/29/96

Quantity	ISBN	Title	Price	Total

Shipping & Handling Charges

	Description	First book	Each additional book	Total
Domestic	Normal	$4.50	$1.50	$
	Two Day Air	$8.50	$2.50	$
	Overnight	$18.00	$3.00	$
International	Surface	$8.00	$8.00	$
	Airmail	$16.00	$16.00	$
	DHL Air	$17.00	$17.00	$

*For large quantities call for shipping & handling charges.
**Prices are subject to change without notice.

Ship to:

Name _____

Company _____

Address _____

City/State/Zip _____

Daytime Phone _____

Payment: ☐ Check to IDG Books Worldwide (US Funds Only)

☐ VISA   ☐ MasterCard   ☐ American Express

Card # _____ Expires _____

Signature _____

Subtotal _____

CA residents add
applicable sales tax _____

IN, MA, and MD
residents add
5% sales tax _____

IL residents add
6.25% sales tax_____

RI residents add
7% sales tax_____

TX residents add
8.25% sales tax_____

Shipping_____

Total _____

Please send this order form to:

IDG Books Worldwide, Inc.
Attn: Order Entry Dept.
7260 Shadeland Station, Suite 100
Indianapolis, IN 46256

Allow up to 3 weeks for delivery.
Thank you!

IDG BOOKS WORLDWIDE, INC.
END-USER LICENSE AGREEMENT

<u>Read This</u>. **You should carefully read these terms and conditions before opening the software packet(s) included with this book ("Book"). This is a license agreement ("Agreement") between you and IDG Books Worldwide, Inc. ("IDGB"). By opening the accompanying software packet(s), you acknowledge that you have read and accept the following terms and conditions. If you do not agree and do not want to be bound by such terms and conditions, promptly return the Book and the unopened software packet(s) to the place you obtained them for a full refund.**

1. <u>License Grant</u>. IDGB grants to you (either an individual or entity) a nonexclusive license to use one copy of the enclosed software program(s) (collectively, the "Software") solely for your own personal or business purposes on a single computer (whether a standard computer or a workstation component of a multiuser network). The Software is in use on a computer when it is loaded into temporary memory (i.e., RAM) or installed into permanent memory (e.g., hard disk, CD-ROM, or other storage device). IDGB reserves all rights not expressly granted herein.

2. <u>Ownership</u>. IDGB is the owner of all right, title, and interest, including copyright, in and to the compilation of the Software recorded on the disk(s)/CD-ROM. Copyright to the individual programs on the disk(s)/CD-ROM is owned by the author or other authorized copyright owner of each program. Ownership of the Software and all proprietary rights relating thereto remain with IDGB and its licensors.

3. <u>Restrictions on Use and Transfer</u>.

   (a) You may only (i) make one copy of the Software for backup or archival purposes, or (ii) transfer the Software to a single hard disk, provided that you keep the original for backup or archival purposes. You may not (i) rent or lease the Software, (ii) copy or reproduce the Software through a LAN or other network system or through any computer subscriber system or bulletin-board system, or (iii) modify, adapt, or create derivative works based on the Software.

   (b) You may not reverse engineer, decompile, or disassemble the Software. You may transfer the Software and user documentation on a permanent basis, provided that the transferee agrees to accept the terms and conditions of this Agreement and you retain no copies. If the Software is an update or has been updated, any transfer must include the most recent update and all prior versions.

4. <u>Restrictions on Use of Individual Programs</u>. You must follow the individual requirements and restrictions detailed for each individual program in the "About the CD" section of this Book. These limitations are contained in the individual license agreements recorded on the disk(s)/CD-ROM. These restrictions may include a requirement that after using the program for the period of time specified in its text, the user must pay a registration fee or discontinue use. By opening the Software packet(s), you will be agreeing to abide by the licenses and restrictions for these individual programs. None of the material on this disk(s) or listed in this Book may ever be distributed, in original or modified form, for commercial purposes.

5. <u>**Limited Warranty**</u>.

   (a) IDGB warrants that the Software and disk(s)/CD-ROM are free from defects in materials and workmanship under normal use for a period of sixty (60) days from the date of purchase of this Book. If IDGB receives notification within the warranty period of defects in materials or workmanship, IDGB will replace the defective disk(s)/CD-ROM.

   (b) IDGB AND THE AUTHOR OF THE BOOK DISCLAIM ALL OTHER WARRANTIES, EXPRESS OR IMPLIED, INCLUDING WITHOUT LIMITATION IMPLIED WARRANTIES OF MERCHANTABILITY AND FITNESS FOR A PARTICULAR PURPOSE, WITH RESPECT TO THE SOFTWARE, THE PROGRAMS, THE SOURCE CODE CONTAINED THEREIN, AND/OR THE TECHNIQUES DESCRIBED IN THIS BOOK. IDGB DOES NOT WARRANT THAT THE FUNCTIONS CONTAINED IN THE SOFTWARE WILL MEET YOUR REQUIREMENTS OR THAT THE OPERATION OF THE SOFTWARE WILL BE ERROR FREE.

   (c) This limited warranty gives you specific legal rights, and you may have other rights which vary from jurisdiction to jurisdiction.

6. <u>**Remedies**</u>.

   (a) IDGB's entire liability and your exclusive remedy for defects in materials and workmanship shall be limited to replacement of the Software, which may be returned to IDGB with a copy of your receipt at the following address: Disk Fulfillment Department, Attn: Dummies 101: Microsoft Office 97 For Windows, IDG Books Worldwide, Inc., 7260 Shadeland Station, Ste. 100, Indianapolis, IN 46256, or call 1-800-762-2974. Please allow 3–4 weeks for delivery. This Limited Warranty is void if failure of the Software has resulted from accident, abuse, or misapplication. Any replacement Software will be warranted for the remainder of the original warranty period or thirty (30) days, whichever is longer.

   (b) In no event shall IDGB or the author be liable for any damages whatsoever (including without limitation damages for loss of business profits, business interruption, loss of business information, or any other pecuniary loss) arising from the use of or inability to use the Book or the Software, even if IDGB has been advised of the possibility of such damages.

   (c) Because some jurisdictions do not allow the exclusion or limitation of liability for consequential or incidental damages, the above limitation or exclusion may not apply to you.

7. <u>**U.S. Government Restricted Rights**</u>. Use, duplication, or disclosure of the Software by the U.S. Government is subject to restrictions stated in paragraph (c) (1) (ii) of the Rights in Technical Data and Computer Software clause of DFARS 252.227-7013, and in subparagraphs (a) through (d) of the Commercial Computer — Restricted Rights clause at FAR 52.227-19, and in similar clauses in the NASA FAR supplement, when applicable.

8. <u>**General**</u>. This Agreement constitutes the entire understanding of the parties and revokes and supersedes all prior agreements, oral or written, between them and may not be modified or amended except in a writing signed by both parties hereto which specifically refers to this Agreement. This Agreement shall take precedence over any other documents that may be in conflict herewith. If any one or more provisions contained in this Agreement are held by any court or tribunal to be invalid, illegal, or otherwise unenforceable, each and every other provision shall remain in full force and effect.

Dummies 101 CD-ROM Installation Instructions

The CD-ROM at the back of this book contains the exercise files that you'll use while you work through the lessons in this book. It also contains a handy installation program that copies the files to your hard drive in a very simple process. See Appendix B for complete details about the CD (especially system requirements for using the CD).

Note: The CD-ROM does *not* contain Windows 95 or any of the Microsoft Office 97 programs. You must already have Windows 95 and the appropriate Microsoft Office 97 programs installed on your computer.

The first thing you need to do is install a couple of icons to the Start menu or Program Manager to make the CD easier to use. Then you install the exercise files, which you learn more about in Appendix B.

With Windows 95 up and running, follow these steps:

on the CD

1 Insert the Dummies 101 CD (label side up) into your computer's CD drive and wait about 30 seconds to see whether Windows 95 starts the CD for you.

If your computer's CD-ROM has the AutoPlay feature, the installation program runs automatically. If the program does not start after 30 seconds, go to Step 2. If it does, go to Step 4.

2 If the installation program doesn't start automatically, click the Start button and click Run.

3 In the dialog box that appears, type d:\setup.exe **(if your CD drive is not drive D, then substitute the appropriate letter for D) and click OK.**

A message informs you that the program is about to install the icons.

4 Click OK in the message window.

After a moment, a program group called Dummies 101 appears on the Start menu, with a set of icons. Then another message appears, asking whether you want to use the CD now.

5 Click Yes to use the CD interface window or click No if you want to use the CD later.

If you click No, you can run the CD later simply by clicking the Dummies 101 - Office 97 For Windows CD icon in the Dummies 101 program group (on the Start menu).

If you have problems with the installation process, you can call the IDG Books Worldwide, Inc., Customer Support number: 800-762-2974 (outside the U.S.: 317-596-5261).

Note: You don't have to do anything with the files yet — I tell you when you need to open the first file (in Unit 1). If you open a file prematurely, you may accidentally make changes to the file, which may prevent you from following along with the steps in the lessons.

IDG BOOKS WORLDWIDE REGISTRATION CARD

RETURN THIS REGISTRATION CARD FOR FREE CATALOG

Title of this book: Dummies 101™: Microsoft® Office 97 For Windows®

My overall rating of this book: ❑ Very good [1] ❑ Good [2] ❑ Satisfactory [3] ❑ Fair [4] ❑ Poor [5]

How I first heard about this book:

❑ Found in bookstore; name: [6] _____

❑ Advertisement: [8] _____

❑ Word of mouth; heard about book from friend, co-worker, etc.: [10] _____

❑ Book review: [7] _____

❑ Catalog: [9] _____

❑ Other: [11] _____

What I liked most about this book:

_____

_____

What I would change, add, delete, etc., in future editions of this book:

_____

_____

Other comments:

_____

Number of computer books I purchase in a year: ❑ 1 [12] ❑ 2-5 [13] ❑ 6-10 [14] ❑ More than 10 [15]

I would characterize my computer skills as: ❑ Beginner [16] ❑ Intermediate [17] ❑ Advanced [18] ❑ Professional [19]

I use ❑ DOS [20] ❑ Windows [21] ❑ OS/2 [22] ❑ Unix [23] ❑ Macintosh [24] ❑ Other: [25]_____

(please specify)

I would be interested in new books on the following subjects:
(please check all that apply, and use the spaces provided to identify specific software)

❑ Word processing: [26] _____

❑ Data bases: [28] _____

❑ File Utilities: [30] _____

❑ Networking: [32] _____

❑ Other: [34] _____

❑ Spreadsheets: [27] _____

❑ Desktop publishing: [29] _____

❑ Money management: [31] _____

❑ Programming languages: [33] _____

I use a PC at (please check all that apply): ❑ home [35] ❑ work [36] ❑ school [37] ❑ other: [38] _____

The disks I prefer to use are ❑ 5.25 [39] ❑ 3.5 [40] ❑ other: [41]_____

I have a CD ROM: ❑ yes [42] ❑ no [43]

I plan to buy or upgrade computer hardware this year: ❑ yes [44] ❑ no [45]

I plan to buy or upgrade computer software this year: ❑ yes [46] ❑ no [47]

Name: _____ Business title: [48] _____ Type of Business: [49] _____

Address (❑ home [50] ❑ work [51]/Company name: _____)

Street/Suite# _____

City [52]/State [53]/Zipcode [54]: _____ Country [55] _____

❑ **I liked this book!** You may quote me by name in future
IDG Books Worldwide promotional materials.

My daytime phone number is _____

IDG BOOKS®

THE WORLD OF
COMPUTER
KNOWLEDGE

❑ YES!

Please keep me informed about IDG's World of Computer Knowledge.
Send me the latest IDG Books catalog.